Stop Sinning and Be
Healed

by Alan P. Ballou

Stop Sinning and Be Healed

Copyright © December 2013 Alan P. Ballou

Author Alan P. Ballou

ISBN 978-0-9891969-2-5

Jedidiah Speak www.jedidiah.org

ဆ)(ဇ

Acknowledgments

All the praise, glory, and honor be to the Lord God almighty! Let him who glories, boast in the Lord! The Lord has gifted me to teach by His grace, and He has given me a wife to help me minister to His people. Praise be to the Lord our God forever!

ഇൗര

Contents

ഇൗൽ

Preface

ഇൗരു

In my last book concerning how to stop sinning, I wrote in such a way as to prove that Christians can indeed stop sinning, in accordance with the Holy Scriptures. However, in this book, I am teaching in such a way, as to minister deliverance, and healing to Christian believers, who want to live by the truth.

I believe that all Christians can be free from sin, and be healed. Praise God. However, few Christians receive either of those from the Lord, and as we begin to dig deeper into the scriptures, you will see obvious reasons for that.

No, I am not insinuating that every Christian who is sick, is not living by faith, and I'm not saying that sin is the cause of all sickness, and with good reason. The Bible doesn't say that.

However, I am teaching Jeremiah 5:25, which says that "Our sins have withheld the good that God has planned for us." We always hear about the good plans that God has for us, but we never hear how our sins block those plans. Any Christian who learns how to control sin, will experience all the good that God intended to give His people.

I will not be teaching anything that the Lord has not enabled me to show you in accordance with His Word. Therefore, if the Bible says that Christians can be totally "Set free from sin," then I will teach it. If the Bible says that we can actually do certain things that would bring healing to our body, I will teach that also, because I believe that all Christians should know these things.

That is what this book is about. I'm here to help God's people who are in need. If you are a believer, who is in need of deliverance, or healing, or if you want to learn how to effectively minister to those who are, then this book is for you.

The Lord has allowed me to minister deliverance, and healing to His people from many different parts of this world, even through emails, and phone calls, through simple instructions found in His Word that work just like they are written. Glory be to God! I would like to show you what the Lord has revealed to me.

There are many today who suffer sickness and disease, due to their lack of knowledge, or the lack of knowing what to do in their situation. These are little things, written in scripture, that make a huge difference.

The Lord has allowed me to minister to many long-time Christians who only needed small changes in their life in order to receive healing from the Lord in the comfort of their own home. Praise be to the Lord God almighty.

Christ died so that we could stop sinning, and be healed. However, we have to position ourself to receive it by faith. In fact, the whole Christian life is lived by faith, from start to finish (Romans 1:17). Everything that I will teach in this book is by faith.

For example, did you know that God has no problem whatsoever with protecting us from the devil (2 Thessalonians 3:3)? How do we position ourself in order to receive it? Quoting Psalm 91 is not the solution, and it doesn't bring about protection just by simply quoting it, but living by faith in Jesus Christ does. I will explain that in this book.

I'm not saying that all sickness can be totally avoided either. The Bible does not say that Christians will never get sick. God even uses affliction for a Christian's benefit, according to the Word of the Lord, written in Psalm 34:19. Check the verse.

However, the more we know about how sin works, and how to position ourself in order to receive healing, and protection from God, the better off we will be. God's people are destroyed for lack of knowledge (Hosea 4:6). That means that not knowing what to do, will certainly lead to destruction in our life, and I want to help you avoid that.

Although not all sickness is caused by sin, still many Christians do not receive healing from the Lord, due to their sins. In other words, sin may have not have made a person sick, but sin is the reason there is no answer to prayer.

I'm here to help you, if you will believe the verses I will show you. Therefore, prepare yourself to learn some very simple spiritual principles which are clearly written in scripture, that will make a big difference in your life and the lives of those you minister to.

In this book, I am using 1000 verses by permission from the New King James Bible, and a few more from the King James Bible. I would like you to read those verses out loud, so that you can hear them in your ears, as you read through this book.

I believe that the New King James Bible is an excellent translation, based on the 1611 Authorized Version, known as the King James Bible. Lord willing, my teachings and my speech, will always be in-line with that version of the Holy Scriptures.

Lord willing, my wife Lucie and I will always pray for, and make ourselves available to those who read this book, and believe the verses contained in it. Peace be with you, and may the Lord bless you!

೩೦೦ಃ

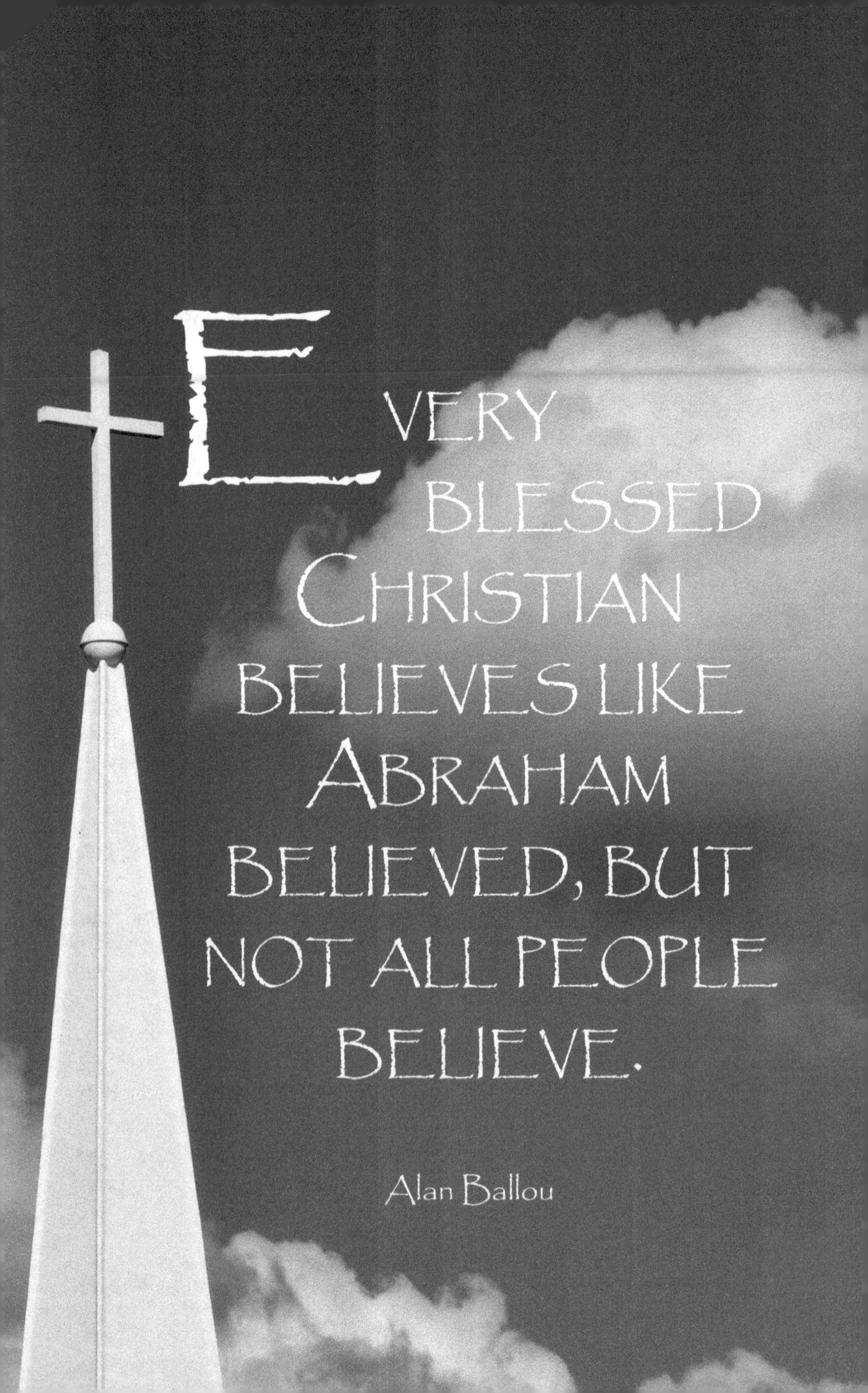
Every blessed Christian believes like Abraham believed, but not all people believe.
Alan Ballou

1

Blessed with Believing Abraham

ಏಂ೦ಜ

According to faith, the evidence of things not seen (Hebrews 11:1), whatever we do not believe, we cannot receive (James 1:5-7). In other words, if we doubt that God is able to do what He has promised, then we can forget about obtaining it.

James 1:5-8
5 If any of you lacks wisdom, let him ask of God, who gives to all liberally and without reproach, and it will be given to him.
6 But let him ask in faith, with no doubting, for he who doubts is like a wave of the sea driven and tossed by the wind. 7 For let not that man suppose that he will receive anything from the Lord; 8 he is a double-minded man, unstable in all his ways.
NKJV

James begins by explaining how to obtain wisdom from God, but in this passage of scripture there is a little known spiritual principle. The person who doubts that God is able to do what He says He can do, will not receive anything from the Lord.

We need to know that because it places a little known condition on every promise we might be relying on in the New Testament. If we do not believe, we will not receive, and therefore, we wait in vain.

Due to their doubts, millions are waiting in vain on promises to materialize today. They may even quote verses daily, but unbelief keeps them in defeat. In this way, the Christian life can become a guessing game, as many begin to wonder if they can rely on what the Lord has promised, because it never comes.

Faith is our assured hope in a promise that God has made (Hebrews 11:1). We believe what He has said to the point of knowing that it is going to happen, if we complete our part of the promise. Without this type of hope in a promise, we cannot possibly have the type of faith needed to make that promise materialize in our life.

In this book, we will discuss many promises, written in the Bible, that work to stop sin, and bring healing to our body. They may seem impossible to you, but do not allow your feelings to rob you of what God has promised. Even if it is against all hope, we must believe.

The same is true of Abraham's faith. Against all hope, Abraham believed what God had promised to the point of being fully convinced that God had the power to do what He said He would do (verse 18 below).

Romans 4:18-21

18 who, contrary to hope, in hope believed, so that he became the father of many nations, according to what was spoken, "So shall your descendants be." 19 And not being weak in faith, he did not consider his own body, already dead (since he was about a hundred years old), and the deadness of Sarah's womb. 20 He did not waver at the promise of God through unbelief, but was strengthened in faith, giving glory to God, 21 and being fully convinced that what He had promised He was also able to perform. NKJV

Against all hope, means that it didn't seem true in the natural, but if God said it, Abraham believed it, point, blank, period. He may not have known how God was going to do what He had promised, but once he believed, he did not allow himself to waver through unbelief regarding what was promised (verse 20 above).

We are called to believe just as Abraham believed (Romans 4:23-24, Galatians 3:7-9). In other words, our faith should match Abraham's faith, and only those who are of faith are blessed along with him (verse 7 below, Romans 4:16).

Galatians 3:6-9

6 just as Abraham "believed God, and it was accounted to him for righteousness." 7 Therefore know that only those who are of faith are sons of Abraham. 8 And the Scripture, foreseeing that God would justify the Gentiles by faith, preached the gospel to Abraham beforehand, saying, "In you all the nations shall be blessed." 9 So then those who are of faith are blessed with believing Abraham. NKJV

We need to ask ourself if we are fully convinced that God has the power to do what He has promised, or do we waver through unbelief regarding what He has promised? That could be the difference between a Christian who has faith that works and one whose faith does not work.

Read the following passage of scripture as the Apostle Paul attempts to bring the Galatians back to "hearing with faith." In other words, the Apostle Paul wanted them to simply believe what they heard to the point of putting faith in it.

Galatians 3:1-5

1 O foolish Galatians! Who has bewitched you that you should

not obey the truth, before whose eyes Jesus Christ was clearly portrayed among you as crucified? 2 This only I want to learn from you: Did you receive the Spirit by the works of the law, or by the hearing of faith? 3 Are you so foolish? Having begun in the Spirit, are you now being made perfect by the flesh? 4 Have you suffered so many things in vain — if indeed it was in vain? 5 Therefore He who supplies the Spirit to you and works miracles among you, does He do it by the works of the law, or by the hearing of faith? NKJV

We don't receive the Spirit by the works of the Law, but by the hearing of faith (verse 2 above). That means that we can receive the Spirit by believing the Word of God as it is spoken, just like it is written.

Also, God works miracles through the hearing of faith (verse 5 above). It is believing the Word of God as we hear it, and then trusting what God has said, that makes things happen supernaturally.

We have to believe the Words written on a page in our Bible to the point of refusing to allow our mind to settle on them not being truth. People with great faith believe to the point of taking God at His Word. For them, whatever God has promised is as good as done.

People who doubt, wonder how God is going to be able to do what He has promised in view of their circumstances. That's not assured hope, but uncertain hope. Faith is our assured hope in something God has said (Hebrews 11:1).

Unbelievers, simply do not accept what is written as truth. If we do not believe, it doesn't matter how God is going to accomplish what He has promised, since we won't be receiving it anyway.

Keep in mind that against "all" hope, Abraham in hope believed. In other words, in view of his circumstances, there wasn't any reason to believe that what he was promised was going to take place. Today we would call that a hopeless situation, but we can and should use God's promises to deliver us from hopeless situations. Our God is a God of hope, even in places where there is no hope.

Father, in the name of Jesus Christ, Thy Word is truth (John 17:17). We believe it, and we receive it, in the name of Jesus. Create in us a new heart, that is receptive to Your Word, that we may walk in Your ways, and bring glory to Your holy name. Amen!

Throughout this book, I will discuss some of the biggest reasons why Christians cannot stop sinning, and the solutions, in accordance with the Word of God. All of these issues stem from real-life problems that Christians from all over the world have had, including myself.

These principles can be used in every area of the Christian life. Deliverance, healing, provisions, and life in general are all directly tied to our sins (verse 25 below). Therefore, the people who have followed these principles have also experienced supernatural changes in every area of their life. Praise be to the Lord God almighty.

Jeremiah 5:25
25 Your iniquities have turned these things away, And your sins have withheld good from you. NKJV

Our sins have withheld the good God intended for us. Therefore, any Christian who turns from sin will experience good. Most Christians will receive healing in their body as they turn away from sin, and simply take a few steps in the right direction.

Now what

Take God at His Word and watch your life change for the better. That's when you will see results.

I believe that unbelief is the number one reason why Christians cannot stop sinning, and do not receive healing from the Lord. Many of the people I have worked with, wanted to pick and choose the parts of the Bible that they wanted to follow, and to ignore the rest. It doesn't work that way.

Without the type of faith that Abraham had, who believed everything God had promised him, our faith will not produce desired results. In order to be blessed with believing Abraham, we must do the works of Abraham (verse 39 below).

John 8:39
39 They answered and said to Him, "Abraham is our father." Jesus said to them, "If you were Abraham's children, you would do the works of Abraham. NKJV

Abraham believed God, and lived by faith in what God said. The entire Christian life is lived by faith (Romans 1:17), and therefore, if our faith is dead, weak, off-track, or shipwrecked, it will have an effect on our whole life.

Read the Bible for yourself, especially if the things we have covered so far seem strange to you. Don't try to fit what you read into what you believe; big mistake. Allow your Bible to paint the picture for you. That's hearing with faith.

Abide in the teachings first. Love the truth, and avoid anything that sounds good, but is against what is written in the Bible, and then you will be safe (2 John 1:9-11).

The type of healing we will discuss in this book is from God, and it can be received at any time, and any place through the hearing of faith. Faith can work anywhere that you will believe, by applying the principles that we will discuss in this book.

All things are possible for those who believe. Nothing is possible spiritually for those who do not (James 1:5-8).

Mark 9:23
23 Jesus said to him, "If you can believe, all things are possible to him who believes." NKJV

We are called to worship God in truth, and in Spirit (John 4:23-24), and the Word itself is truth (John 17:17).

John 4:23-24
23 But the hour is coming, and now is, when the true worshipers will worship the Father in spirit and truth; for the Father is seeking such to worship Him. 24 God is Spirit, and those who worship Him must worship in spirit and truth." NKJV

The will of God is our sanctification (1 Thessalonians 4:3-5). That means that we should be holy in conduct. We are already sanctified by the blood of Christ (Hebrews 10:10, 14, 29), and we are now being sanctified by the truth (verse 17 below), and by the Spirit (verse 16 below). Therefore, those who worship God, must worship Him in truth and Spirit.

John 17:17
17 Sanctify them by Your truth. Your word is truth. NKJV

Romans 15:16
16 that I might be a minister of Jesus Christ to the Gentiles, ministering the gospel of God, that the offering of the Gentiles might be acceptable, sanctified by the Holy Spirit. NKJV

When the truth is taken out of the way, then the door will be opened to deceiving spirits and the doctrine of demons, since at that point, no one will compare what they believe with the Word of God to make sure that it is truth (2 Corinthians 10:3-5).

In the last days, there will even be miracles among those who will perish, to draw them away because they did not "love the truth." Therefore, look for truth first and foremost, and then you will not be tricked.

Do not run with the crowd that chases miracles, signs, and wonders, but rejects what is written in the Bible. Signs and wonders will be used to deceive those who do not believe the truth (verses 11-12 below).

2 Thessalonians 2:9-12
9 The coming of the lawless one is according to the working of Satan, with all power, signs, and lying wonders, 10 and with all unrighteous deception among those who perish, because they did not receive the love of the truth, that they might be saved. 11 And for this reason God will send them strong delusion, that

they should believe the lie, 12 that they all may be condemned who did not believe the truth but had pleasure in unrighteousness. NKJV

Matthew 24:24
24 For false christs and false prophets will rise and show great signs and wonders to deceive, if possible, even the elect. NKJV

If you do not believe what is written in your Bible, and you are rushing from place to place chasing any sign that you can see, then let the verses above be a warning to you. God, Himself will send a strong delusion among those who do not believe the truth, but delight in unrighteousness (verses 11-12 above). Therefore, love the truth, as it is written in the Bible, so that you will not be deceived with those who will perish.

That is already happening today. Signs and wonders are drawing people away from the faith. They will perish because they do not love the truth, but delight in doing what is wrong (verse 12 above).

Father, in Jesus' name, I pray for myself, and everyone who reads this book, that You will have mercy upon us. Forgive us for our sins, and wash us clean with the blood of Christ. Open our eyes, so that we can see, and turn us from the power of darkness, to the power of light. Reveal to us where we are in the faith that You have given us, and give us what we need to continue in it. Save us from the things that we cannot see. Enable those who have not come to You, and bless those who have. For You alone are worthy to be praised. To You be glory, and honor forever, and ever. Amen.

I'm Alan Ballou; a servant. My wife Lucie and I serve free of charge. If we may be of service to you, please contact us.

www.HowToStopSinning.com

෨෬

2

Through Their Word

༄ ༅

It's not just our belief that counts, but also the belief of those around us. Jesus could not do many miracles when He was among those who did not believe (Matthew 13:58). Their unbelief hindered what Jesus could do around them.

Unbelievers will hinder your spiritual ability too. Therefore, if you gather with a group of unbelievers and doubters, your faith may not work, even though you might be on the right path. Imagine that.

I'm not saying, pack your bags and never speak to them again, but you need to know the truth so that you can make decisions based on truth, and not on feelings. Let your feelings follow your faith, and not the other way around.

Always make spiritual decisions based on truth, and never on feelings. Use your feelings to help you decide if you want pizza for supper, but when it comes to your faith, you must live by "every" Word that proceeds from the mouth of God (Deuteronomy 8:3).

Matthew 4:4
4 But He answered and said, "It is written, 'Man shall not live by bread alone, but by every word that proceeds from the mouth of God.'" NKJV

Decide today to take God at His Word, since He is the one Who can heal us, and keep us from sinning, which we will be explaining in detail throughout this book. Believe every Word, regardless of how it makes you feel.

I want you to know that part truth and part human wisdom is not going to work, since human wisdom takes away from the power already contained in the Word of God (1 Corinthians 1:17, Hebrews 4:12). Therefore, our faith should never rest on how the Word makes us feel, or the wisdom of men (verses 4-5 below).

1 Corinthians 2:4-5
4 And my speech and my preaching were not with persuasive words of human wisdom, but in demonstration of the Spirit and of power, 5 that your faith should not be in the wisdom of men but in the power of God. NKJV

There is a huge crowd of Christians out there today, who do not believe every Word of God, and you may have been a part of that group. I know that they all have their reasons, but what you need to know is that your faith is not going to work as it should, if you decide to be partners with them.

Christians, who are caught up in human wisdom, and philosophy, usually don't accept certain passages of scripture in the Bible, or they may even reject entire books. Yes, they trusted God's Word to save them, believing the very Words written on one page (hearing with faith), but they may not believe the very next page (unbelief).

They want to be known as believers, but there is no such thing as a believer who does not believe. Believers believe the whole message (Ephesians 1:13). Either we are believers, or unbelievers (2 Corinthians 4:3-4). Let me tell you right now that the things we will discuss in this book will not work for unbelievers.

If that describes you, repent of the past and start over. Ask God our Father to forgive you for rejecting His Word in the past, and to give you a new heart that is receptive to His Word in Jesus' name. Amen.

Father, in Jesus' name, You alone are worthy of our praise. According to Your great mercies, forgive us of our sins, and wash us clean with the blood of Jesus Christ. Give us the grace we so desperately need in order to do Your will. Give us eyes that can see, and ears that can hear, that we may understand Your Word, and create in us a pure heart, that we may accept it as truth. In the name of Jesus Christ, we pray. Amen. May the Lord bless all who read this book.

I had a man ask me if I received my Gospel from Jesus or from James, after I used a verse from that book to prove a point. He didn't believe the book of James, which was his main problem, and so he decided to ignore it altogether, as well as other books of the Holy Bible.

Like so many who reject different parts of the Bible, his reason for rejecting the book of James was also based on human wisdom. He declared, "I trust in Jesus Christ and Him alone!"

That certainly sounds spiritual, and it could easily draw away young Christians, who do not know the truth for themself, especially when it is mixed with a little emotion. Many Christians, who do believe, are entangled with the teachings of unbelievers, who may sound spiritual, but they are actually ungodly (Ephesians 4:12-14). Test everything you hear (1 Thessalonians 5:21)!

We should trust in Jesus, and if we trust in Jesus Christ, we would believe what He said in John 17:19-23 below.

John 17:19-23
19 And for their sakes I sanctify Myself, that they also may be

sanctified by the truth. 20 "I do not pray for these alone, but also for those who will believe in Me through their word; 21 that they all may be one, as You, Father, are in Me, and I in You; that they also may be one in Us, that the world may believe that You sent Me. 22 And the glory which You gave Me I have given them, that they may be one just as We are one: 23 I in them, and You in Me; that they may be made perfect in one, and that the world may know that You have sent Me, and have loved them as You have loved Me. NKJV

Jesus prayed for us today, that we would believe in Him through the Words of His disciples (verse 20 above). Therefore, if we trust Jesus, we would believe not only His Words, spoken through His disciples, but we would also believe His disciples.

Even the Gospels of Matthew, Mark, Luke, and John were written by disciples as they were moved by the Holy Spirit.

2 Peter 1:20-21
20 knowing this first, that no prophecy of Scripture is of any private interpretation, 21 for prophecy never came by the will of man, but holy men of God spoke as they were moved by the Holy Spirit. NKJV

2 Timothy 3:16-17
16 All Scripture is given by inspiration of God, and is profitable for doctrine, for reproof, for correction, for instruction in righteousness, 17 that the man of God may be complete, thoroughly equipped for every good work. NKJV

How can we become Christians without believing the Word spoken by disciples of Jesus Christ? We can't. We use Romans chapter ten, written by the Apostle Paul, to get people saved. Was he a disciple? Yes. Was Peter a disciple of Jesus? Yes! Was James a disciple? Yes!

Therefore, when people say that they only believe the Words spoken by Jesus, what they are actually saying is that they believe the disciples who wrote what Jesus spoke. By their testimony, they believe that God spoke through disciples, but again they simply reject the parts that they do not like, which shows that their problem is unbelief.

Therefore, when someone says, "I trust in Jesus Christ and Him alone," in such a way as to say that it is okay to reject God's Word spoken by other disciples of Jesus Christ, then you should recognize that for what it really is; an excuse to reject God's Word. In situations like this, many end up following talented speakers, who are actually deceivers rather than preachers of the Gospel (Acts 20:29-32).

Things that sound spiritual may indeed be spiritual, since in the last days many will follow deceiving spirits and the doctrines of demons according to 1 Timothy 4:1-2 below. However, even though something seems to be spiritual, it doesn't mean that it is godly.

1 Timothy 4:1-2

1 Now the Spirit expressly says that in latter times some will depart from the faith, giving heed to deceiving spirits and doctrines of demons, 2 speaking lies in hypocrisy, having their own conscience seared with a hot iron, NKJV

Many today follow deceiving spirits, and the doctrines of demons (evil spirits). I don't mean to shock you, but you need to know the truth.

Get this. We cannot be right with God, and not believe God. There is no such thing as a righteous person who does not believe God's Word. Abraham believed God and it was counted to him as righteousness (Romans 4:3); right standing with God. The same is true for us (Romans 4:20-24).

Concerning the Christian life, there are a few things that are not optional, and I'm not talking about before we get saved, but after. We must believe Jesus, hear God's Word, and follow Jesus.

John 3:36

36 He who believes in the Son has everlasting life; and he who does not believe the Son shall not see life, but the wrath of God abides on him." NKJV

Find me a Christian who does not believe Jesus, and I will show you someone who doesn't have eternal life abiding in him. Believing in Jesus includes believing the Words that He spoke (verse 24 below).

John 5:24

24 "Most assuredly, I say to you, he who hears My word and believes in Him who sent Me has everlasting life, and shall not come into judgment, but has passed from death into life. NKJV

Therefore, show me someone who rejects John 17:19-23 above, and I will show you someone who needs to repent ASAP. Those who belong to God, hear God's Word.

John 8:47

47 He who is of God hears God's words; therefore you do not hear, because you are not of God." NKJV

Show me someone who refuses to hear God's Word, and I will show you someone who does not belong to God. It's just that simple. Now, do you see how easy it would be to spot an unbeliever, if we knew the verses?

Satan's ministers transform themselves into ministers of righteousness according to 2 Corinthians 11:14-15. Therefore, the only way to recognize them is by their fruit, which includes their words (Matthew 7:16-20). The one thing that they will never be able to do is to continually speak in accordance with the doctrine of Jesus Christ, written in the Bible.

Matthew 12:34-35
34 Brood of vipers! How can you, being evil, speak good things? For out of the abundance of the heart the mouth speaks. 35 A good man out of the good treasure of his heart brings forth good things, and an evil man out of the evil treasure brings forth evil things. NKJV

Jesus said that whoever did not believe Him, would not have His Word abiding (remaining) in them (verse 38 below). A sure sign of those who do not believe Jesus is that they will not have His doctrine living in them, and consequently, they cannot possibly speak in-line with His teachings.

John 5:38
38 But you do not have His word abiding in you, because whom He sent, Him you do not believe. NKJV

Those who do not accept and believe the doctrine of Jesus Christ, will not have the Word abiding in them, and they shall not see life, but those who hear His Words, have everlasting life. Those who belong to God, hear God's Words spoken through Jesus (John 12:49), and they follow Him.

The sheep that belong to Jesus, hear His voice, and follow Him (verse 27 below). They shall never be snatched out of Jesus' hand.

John 10:26-28
26 But you do not believe, because you are not of My sheep, as I said to you. 27 My sheep hear My voice, and I know them, and they follow Me. 28 And I give them eternal life, and they shall never perish; neither shall anyone snatch them out of My hand. NKJV

If we only hear verse 28 (above) without the verses that come before it , then this passage of scripture would mean something totally different than what it says.

The disciples that cannot be snatched out of Jesus' hands, hear Him, and follow Him (verse 27 above). Can we refuse to hear Jesus' Words, and stop following Him, but still claim what is promised in verse 28 above? No, we cannot.

Some might say that they are saved, and we are. Praise God! However, according to John chapter 6, many of Jesus' disciples stopped following Him after He taught them something that they did not like, and so it is today. Many accept Jesus because they do not want to burn in hell, but later reject Him after they hear His teachings (verse 66 below).

John 6:60-66
60 Therefore many of His disciples, when they heard this, said, "This is a hard saying; who can understand it?" 61 When Jesus knew in Himself that His disciples complained about this, He said to them, "Does this offend you? 62 What then if you should see the Son of Man ascend where He was before? 63 It is the Spirit who gives life; the flesh profits nothing. The words that I speak to you are spirit, and they are life. 64 But there are some of you who do not believe." For Jesus knew from the beginning who they were who did not believe, and who would betray Him. 65 And He said, "Therefore I have said to you that no one can come to Me unless it has been granted to him by My Father." 66 From that time many of His disciples went back and walked with Him no more. NKJV

Christians who reject Jesus' teachings today do not necessarily stop attending weekly church services, but they simply seek out a message that fits their beliefs. That's not a surprise, since it is predicted that in the last days, people will turn away from sound doctrine, and turn aside toward teachers who willingly tell them what they want to hear (2 Timothy 4:3-4).

2 Timothy 4:3-4
3 For the time will come when they will not endure sound doctrine, but according to their own desires, because they have itching ears, they will heap up for themselves teachers; 4 and they will turn their ears away from the truth, and be turned aside to fables. NKJV

People who reject certain verses in their Bible, turn to teachers who never mention those verses. However, God's people are destroyed for lack of knowledge (Hosea 4:6), and not because we aren't attending church services.

Therefore, never follow someone who only tells people what they want to hear, in keeping with 2 Timothy 4:3-4 above, since that could very well be the reason why your faith is not working.

Teachers who tell people what they want to hear, leave out anything that doesn't sound good to them, or that doesn't get the crowd going, which reveals their desires; more people. Consequently, there may be hundreds of verses written in the Bible that the unsuspecting listeners never learn, which means that they are never free from the destruction caused by their lack of knowledge.

That's the tradeoff. The desire for more people can lead to a lack of knowledge due to avoiding the truth, and avoiding the truth, will lead to a life full of destruction.

Now what

Take a good look at your surroundings to make sure that you are amongst believers, and not unbelievers. I'm not telling you to change churches, but by making a judgment call in accordance with the truth (1 Corinthians 2:15), you may need to spend more time worshiping God in your closet, in order that your faith will work like it should.

On the other hand, it's not good to reject parts of the Bible, and at the same time, receive the teachings of men who speak against what is written in God's Word (1 Corinthians 4:6, John 5:43-44, Acts 20:29-32).

John 5:43-44
43 I have come in My Father's name, and you do not receive Me; if another comes in his own name, him you will receive. 44 How can you believe, who receive honor from one another, and do not seek the honor that comes from the only God? NKJV

Know that, because we can't live by part of the truth, and reject the rest. Trust what is written in the Bible, and test everything you hear to make sure that it is in-line with it (1 Thessalonians 5:21, 2 Corinthians 10:3-5).

Take God at His Word. Hearing God's Word is evidence that we belong to God (John 8:47). Rejecting God's Word is evidence of the opposite.

Don't live under peer pressure, but by faith. It's far better to gather with one believer than a church full of unbelievers, and doubters, and wherever two or three gather, there you have a church (Matthew 18:20). Therefore, your faith in what God has said in His Word will lead you to achieve better results away from a crowd of people who do not want to hear it.

People who believe in Jesus Christ come out of darkness (verse 46 below), rather than distort the truth, in order to make it sound as if grace can be used as a license for sinning (Jude 1:4). This is another sign that you are among those who believe every Word of God.

John 12:46
46 I have come as a light into the world, that whoever believes in Me should not abide in darkness. NKJV

I used to gather in a place that welcomed practicing prostitutes, and the like. Don't misunderstand me here because I'm not saying that I am any better than the worst sinner in the world.

However, when the Word of God is avoided and rejected, that means that people who need to change, never change. In this way, grace is simply received in vain, and the people never learn righteousness (Isaiah 26:10).

2 Corinthians 6:1-2
1 We then, as workers together with Him also plead with you

not to receive the grace of God in vain. 2 For He says: "In an acceptable time I have heard you, And in the day of salvation I have helped you. NKJV

When Christians are taught that they can avoid and reject the truth, then even church gatherings can become a place to simply hang out, which is exactly what I experienced. However, a church gathering was never intended to be that way.

If you are trying to change your habits, the last place you need to gather is in a crowd of people who condone what you are trying to change, regardless if they are singing their hearts out to God. Contrary to popular belief, we can't sing our way into stopping sin from controlling us. No, somebody is going to have to preach the Word of God (John 17:17, 8:31-37).

2 Thessalonians 3:6
6 But we command you, brethren, in the name of our Lord Jesus Christ, that you withdraw from every brother who walks disorderly and not according to the tradition which he received from us. NKJV

2 Thessalonians 3:14-15
14 And if anyone does not obey our word in this epistle, note that person and do not keep company with him, that he may be ashamed. 15 Yet do not count him as an enemy, but admonish him as a brother. NKJV

If we followed God's instructions written above, what would we need to change about ourself? We could use philosophy, or human wisdom to say that we are all sinners in the same boat, and that may be true, but God looks at it differently.

God doesn't want us to keep company with Christians who are headed in the wrong direction. How can we tell who is headed in the wrong direction? When we reach a point where the Word of God cannot even be mentioned to admonish (warn) a brother who has taken the wrong path, in accordance with verse 15 above, then surely we are among those in whom we are to avoid.

What if you are on the list of people that should be avoided? That's one of the reasons why I am writing this book; to help you. I will explain what you need to do in order to come out of darkness, stop sinning, and position yourself to never stumble again; verses included.

However, know that our sinfulness does not change the message, and that's what is wrong with the church today. The message is changing in order to fill the building. We all need God's help to stop sinning, but how can we receive God's help if we reject God's ways?

Think about this. We all need more of something that only God can give us; grace. Therefore, it's not a good idea to disrespect His Word. We gain access into grace by faith (Romans 5:2). No faith, means no more grace (ability).

Some people actually believe that we can take a stand against God's Word, and He will still answer our cry for help in our time of need, but that is far from the truth according to Proverbs 1:22-33. Let us repent and return to the Lord our God.

Father, in Jesus' name, it's only because of Your mercy that we are still here. Forgive us for our great transgressions. Have mercy on us, as You have in the past, and wash our sins away with the blood of Jesus Christ our Lord. Amen.

Can light have any fellowship with darkness? Unbelievers have no fellowship with believers (2 Corinthians 6:14-18), just as people who walk in the light have no fellowship with those who remain in darkness (1 John 1:5-7). Don't reject God's ways, but simply repent of the past.

1 John 1:5-7
5 This is the message which we have heard from Him and declare to you, that God is light and in Him is no darkness at all. 6 If we say that we have fellowship with Him, and walk in darkness, we lie and do not practice the truth. 7 But if we walk in the light as He is in the light, we have fellowship with one another, and the blood of Jesus Christ His Son cleanses us from all sin. NKJV

If we walk in the light, we have fellowship with God, and one another, and the blood of Jesus Christ cleanses us from all sin (verse 7 above). However, those who walk in darkness do not practice the truth (verse 6 above), and need to confess their sins in order to be forgiven, according to 1 John 1:9. That's a big difference.

Keeping company with people who walk in darkness, and do not believe what is written in the Bible will only serve to hinder you (1 Corinthians 15:33-34 below). A righteous person is very cautious in friendships (Proverbs 12:26 below).

1 Corinthians 15:33-34
33 Do not be deceived: "Evil company corrupts good habits." 34 Awake to righteousness, and do not sin; for some do not have the knowledge of God. I speak this to your shame. NKJV

Proverbs 12:26
26 The righteous should choose his friends carefully, For the way of the wicked leads them astray. NKJV

As we have already learned according to John 12:46 above, believers come out of darkness. That's the biggest difference between those who believe every Word of God, and those who reject bits and pieces of it, and many never seem to put two and two together. We will not have the intended results, until we accept the method, or path that we are supposed to take. Only believers come out of darkness.

The truth sanctifies us (John 17:17). We cannot reject the truth, and be holy (sanctified) in our conduct at the same time. Therefore, we should expect an unbeliever to be caught up in all kinds of sins. In fact, we should be totally shocked to find a Christian who rejects different parts of the Bible, who is able to keep his sin from ruling over him. If we could possibly sanctify ourself, why would we need Jesus?

Some will ask, "How are we supposed to help people who are given over to sin's control if we don't gather with them?" It doesn't say that we cannot minister (help) to them. I'm writing this book to help people who are controlled by sins. The Word of God changed me, and therefore, I know it will change even the worst of sinners out there.

It says that evil company will have an adverse effect on our habits, and we need to be aware of that. In other words, keeping company with people who walk in darkness will eventually change our conduct for the worse.

If they are repenting of their sins, and not avoiding the pure Word of God, fine, but the absolute worse place to try and stop sinning is in a group of Christians who do not believe that Christians can stop sinning. That would be disregarding God's advice, and rejecting His ways.

Church was never intended to be a place where sinners could continue in sins that lead to death. The instructions above say to withdraw from every "brother" who does not walk (live) according to the traditions he received (2 Thessalonians 3:6 above), and do not keep company with anyone named a brother, who does not obey the Word in that letter (epistle, 2 Thessalonians 3:14 above).

That may be a shock to you, but I'm sure that we will cover many things that you have never heard before, which is very common with the people I have worked with in the past. The little things that we deem insignificant, are the very things that give us over to the bigger things (Romans 6:16).

In other words, the things that we can do something about, but we ignore due to peer pressure, or our feelings, are the things that place us under the control of sins that we cannot do anything about. Ironically, we focus on the sins that we are given over to, and we call them addictions (uncontrollable desires), but we never focus on the sins that can stop this process.

All sin entangles us, or it ensnares us (Hebrews 12:1). Every little sin has some type of effect on our life. We can be forgiven, but we still reap what we have sown (Galatians 6:7-10). Therefore, don't worry about the sins that you cannot do anything about until you stop the sins that you can control.

I never tell an alcoholic to stop drinking because drinking is not his problem. The sins that have given him over to alcohol is his problem, and once we stick him in a group that only focuses on the alcohol, he may never learn the truth. There is not a different method in the Bible for every type of sin.

No, the same method that will deliver a person caught up in sexual sins, is the same method that will deliver someone who abuses drugs, or who is in need of healing. Separating people by the sins they are given over to, is a death trap, because they never learn how to be set free from sin (Romans 6:1-22).

The only solution is to take God at His Word, accepting His advice, His counsel, and His ways, and then He will help you (Proverbs 1:22-33, 3:5, Romans 5:2), but if you reject God's advice, He will reject your cry for help (Proverbs 1:22-33).

Most people experience healing in their body while learning these things, even in the comfort of their own home. Praise the Lord God almighty. I will even answer any questions you may have along the way through email, Lord willing, but I will not argue with unbelievers.

If this book does not work for you, it will be because you do not accept and believe the verses I will show you, or you are unwilling to do what they say to do. We're going to be reading a great amount of scripture in this book, and I'm going to expect you to believe those verses, just like they are written.

Everything that I tell you will be backed up with a verse or two. You don't have to believe me, but believe the verses, even without understanding them (Proverbs 3:5), and read them out loud (Romans 10:17).

I can only use one-thousand verses from the New King James Version of the Bible, by permission from the publisher, in this one book. Therefore, I have added some verses from the King James Version.

Like so many, you may have come to believe something different. Set your beliefs aside while you are reading this book, and simply take God at His Word. Believe the verses, just as Abraham believed and you will experience the results that God has promised. Then you will know that many today forfeit the best that God has to give us, simply because they refuse to accept and believe His Word.

Father, in Jesus' name, we love You, and we thank You for Your Word. Enable us to receive it, and make it grow on the inside of us, that it may change us from the inside out. Forgive us for the sins that we have committed against You, and wash our conscience clean with the blood of Jesus that we may serve You with a clear conscience. For You alone are worthy of all the praise, glory, and honor forever and ever. Amen.

I'm Alan Ballou; a servant. My wife Lucie and I serve God's people free of charge. If we may be of service to you, please contact us.

www.HowToStopSinning.com

୫୬୯୧

GOD HAS GIVEN US EVERYTHING WE
NEED TO SUSTAIN LIFE, AND TO BE
GOD-LIKE HERE ON EARTH, BUT WE CAN ONLY
RECEIVE WHAT HE HAS GIVEN US, AS WE
COME TO KNOW HIM THROUGH HIS WORD,
AND PARTICIPATE IN HIS PROMISES.

Alan Ballou

3

His Promises

ഇൽരു

God is able to do far above all that we would ever ask or even think, according to His power that is at work "in us." God is able. Nothing is too hard for Him.

your *you* *you*

Ephesians 3:20
20 Now to Him who is able to do exceedingly abundantly above all that we ask or think, according to the power that works in us NKJV

God's power works through believers; that's His power at work "in us" (verse 20 above). Our faith should be in what God can do through His power, and not in man's wisdom (1 Corinthians 2:4-5). The Kingdom of God is not about talk, but about power (1 Corinthians 4:20).

God's way begins with believing what He has said, and then using His promises to receive what He has already given us.

2 Peter 1:3-4
3 as His divine power has given to us all things that pertain to life and godliness, through the knowledge of Him who called us by glory and virtue, 4 by which have been given to us exceedingly great and precious promises, that through these you may be partakers of the divine nature, having escaped the corruption that is in the world through lust. NKJV

Let this sink in. God has already given us everything we would ever need for this life, and it comes through our knowledge of Him (verse 3 above). That means that we need to know God in accordance with His Word, in order to receive what He has given us.

We participate in the divine (heavenly) nature through the promises (verse 4 above). It is through God's promises that we will receive what He has already given us pertaining to this life and godliness.

To sum all that up we would say, God has given us everything we need to sustain life, and to be God-like here on earth, but we can only receive what He has given us, as we come to know Him through His Word, and participate in His promises.

Therefore, our problems never stem from God's lack of ability, His lack of power, or His lack of providing what we need, but from our unwillingness to use God's power, God's way. Therefore, we need to learn how to use God's promises, and how to use them in such a way as to receive the things that He has already given us. That is what this chapter is about.

Absolutely nothing is too difficult for God. He can heal who He wants to heal, when He wants to heal them, but not everyone receives healing. Why? God can deliver who He wants to deliver, when He wants to, but not everyone is delivered. Why is that? God can feed and clothe who He wants to, but people are still starving to death.

God's people are destroyed for lack of knowledge (Hosea 4:6). Therefore, being God's people, we know upfront that the reason we experience destruction in our life, is because we don't know what we should know, and not because God cannot heal us, deliver us, feed us, clothe us, provide our needs, or even keep us from sinning.

Can any of us say that we have wholeheartedly followed the promises written in the Bible concerning healing, deliverance, or whatever else, but they did not work? No, we cannot, and all we mainly focus on is how big our problems are. We're sick. We've made a mess of things again. We have a drug problem, or an alcohol problem, or this condition, or that condition.

We hardly ever talk about the promises, and spiritual principles that we should follow in order to receive what we need by faith. God has finished His work concerning what we need for this life, and He is expecting us to use His power through His promises in order to receive what He has given us.

The whole Christian life is lived by faith from start to finish (Romans 1:17), and God gave us the faith that we needed to start with as a gift (verse 8 below). Therefore, God has already given us what we need to use in order to receive everything we need for this life. We need to learn how to use it.

Ephesians 2:8
8 For by grace you have been saved through faith, and that not of yourselves; it is the gift of God, NKJV

Romans 12:3
3 For I say, through the grace given to me, to everyone who is among you, not to think of himself more highly than he ought to think, but to think soberly, as God has dealt to each one a measure of faith. NKJV

Faith is the reason for our hope, or our assured hope combined with the evidence of things not seen (verse 1 below). Our responsibility is to use our faith, or to mix the faith that we have been given with God's Word.

Hebrews 11:1
1 Now faith is the substance of things hoped for, the evidence of things not seen. NKJV

Just as believing makes all things possible (Mark 9:23), mixing faith with what is promised will make it materialize (Hebrews 4:2 below). We even have to mix faith with the Gospel, or it will not profit us (verse 2 below).

Hebrews 4:2
2 For indeed the gospel was preached to us as well as to them; but the word which they heard did not profit them, not being mixed with faith in those who heard it. NKJV

Many people hear the Word, but few mix faith with what they hear. In other words, now that we believe as Abraham believed, we are going to act upon what we read in God's Word, accepting it as unquestionable truth (Luke 3:8-9, Acts 26:20, James 2:17).

For example, God has already given us, all the food, clothing, and shelter that we would ever need, but why doesn't every Christian in the world have daily necessities? Could it be that we focus on the problem, rather than focusing on the promise that can solve the problem?

Matthew 6:30-34
30 Now if God so clothes the grass of the field, which today is, and tomorrow is thrown into the oven, will He not much more clothe you, O you of little faith? 31 "Therefore do not worry, saying, 'What shall we eat?' or 'What shall we drink?' or 'What shall we wear?' 32 For after all these things the Gentiles seek. For your heavenly Father knows that you need all these things. 33 But seek first the kingdom of God and His righteousness, and all these things shall be added to you. 34 Therefore do not worry about tomorrow, for tomorrow will worry about its own things. Sufficient for the day is its own trouble. NKJV

We have to receive that by faith. If we were to mix faith with the passage of scripture above, we would seek God's Kingdom and His righteousness first place in our life and all the things we might have a tendency to worry about will be given to us (verse 33 above).

If our hope is to receive what is promised, then we will receive it according to the written evidence, which is unseen. That's faith. Faith is our assured hope in the written evidence (Hebrews 11:1).

For example, I know that God is able to give me the things that I worry about if He wanted to (belief), but I also know that if I would seek God's Kingdom and His righteousness first place in my life, according to the evidence written in Matthew 6:30-34 above, then He would make sure that I had everything that I might have a tendency to worry about.

In fact, I am sure that if I follow the instructions written in Matthew 6:33 above, I would receive what is promised. That's faith; the assurance of things hoped for, the evidence of things not seen (Hebrews 11:1 above).

That's the difference between believing, and the hearing with faith. We have to believe what God has promised in His Word in order to use faith to receive it, but it is possible to believe Matthew 6:30-34 (above), and never seek God's Kingdom and His righteousness first place in our life.

It's one thing to believe Matthew 6:30-34 above, but it is another to believe, and mix faith with it. If we decided to mix faith with those verses, we would "seek first the Kingdom of God and His righteousness." Doing that would make what is promised materialize.

I have worked with many Christians who had a belief problem. Actually, most of us don't necessarily have a problem believing, but we believe everything we are told, even if it is against what is actually written in the Bible. Once we get what we believe, in-line with what God has said, then the next hurdle to overcome is to mix faith with what we believe. In other words, now that we believe as Abraham believed, we are going to mix faith with everything we believe.

I know plenty of people who feed the homeless, and praise God for that, since that is a part of what Christians should be doing. Love your neighbor as you love yourself (Romans 13:8-10). However, if we could teach homeless people to believe as Abraham believed, and how to live by faith, God would feed them through their faith.

God has already set aside every meal that they would ever need in their lifetime. However, they will not receive it for themselves through faith, if they never learn to live by faith.

Now, imagine teaching people in Third World countries how to live by faith in order to solve their problems. Would there be a food shortage in the world? My God fed a nation in the desert for forty years, and His arm has not been shortened. Praise God, halleluiah!

Can we trust Him? If we can trust Him, then we need to teach others to place their hope in Him. Amen.

Father, in Jesus' name, have mercy on us. We are full of all kinds of teachings that are based on man's wisdom. Help us to sort through what we believe in our heart, and rid ourselves of anything that is not according to Your Word. Teach us through the power of Your Holy Spirit, that we may know You according to Your Word, and walk in Your ways, that we may receive the things we need for this life. You alone are able, and You alone are worthy of praise. Amen.

Again, can anyone say that they have wholeheartedly followed His promises, but they did not work? Nope. No one can testify that God is a liar.

In the same way, I know God can heal me if He wanted to (belief), but I also know that if I die to sins and live for righteousness, He "will" heal me (faith). Knowing God can, and knowing God will is two different things.

1 Peter 2:24-25
24 who Himself bore our sins in His own body on the tree, that we, having died to sins, might live for righteousness — by whose stripes you were healed. 25 For you were like sheep going astray, but have now returned to the Shepherd and Overseer of your souls. NKJV

Some people declare "By His stripes, so and so is healed" all the way to the funeral, and the Lord may have compassion on some people depending on what they have heard (Hosea 7:12), or when He sees that their power (strength) is gone (Deuteronomy 32:36). However, only a few mix faith with His promises, and then receive a guaranteed outcome.

Don't get me wrong, since God does heal backsliders from time to time (Isaiah 57:14-21), but once our sinful nature is fully grown, it will put us to death (James 1:15). It is far better to die with Christ, and to live by faith before we need healing, since then the Spirit will give life to our body (verses 10-11 below).

Galatians 2:20
20 I have been crucified with Christ; it is no longer I who live, but Christ lives in me; and the life which I now live in the flesh I live by faith in the Son of God, who loved me and gave Himself for me. NKJV

Romans 8:10-11
10 And if Christ be in you, the body is dead because of sin; but the Spirit is life because of righteousness. 11 But if the Spirit of him that raised up Jesus from the dead dwell in you, he that raised up Christ from the dead shall also quicken your mortal bodies by his Spirit that dwelleth in you. KJV

Therefore, why not repent of the past, die to sins, live for righteousness, and be healed (John 5:14, James 5:14-16)? Those who keep Jesus' Word will never see death, so why not be healed by faith?

John 8:51
51 Verily, verily, I say unto you, If a man keep my saying, he shall never see death. KJV

What an awesome promise! Praise the Lord, oh my soul! Do you believe that? If not, then don't worry about receiving it.

Now what

Many people say, "I know God can" in such a way as if to say, "But will He?" They believe God is able, but there is no faith in what they are saying.

Yes, God can do anything He wants to do, but His work concerning what we need for life and godliness here on earth is finished. We will receive what we need through faith. Our faith is what needs to grow, and be perfected (2 Timothy 2:22, 1 Timothy 6:11, Hebrews 12:2, James 1:2-4, 1 Peter 1:6-7).

Therefore, whether God is able to deliver what He has promised is not the question. The question is, do we believe, do we trust Him, and are we willing to learn to use His promises in order to receive what He has given us? That's God's power, God's way.

Whenever I teach a new group of people, I always ask them to name the promises that they are living by. Very few can name even one promise, and that is the reason why many are still tangled up in the corruption of the world (2 Peter 1:4). Let's put two and two together and associate one with the other.

Imagine Christians trying to stop sinning without knowing a single promise to mix faith with, in order to help them stop sinning. We will cover many promises throughout this book that can and should be used to control sin, and promote healing in our life. Learn them as you go, believe them as Abraham believed, and mix faith with them in order to receive what is promised.

Kingdom teaching is found in the New Testament (Luke 16:16), and God's righteousness is also revealed in our new agreement with God (Romans 1:16-17). Therefore, if you decide today to receive the things you need for life and godliness from God, read the New Testament out loud, every day. Seek these things first place in your life and God will do His part.

May the Lord bless you and keep you, in Jesus' name. Amen.

I'm Alan Ballou; a servant. My wife Lucie and I serve God's people free of charge. If we may be of service to you, please contact us.

www.HowToStopSinning.com

Alan's email alan@howtostopsinning.com

Lucie's email lucie@howtostopsinning.com

℘℘℘

4

Obedience from Faith

Y ou know the story of Noah and the Ark, since you've heard it a thousand times. Now look at it with your eyes of faith to see if you can tell what happened behind the scenes. Faith is our assured hope, combined with the evidence of things not seen (Hebrews 11:1).

Hebrews 11:7
7 By faith Noah, being divinely warned of things not yet seen, moved with godly fear, prepared an ark for the saving of his household, by which he condemned the world and became heir of the righteousness which is according to faith. NKJV

Noah's belief in what God told him made him spring into action. God told him what was going to happen, and what he needed to do in order to save his family. Noah's hope was to save his family, and he was going to achieve that by following the instructions; build the ark.

God not only told Noah that a flood was coming, but He also told him how to build the ark so that he would survive the flood. Therefore, the instructions were also a part of the evidence of things not seen (faith).

God didn't build the ark for Noah, but He told him exactly what he needed to do. In the same way, God is not going to do our part, but He has left us specific instructions pertaining to all areas of life. We can certainly choose to ignore those instructions, or substitute them with something else, which is a very common mistake.

For example, instead of seeking God's Kingdom and His righteousness first place in our life in order to receive the things we worry about, we can pray, sing halleluiah, fast for 40 days, beat our chest, blow a horn, and march around the church seventy times, but until we seek God's Kingdom and His righteousness we will be filled with anxiety, and not have the things we need for this life, or godliness.

There is no such thing as a Christian who has everything that he might worry about, if he does not seek God's Kingdom, and God's righteousness first place in his life. In the same way, there is no such thing as a godly person, who does not have time to put God first.

Worrying and godliness are directly connected to how much time we spend seeking God through His Word. Think about that.

Noah obeyed his instructions, and received what he hoped for, which was to save his family. In the same way, we can obey the instructions and receive what is promised to us, concerning sin, healing, provisions, deliverance, and so on.

In this way, obedience comes from faith (Romans 1:5). Noah's faith in God, made him obey God, just as our faith in Jesus Christ will make us obey Him.

Genesis 6:22
22 Thus Noah did; according to all that God commanded him, so he did. NKJV

Take Matthew 6:14-15 as an example. Christians who believe in Jesus Christ also forgive everyone, because just as faith in God made Noah build a boat, faith in Jesus will make us forgive people.

Matthew 6:14-15
14 "For if you forgive men their trespasses, your heavenly Father will also forgive you. 15 But if you do not forgive men their trespasses, neither will your Father forgive your trespasses. NKJV

The same type of faith that made Noah build the ark, after believing what God had said, is the same type of faith that will make us forgive everyone, in accordance with what Jesus said, if we believe Him.

There is a difference between hearing and believing, and hearing with faith. Hearing with faith makes believers spring into action. After reading Matthew 6:14-15 above, believers, who live by faith in Jesus Christ, will forgive everyone. Therefore, living by faith in Jesus will make us obey Jesus.

In this way, we don't just call Jesus Lord, but we allow Him to be the Lord over our life (2 Timothy 2:19).

Luke 6:46
46 "But why do you call Me 'Lord, Lord,' and not do the things which I say? NKJV

By saying, "Why do you call Me Lord and not do the things that I say," Jesus is clearly expecting those who call Him Lord to allow Him to be their Lord.

Many people believe that Jesus Christ exists, but few believe in Him to the point of allowing Him to tell them what to do. Calling Jesus Lord is one thing, but believing in Him, or trusting Him will make us place faith in the things that He has said, which in turn will lead to obedience.

Everything we need for this life, and godliness has already been given to us, including the ability to stop sinning. What would happen if we placed faith in a few promises that work to control sin? Would we all obey?

Proverbs 3:5-6
5 Trust in the Lord with all your heart, And lean not on your own understanding; 6 In all your ways acknowledge Him, And He shall direct your paths. NKJV

Will those who do not trust in the Lord with all their heart, and acknowledge him in all their ways have their paths directed by the Lord? They would if they placed faith in that passage of scripture. Consequently, what would happen if all Christians lived by faith? Wouldn't they all have their paths directed by the Lord?

We have to trust Him, and acknowledge Him, even without understanding everything, and then He will direct our paths. In order to follow God's instructions contained in His Word without understanding everything, we must take Him at His Word.

That's why the first thing we covered in the book was believing as Abraham believed. I know that many people do not always start reading books with the first chapter, but if we do not believe as Abraham believed, nothing will work out for us.

Like Abraham, we have to take God at His Word, and then we have to mix faith with the promises that are associated with our particular situation. Like Noah, we have to get the instructions right, and then receive our hope.

Read the following passage of scripture as another example of promises that work to control sin in our life.

1 John 3:6-9
6 Whoever abides in Him does not sin. Whoever sins has neither seen Him nor known Him. 7 Little children, let no one deceive you. He who practices righteousness is righteous, just as He is righteous. 8 He who sins is of the devil, for the devil has sinned from the beginning. For this purpose the Son of God was manifested, that He might destroy the works of the devil. 9 Whoever has been born of God does not sin, for His seed remains in him; and he cannot sin, because he has been born of God. NKJV

Whoever abides in Jesus does not sin (verse 6 above). It only takes about thirty minutes to teach a new convert to abide in Jesus, so why is the church full of people who do not know how to abide in Jesus?

I don't mean to be hurtful, but at some point in this book, you will realize that God has already given us what we need to stop sinning, and be healed, but we got off track somewhere. One of the first things we ought to learn as Christians should be abiding in Jesus, but that is not exactly what happens this day and age (John 15:1-17, 14:21-23).

What happened? We got saved, baptized, and then we were told that we would never be able to completely stop sinning, which is in direct opposition to "Trust in the Lord with all your heart, and lean not on your own understanding." Right at the start of our Christian walk of faith, we were taught to distrust the Lord, Who is the Word made flesh (John 1:14). Imagine that.

My friend, Jesus came to destroy the devil's work in us (verse 8 above), and not so that we could use grace as a license to continue in sin (Jude 1:4). It's time to repent and start over.

Father, in the name of Jesus Christ, have mercy upon us. Forgive us for not trusting in our Lord Jesus. Forgive us for not taking You at Your Word, or relying on Your power to deliver us from sin. We have even taken a stand against the things You have said. O' Lord, have mercy upon us and forgive us of this great transgression. Wash us clean with the blood of Christ, that we may now walk in Your ways, and use Your power to deliver us from our sins through what You have promised. Amen!

The things we have covered so far are very basic, but many Christians do not have these verses living in them because they have rejected them (Mark 4:24-25), or they speak against them (1 Timothy 6:20-21).

If you are like me, then you didn't necessarily reject the truth, but you never heard it because it was not taught. Be careful not to reject it now that you can see it, since there is no guarantee that you will ever be able to see it again, once you reject it.

It is far better to say that we have not stopped sinning rather than testifying that we cannot stop sinning according to God's Word. Those who speak in opposition to God's Word cannot possibly have God's Word living in them (1 Timothy 6:20-21, Mark 4:24-25, John 5:38).

Does anyone ever testify that they have wholeheartedly followed the promises written in the Bible concerning sin, but they did not work? No, we never hear anyone say that, but what we hear is, "I've got this sin problem," or that sin problem, and after being given over, what we hear is, "I've got an addiction," I'm an alcoholic," "I am gay," I'm bipolar, or I can't stop doing this or that.

Get this. We stumble because we disobey the message (1 Peter 2:8). The Bible explains in detail how to stop sinning in several places, and in several different ways, which we will be covering throughout this book. Obeying the message will keep us from stumbling (2 Peter 1:10-11).

If Christians could "not" stop sinning, why are we instructed to withdraw from the ones who continue in certain sins? Needing help is one thing, but to take a direct stand against God's Word is something else. We cannot rely on God's promises to stop sinning, and at the same time testify that His Word is not true.

1 Corinthians 5:9-13
**9 I wrote to you in my epistle not to keep company with sex-
ually immoral people. 10 Yet I certainly did not mean with the
sexually immoral people of this world, or with the covetous,
or extortioners, or idolaters, since then you would need to go
out of the world. 11 But now I have written to you not to keep
company with anyone named a brother, who is sexually immoral, or covetous, or an idolater, or a reviler, or a drunkard, or an
extortioner — not even to eat with such a person. 12 For what
have I to do with judging those also who are outside? Do you
not judge those who are inside? 13 But those who are outside
God judges. Therefore "put away from yourselves the evil person." NKJV**

Christians are instructed not to keep company with anyone named a brother
who is caught up in these sins, and this isn't the only list (Ephesians 5:3-7). Some
will be quick to say that Jesus ate with sinners, but read verses 9 and 10 again.

It is the person who claims to be a brother, but is caught up in these sins
that we are instructed not to eat with. We don't judge those outside the church
(verses 12-13 above). Jesus ate with sinners in order to call them to repentance,
and that would not be any different today (Mark 2:17).

Do you need help? We all need help living the Christian life that we have
been called to live, and the Lord's arm is not too short to help us. Praise the Lord
God almighty.

However, some of us seek God's help in accordance with His Word and
receive it by faith, and some of us take a stand against God's Word, rejecting any
correction from it, and at the same time we proclaim that we can't do it. We can't
do it because we reject the method (process) that God has given us to do it with.

God says to stop eating with Christians, who are caught up in the sins listed
above (1 Corinthians 5:9-13 above). What if you are on that list? I'm going to
show you what to do, and I have already started showing you, but be careful not
to reject the message.

Start by repenting of the past, and begin following the instructions. Obedience will come if we place faith in the message, but if we reject the message we
will not be able to live the Christian life.

If you have tried to stop sinning, but you have never heard the verses that
we have covered so far, then you have not received the right message. Obedience
comes from faith, and not by following a man-made set of rules (Colossians
2:20-23).

The Lord knows how to deliver us from every temptation we may face so
that we will not follow our sinful nature, but He will "not" do that for those who
walk according to the flesh, those who despise authority, those who are self-
willed (stubborn, pig-headed), and those who are presumptuous (arrogant, rude,

disrespectful). If that describes you, begin with repentance.

2 Peter 2:9-10
9 then the Lord knows how to deliver the godly out of tempta-tions and to reserve the unjust under punishment for the day of judgment, 10 and especially those who walk according to the flesh in the lust of uncleanness and despise authority. They are presumptuous, self-willed. They are not afraid to speak evil of dignitaries NKJV

The Lord can deliver the godly out of temptations (verse 9 above), but He resists, or opposes the proud. That means that He will fight against those who walk according to the flesh, and who despise authority.

Now, will we trust in the Lord with all of our heart, acknowledging Him in all of our ways in order to receive His guidance and grace (ability), or will we reject Him? Contrary to popular belief, God only gives grace to the humble (James 4:6, 1 Peter 5:5), but the face of the Lord is against those who do evil. Therefore, be sure to repent.

1 Peter 3:12
12 For the eyes of the Lord are on the righteous, And His ears are open to their prayers; But the face of the Lord is against those who do evil." NKJV

Now what

The church was never intended to be a place where Christians, who continue in sins that lead to death, could hang out (1 Corinthians 5:9-13 above). It is supposed to be a place where people go to be delivered from sin, by continuing in their faith, but this day and age we are just getting people saved without teaching them how to live the Christian life.

We are assuming that God, Who began a good work in them, will carry it on to the day of completion (Philippians 1:6). That verse is true, but the people that the Apostle Paul was referring to, accepted the Gospel message (verse 5 below), and they were partakers with him in receiving grace, which was the confirmation that God's work had started in them (verse 7 below).

Philippians 1:3-7
3 I thank my God upon every remembrance of you, 4 always in every prayer of mine making request for you all with joy, 5 for your fellowship in the gospel from the first day until now, 6 be-ing confident of this very thing, that He who has begun a good work in you will complete it until the day of Jesus Christ; 7 just as it is right for me to think this of you all, because I have you in my heart, inasmuch as both in my chains and in the defense

and confirmation of the gospel, you all are partakers with me of grace. NKJV

When God enables a person to come to Jesus, they accept the Gospel (John 6:44), but a person who has only been man-enabled to come, does not accept the Word of God according to John 6:60-69, and John 8:47. If you believe every Word in the Bible, then surely God has enabled you to accept Jesus Christ, but if you cannot accept the verses we have covered so far, I would advise you to call on Jesus to save you.

Many people today accept part of the Gospel message that describes being saved, but afterwards they have little fellowship with the Gospel. How can I make such a statement? My friend, if we welcomed the Gospel with open arms, then every Christian in the world would know how to abide in Jesus, and if we abide in Jesus, we will not sin.

1 John 3:6
6 Whoever abides in Him does not sin. Whoever sins has neither seen Him nor known Him. NKJV.

According to the Word of God, our instructions are to not even greet the person who comes to us and does not bring the doctrine of abiding in Jesus (verse 10 below), but we have ignored those instructions long before I was born, and that is why the church is in the situation that it is in today.

2 John 9-11
9 Whoever transgresses and does not abide in the doctrine of Christ does not have God. He who abides in the doctrine of Christ has both the Father and the Son. 10 If anyone comes to you and does not bring this doctrine, do not receive him into your house nor greet him; 11 for he who greets him shares in his evil deeds. NKJV

Therefore, God may have enabled you to accept Jesus Christ, but you may not have ever heard the truth. Many are in this situation today because of peer pressure, and man-made traditions (1 Peter 1:18). Lack of knowledge is our fault, but God will have mercy on us if we return to Him in accordance with His ways.

If we do not abide in the doctrine of Jesus Christ, we do not have God (verse 9 above). This is why many of us cannot obtain God's help to stop sinning. We need to place our faith in God's instructions in order to receive what He has promised. Let us return to the Lord our God in accordance with His Word, and reject those who reject Him, unless they repent.

The instructions in 2 John 1:9-11 above, reveal to us just how important the doctrine of abiding in Christ is, which we can read for ourself in John 15:1-17. We need God's help to stop sinning, and therefore, we cannot sit in the seat of those who oppose Him (the scornful).

Psalm 1:1-3
1 Blessed is the man Who walks not in the counsel of the ungodly, Nor stands in the path of sinners, Nor sits in the seat of the scornful; 2 But his delight is in the law of the Lord, And in His law he meditates day and night. 3 He shall be like a tree Planted by the rivers of water, That brings forth its fruit in its season, Whose leaf also shall not wither; And whatever he does shall prosper. NKJV

If God has begun a good work in us, can we now oppose God and continue? We say the name "Jesus," and we call on Jesus, but if the doctrine of abiding in Jesus is not being taught, then we are not helping God's people in the way that God has instructed us. We may be saved, but unlike the Philippians, we have no fellowship with the message.

Get this. We will never be able to bear the right kind of fruit unless we abide (remain) in the vine; never. Obedience comes from faith. If we do not place our faith in the message, we will never be able to obey, and the church will be full of people who will never be able to stop sinning, or receive the healing that comes as a result of it.

We can try whatever man-made method we want to try, but until the church returns to the instructions we were given by our Lord Jesus, we will never have the right outcome. Apart from Jesus, we can do nothing (verse 5 below).

John 15:5-6
5 "I am the vine, you are the branches. He who abides in Me, and I in him, bears much fruit; for without Me you can do nothing. 6 If anyone does not abide in Me, he is cast out as a branch and is withered; and they gather them and throw them into the fire, and they are burned. NKJV

How do we abide in Jesus? We abide in Jesus by keeping His commands.

John 15:10
10 If you keep My commandments, you will abide in My love, just as I have kept My Father's commandments and abide in His love. NKJV

1 John 3:24
24 Now he who keeps His commandments abides in Him, and He in him. And by this we know that He abides in us, by the Spirit whom He has given us. NKJV

I don't believe that a new convert would conclude that he needed to obey Jesus, if all he was told was to "Go have a personal relationship" with Jesus. "Go have a personal relationship with Jesus" is not written in the Bible, but obeying Jesus is, and those who do not obey Him will not be able to do anything (John

15:5 above).

Many fall away from the faith a few months after they accept Jesus as Lord. I believe that it is because they are not taught the truth, but a delusional message. Actually, Jesus is ashamed of those who are not in the process of being sanctified; made holy (Hebrews 2:11).

If you cannot stop sinning, and you have never heard that we have to obey Jesus in order to bear the right type of fruit, then that is the first problem that needs to be resolved. Not only will that one thing solve many sin problems and bring health to the body of millions of Christians, but it will also save the souls of millions who believe that they are Heaven bound, even if they do not abide in Jesus according to John 15:6 above. Those who do not abide in the vine end up burning in the fire.

The Philippians, whom the Apostle Paul referred to in Philippians 1:3-7 above, were obedient, even in Paul's absence. They were abiding in the vine, and therefore, they were receiving God's help (2 John 1:9). They were following the instructions given to them, and consequently, God was working in them what was promised (verse 13 below).

Philippians 2:12-13
12 Therefore, my beloved, as you have always obeyed, not as in my presence only, but now much more in my absence, work out your own salvation with fear and trembling; 13 for it is God who works in you both to will and to do for His good pleasure. NKJV

That was evidence that the good work started in them, would continue until the end, but Philippians 1:6 cannot be used for those who reject God's Word. No, Jesus promised that if we did not abide in Him, God would indeed cut us off (verse 2 below).

That is a part of the doctrine of Jesus Christ, and that is a promise just like any other promise He made. Those who do not believe what Jesus Christ taught according to the verses below, cannot possibly have His doctrine living in them (John 5:38), and therefore, they easily accept and then proclaim false doctrines.

John 15:1-6
1 "I am the true vine, and My Father is the vinedresser. 2 Every branch in Me that does not bear fruit He takes away; and every branch that bears fruit He prunes, that it may bear more fruit. 3 You are already clean because of the word which I have spoken to you. 4 Abide in Me, and I in you. As the branch cannot bear fruit of itself, unless it abides in the vine, neither can you, unless you abide in Me. 5 "I am the vine, you are the branches. He who abides in Me, and I in him, bears much fruit; for without Me you can do nothing. 6 If anyone does not abide in Me, he is

cast out as a branch and is withered; and they gather them and throw them into the fire, and they are burned. NKJV

The promise made to the Philippians cannot be made to those who do not obey, since those who do not obey Jesus, do not abide in Jesus (John 15:10). If you did not know that before now, then repent of the past, and return to the Lord your God.

Notice in verse 4 above that a branch cannot bear fruit without abiding in Jesus, Who is the vine. There isn't any way for Christians to be able to do what we are supposed to be doing, unless we learn how to abide in Jesus (verse 5 above). We cannot live the Christian life any other way. Jesus is the only way.

Therefore, shouldn't every Christian know those verses? Yes, we should. Wherever I go, I always ask the audience "How do we abide in Jesus?" I have never received a correct answer in accordance with what is written in the Bible. Therefore, it is obvious why sin and sickness are common among Christians today. Let us return to the Lord our God!

Father, in Jesus' name, have mercy upon all of us. We don't know Your ways and we followed those who did not know. Have mercy upon all of us, and forgive us for taking our stand against Your Word. Allow us to start over, trusting in You with our whole heart, and without leaning on our own understanding that we may walk in Your ways, and receive the things that You have already provided for us. As You did with the Philippians, cause in us what is pleasing to You. For You alone are worthy to be praised. Amen!

If I had learned how to abide in Jesus, the first week I accepted Jesus as Lord, I would have avoided tons of destruction over the past twenty years, since those who abide in Jesus do not continue in sin. Better yet, if I had known that church was the place to go to in order to learn how to stop sinning, I probably would have accepted Jesus as a teenager, when most of my problems started.

For many years I followed the teachings that everybody else was following, thinking that surely the vast majority of Christians cannot be wrong. However, there are many more who enter the broad gate compared to those who enter by the narrow gate (Matthew 7:13-14). In other words, many more people will head in the wrong direction, than in the right direction.

That may be a shock to you, but according to the Word of Jesus Christ, many will seek to enter, but will not be able (Luke 13:24-28). One day I decided to believe Jesus Christ above what I was hearing, and I advise you to do the same.

You will recognize those who support the wrong message, because they will oppose the doctrine of Jesus Christ. Imagine that. Jesus, Himself would not be able to preach His doctrine in many church buildings today, even if He was the guest preacher.

I'm Alan Ballou; a servant. My wife Lucie and I serve God's people free of charge. We work as a team, and teach at church events, small group meetings, homeless shelters, and from house to house. If we may be of service to you, please contact us.

www.HowToStopSinning.com

Alan's email alan@howtostopsinning.com

Lucie's email lucie@howtostopsinning.com

ഇൗരു

If we do not abide in Jesus, we will not be able to live the Christian life (John 15:5-6).

The only way to abide in Jesus is by keeping His commands (John 15:10).

Just about anything can be used for good, or to promote evil. If you have a twitter account, and would like to receive godly reminders, with the verses included, please join me. @AlanBallou

WE MAY NOT DO EVERYTHING RIGHT. HOWEVER, WE DON'T HAVE TO LIVE IN TOTAL OPPOSITION TO THE WORD OF GOD EITHER. WE ARE SUPPOSED TO LIVE UP TO WHAT WE KNOW IS RIGHT (PHILIPPIANS 3:16). LET US REPENT AND RETURN TO THE LORD OUR GOD.

Alan Ballou

5

According to His Instructions

ೞ಄಄ಅ

If we don't get the instructions right, it is our fault. Don't blame God. By faith Noah didn't build a pontoon boat, a fishing boat, a cruise ship, or anything else besides what God commanded him to build, and so it should be with us.

The Bible is loaded with instructions, that we cannot ignore, even in repentance. In other words, we can't just say "I'm sorry for not following the instructions," and be exempt from following them.

We can be forgiven, but forgiveness is not a license to avoid God's will. We are expected to repent, and then continue in our faith. What good is it if we are sorry for not following God's instructions, if we ignore and reject His instructions, which describe what we should be doing as Christians, and how to do it?

Many of us talk about what God can do without ever mentioning that He has saved us and called us to be holy, for His own purposes (2 Timothy 1:9). As we have discussed already, just because God can do something, it doesn't mean that He is going to do it for those who ignore His ways.

For example, God can actually keep us from stumbling, and make us stand to the point of being blameless.

Jude 24
24 Now to Him who is able to keep you from stumbling, And to present you faultless before the presence of His glory with exceeding joy NKJV

1 Thessalonians 5:23-24
23 Now may the God of peace Himself sanctify you completely; and may your whole spirit, soul, and body be preserved blameless at the coming of our Lord Jesus Christ. 24 He who calls you is faithful, who also will do it. NKJV

Romans 14:4
4 Who are you to judge another's servant? To his own master he stands or falls. Indeed, he will be made to stand, for God is able to make him stand. NKJV

The obvious question is why aren't all Christians kept from sinning just as soon as we accept Jesus as Lord? We are, or I should say, we were delivered from the power of darkness (Colossians 1:13 below), and given the ability to live a new life without sin (Romans 6:1-7 below), but we did not wholeheartedly follow the instructions. In fact, as you will soon see, most of us were taught to live in opposition to God's Word.

Colossians 1:13
13 He has delivered us from the power of darkness and conveyed us into the kingdom of the Son of His love, NKJV

Romans 6:1-7
1 What shall we say then? Shall we continue in sin that grace may abound? 2 Certainly not! How shall we who died to sin live any longer in it? 3 Or do you not know that as many of us as were baptized into Christ Jesus were baptized into His death? 4 Therefore we were buried with Him through baptism into death, that just as Christ was raised from the dead by the glory of the Father, even so we also should walk in newness of life.

5 For if we have been united together in the likeness of His death, certainly we also shall be in the likeness of His resurrection, 6 knowing this, that our old man was crucified with Him, that the body of sin might be done away with, that we should no longer be slaves of sin. 7 For he who has died has been freed from sin. NKJV

How shall we who died to sin live in it any longer (verse 2 above)? Does that one question reveal anything about why most Christians are still caught up in sin? We haven't died to sin yet.

We should be walking, or living a new life (verse 4 above), but somehow we got the instructions wrong. He who has died with Christ, "has been" (past tense) freed from sin (verse 7 above).

The Word of God is asking, how can we continue in sin? At the same time, most of us are boldly proclaiming that Christians cannot stop sinning. Whose viewpoint is that, and are the people who say things like that, relying on God's power to help them stop sinning?

God says that He can keep us from stumbling (Jude 1:24 above), make us stand (Romans 14:4 above), sanctify us (1 Thessalonians 5:23-24 above), and deliver us out of temptations (2 Peter 2:9-10). Who would dare say any different, except an unbeliever? If you are a believer, why do you support the doctrine of unbelievers (1 Timothy 4:1-2, 1 Corinthians 10:20-22)?

It's not good to take a stand against God, and that is what we do when we speak in opposition to His Word, or support those who do (2 John 1:10-11). If you do not hear anything else I say, hear this. In accordance with 2 Corinthians 6:17 - 7:1, get away from the crowd that has rejected God's Word through unbelief.

There is no hope for an unbeliever. There is more hope for the worst sinner in the world, who accepts and believes God, and does not reject His Word, than for an unbeliever. May He have mercy upon us.

Hebrews 3:12
12 Beware, brethren, lest there be in any of you an evil heart of unbelief in departing from the living God; NKJV

God so loved the world that He gave His only begotten Son to die for us (John 3:16), and Jesus died for everyone's sins (verse 2 below), but those who do not believe, will be punished in flaming fire, and everlasting destruction (verses 8-10 below).

1 John 2:2
2 And He Himself is the propitiation for our sins, and not for ours only but also for the whole world. NKJV

2 Thessalonians 1:8-10
8 in flaming fire taking vengeance on those who do not know God, and on those who do not obey the gospel of our Lord Jesus Christ. 9 These shall be punished with everlasting destruction from the presence of the Lord and from the glory of His power, 10 when He comes, in that Day, to be glorified in His saints and to be admired among all those who believe, because our testimony among you was believed. NKJV

Father, in Jesus' name, have mercy upon us. Forgive us of our great transgressions. Forgive us for siding with those who do not believe Your Word, and have rejected Your ways. Have mercy on us, I pray. Fill us with the ability to live the life You have laid out for us. We will trust in You. We may not know what to do, but our eyes are on You to save us, and deliver us from the wickedness we have participated in. Hear our prayer, and rescue us, as only You can. You alone are worthy of our praise. In the mighty name of Jesus Christ we pray. Amen.

What happened? We were supposed to abide in Jesus, and die to sin after we got saved, but we didn't. Don't panic, but repent of the past, and get started with the future. Only this time, let's place faith in God's promises written in His Word. God is able to keep us from sinning, but we can't ignore His instructions.

If God's Word says that He will do something, then He will do it. However, He cannot lie. Therefore, if His Word says that He will do something under certain conditions, then those conditions must be met, or the instructions must be followed before we will receive what He has promised. It's just that simple.

For example, have you tried following the instructions found in 2 Peter 1:5-9 so that you will never stumble again? God has promised that if you do those things, you will never stumble. Speaking against that is the same as testifying that God's ways are not right, and that He is a liar.

2 Peter 1:10-11
10 Therefore, brethren, be even more diligent to make your call and election sure, for if you do these things you will never stumble; 11 for so an entrance will be supplied to you abundantly into the everlasting kingdom of our Lord and Savior Jesus Christ. NKJV

If we do these things we will never stumble (verse 10 above); some Bibles say "Never fall." Yes, we have all stumbled, or fallen short, but obviously we can reach a point where we will never stumble again according to the Word of God above, if we follow the instructions.

Most of us speak directly against what God has said in that passage of scripture, and we need to repent of that, if we ever plan on having God help us with our sin problem. We can't reject God's ways, and at the same time receive His help according to Proverbs 1:22-33.

We cannot reject what is written, and keep what is written living on the inside of us (John 5:38, Mark 4:24-25). Therefore, those who reject what is written, cannot possibly know what is written, and consequently, it is much easier for them to speak, and live in opposition to it (Ephesians 4:13-14).

Another example of God's instructions, that every Christian needs to know is repenting of sins. Repentance is not optional (Acts 17:30 below), and repenting of dead works is considered an elementary teaching according to Hebrews 6:1. We should always teach repentance toward God and faith toward Jesus Christ (Acts 20:20-21 below).

Acts 3:19
19 Repent therefore and be converted, that your sins may be blotted out, so that times of refreshing may come from the presence of the Lord, NKJV

Acts 17:30-31
30 Truly, these times of ignorance God overlooked, but now commands all men everywhere to repent, 31 because He has appointed a day on which He will judge the world in righteousness by the Man whom He has ordained. He has given assurance of this to all by raising Him from the dead." NKJV

Acts 20:20-21
20 how I kept back nothing that was helpful, but proclaimed it
to you, and taught you publicly and from house to house, 21
testifying to Jews, and also to Greeks, repentance toward God
and faith toward our Lord Jesus Christ. NKJV

I don't mean to be ugly, but we can either repent, or perish (Luke 13:3). In fact, when Christians fall away from the faith, they simply stop repenting of acts that lead to death (Hebrews 6:4-6), but the righteous person, who lives by faith in Jesus Christ (Romans 1:17, 3:21-22), needs no repentance (Luke 15:7).

Father, in Jesus' name, Your compassions, they fail not, and Your mercies are new every morning. In Your loving kindness have mercy upon us. Forgive us for our sins, and deliver us from our destructions. Teach us to continue in our faith, and send Your Word to heal us. Amen.

Another example of God's instructions that all Christians should be following is Colossians 1:21-23 below. Here is a passage of scripture that describes someone who was saved, or reconciled to God through Christ, and consequently now they are presented holy, and blameless, and above reproach in His sight, but there is a condition. Read this passage out loud and see if you can recognize the condition.

Colossians 1:21-23
21 And you, who once were alienated and enemies in your
mind by wicked works, yet now He has reconciled 22 in the
body of His flesh through death, to present you holy, and
blameless, and above reproach in His sight — 23 if indeed
you continue in the faith, grounded and steadfast, and are not
moved away from the hope of the gospel which you heard,
which was preached to every creature under heaven, of which
I, Paul, became a minister. NKJV

We can say that Christ died for us in order to make us holy in God's sight, but that would not be the full story if we didn't also mention the condition. "If we continue in our faith" we will remain holy, blameless, and above reproach in God's sight (verse 23 above), and faith comes by hearing the Word of God (Romans 10:17).

Yes, if the worse sinner in the world became a Christian he would be holy, blameless, and above reproach in God's sight. However, if he did not continue in his faith, which was given to him as a gift when he got saved (Ephesians 2:8, Romans 12:3), then he will not remain holy in God's sight.

Very few people mention that, and that's another reason why many have turned away from what is actually written in the Bible, and turned aside to doctrines that are not written. In fact, many will take a stand against what is written in order to support something that is not written in their Bible, which is evidence that we are in the very last days (2 Timothy 4:1-4).

I have seen people who were addicted to drugs, alcohol, sick, afflicted, and that had mental disorders healed in a few days, just by believing as Abraham believed, and continuing in their faith. They didn't have to get up in front of the church, or do anything special other than ask God to forgive them for not doing what they were supposed to be doing as Christians, and then continue in their faith on a daily basis. Faith comes by hearing the Word (Romans 10:17).

All they really needed to know was the solution to their problem in accordance with God's Word, without it being mixed with philosophy, or worldly wisdom. God's Word works just like it is written.

Here is the scenario again. We got saved, delivered from the power of darkness (Colossians 1:13 above), and given the ability to live a new life without sin, but we did not continue in our faith for whatever reason.

Most of us were never taught the truth, and some of us didn't like what we heard, and turned away from it. Either way, what happened next is just what the doctrine of Jesus proclaims in John 15:6, we were cut off (verse 22 below), and a person who has been cut off cannot possibly live the Christian life (John 15:5).

Romans 11:20-23
20 Well said. Because of unbelief they were broken off, and you stand by faith. Do not be haughty, but fear. 21 For if God did not spare the natural branches, He may not spare you either. 22 Therefore consider the goodness and severity of God: on those who fell, severity; but toward you, goodness, if you continue in His goodness. Otherwise you also will be cut off. 23 And they also, if they do not continue in unbelief, will be grafted in, for God is able to graft them in again. NKJV

Here again don't panic, but repent of the past, and simply start doing what every Christian is supposed to be doing according to the Word of God, and you will experience results. It's just that simple.

Faith comes by hearing the Word (Romans 10:17). If you start reading your Bible out loud from the New Testament, at least 10 to 15 chapters a day, you will again experience grace. Be careful to accept and believe what you hear; hearing with faith.

We "gain access by faith into grace" (verse 2 below). Therefore, by simply repenting of the past and turning toward God in accordance with His instructions, we will see results, point, blank, period.

Romans 5:2
2 By whom also we have access by faith into this grace wherein we stand, and rejoice in hope of the glory of God. KJV

I'm sure that verse doesn't match what you have come to believe about grace, but there it is in black and white. Without faith, we do not have access to grace. Believe God, as Abraham did, and receive the promised results.

Grace only reigns for a righteous person (Romans 5:21), and the righteous believe like Abraham believed (Romans 4:20-24). Therefore, if we take a Christian, who does not have access to more grace because of his beliefs, and teach him how to believe as Abraham believed, suddenly he will have the ability (grace) to live the Christian life. Praise God, halleluiah!

Actually, any promise written in Romans chapter five and beyond, assumes that we have been justified by faith, just as Abraham was (Romans 5:1), which is described in Romans chapter four. Any promise beyond Romans chapter one, assumes that we are already continuing in our faith, which is described in Romans 1:28-32 below.

You have probably known Christians in the past, who were on the wrong path, that suddenly started doing what was right, but no one could figure out why. If you dig into their life, you will see where they simply accepted what was written in the Bible, believing as Abraham did, or they started reading scripture for themselves, which is a form of continuing in the faith. Either one, repositioned them to receive grace, which is our God-given ability to live the Christian life.

Therefore, if believing God as Abraham believed Him was your only problem, or if you have not been actively reading scripture on your own before you started reading this book, then you have already started experiencing results. All the praise, glory, and honor be to the Lord God almighty!

Read the following passage of scripture and count the number of sins a person can be given over to, simply because they do not like to retain God in their knowledge (verse 28 below). In other words, they did not want to continue in their faith, which includes renewing their mind with the truth to the point of being transformed (Romans 12:1-2), therefore God gave them over to a debased (corrupted, depraved, reprobate) mind.

A debased mind does things that are not fitting (verse 28 below). In other words, Christians with a debased (corrupted, wicked, good-for-nothing) mind, do things that they should not do, and the solution, or the cure is the Word of God living on the inside of them.

Romans 1:28-32
28 And even as they did not like to retain God in their knowledge, God gave them over to a debased mind, to do those things which are not fitting; 29 being filled with all unrighteousness, sexual immorality, wickedness, covetousness, maliciousness; full of envy, murder, strife, deceit, evil-mindedness; they are whisperers, 30 backbiters, haters of God, violent, proud, boasters, inventors of evil things, disobedient to parents, 31 undiscerning, untrustworthy, unloving, unforgiving, unmerci-

ful; 32 who, knowing the righteous judgment of God, that those who practice such things are deserving of death, not only do the same but also approve of those who practice them. NKJV

How many sins are on that list, and in how many different areas of life? The solution is to read the Word of God out loud (faith comes by hearing) to the point of retaining it. That would be continuing in our faith.

Don't focus on the sin, but on the solution. That huge list of sins can be cured by the same solution. As I have mentioned, telling a person to stop doing the sins that they are given over to is of little value. However, teaching them the cure, in accordance with God's Word, works every time.

People say, "I can't believe that so and so did this or that, and he is a Christian." My friend, if he became a Christian, but he refused to continue in his faith, (hearing the Word of God to the point of retaining it), then I can believe it, and I would expect things like that to happen, because it is written that it will happen, according to the verses above. However, once that person repents, and starts continuing in their faith, all of those sins will fall off like water on a duck's back.

When a person is given over to a debased mind, they will do things that they should not do (verse 28 above). Reading the Word of God to the point of retaining it, is the solution. Take any Christian, who people would consider to be of good character, and position him where he never hears the pure Word of God, and he will eventually do things that are out of character for him.

Renewing our mind with the truth is our reasonable service back to God for what He has done for us (Romans 12:1-2). Those who get saved and go about their own business, refusing to continue in their faith, as well as those who hear the Word and believe it, at some point in their life, but do not continue in their faith, quickly find themselves in a situation where they need God.

Get this. God, Who is able to keep us from sinning, is the same God Who will give us over to a depraved mind because we are not following His instructions (verse 28 above). Many people focus on the type of sins a person may commit, but faith, and continuing in our faith is the solution for all of them.

In the same way, many people focus on what God can do, rather than focusing on following His instructions so that He will do what He has promised to do for us. The same solution solves both problems.

By simply turning toward Him in repentance, He will reach out to us, and help us just like He did with the prodigal son (Luke 15:11-31), who didn't really do anything besides make up his mind to turn toward his father in repentance. We don't have to reach the place which we fell from in one day, but we do need to turn.

After turning back, then we need to follow God's instructions, and continue in our faith. This will bring results every time. Many do not realize that while the prodigal son was away, he was dead, but when he returned he was "alive again" (verse 32 below). Being given over (verse 28 above), or cut off as it is written in Romans 11:22 (above), doesn't have to be a permanent thing, but we need to return, and continue ASAP.

Luke 15:32
32 It was right that we should make merry and be glad, for your brother was dead and is alive again, and was lost and is found.'" NKJV

Recently, I had a preacher ask me a loaded question. He said, "Did Christ die for our past sins, present sins, and any sins that we might commit in the future? Before I had finished saying the word "Yes," he said, "Then we are forgiven for all of our sins, past, present, and future."

That was his way of rejecting what I was teaching, but we don't use scripture against scripture. No, we use scripture with scripture in order to allow it to explain itself.

Yes, Jesus died for the sins of the whole world, and not just the sins of those who believe in Him, as I have already mentioned above (1 John 2:2 above). Yes, Jesus died for everyone's sins, past, present, and future, by which God saved all men (1 Timothy 4:10). In other words, He doesn't have to die again, and again, for the sins that we will be forgiven for in the future.

However, the blood of Jesus Christ only cleanses those who walk in the light, and not those who remain in darkness.

1 John 1:5-7
5 This is the message which we have heard from Him and declare to you, that God is light and in Him is no darkness at all. 6 If we say that we have fellowship with Him, and walk in darkness, we lie and do not practice the truth. 7 But if we walk in the light as He is in the light, we have fellowship with one another, and the blood of Jesus Christ His Son cleanses us from all sin. NKJV

If we walk in the light, the blood of Jesus Christ cleanses us from all sin (verse 7 above). If we continue in darkness, we are not practicing the truth (verse 6 above), and consequently, we need to confess our sins (1 John 1:9). As I have already mentioned, just because God can do something, or has done something for us, it doesn't mean that we are in the position to receive it. We need to get the instructions right, and then our results will be right.

Many Christians live in destruction, and even die in sickness simply because they never practice the truth (verse 6 above), and they never repent of their sins. They never turn in faith, probably because they were never taught to repent of dead works, which is considered an elementary teaching (Hebrews 6:1).

Therefore, yes, Jesus died for the sins of the whole world, but the whole world is not going to make it. Why? They do not follow the instructions.

Jesus, Himself said that not everyone who calls Him, "Lord" will be able to enter the Kingdom of Heaven, according to Matthew 7:21-23, and 2 Thessalonians 1:8-9 above, says that those who do not know God, and do not obey the Gospel will suffer everlasting punishment in flaming fire. Were they forgiven at some point, and then turned away from God in unbelief according to Hebrews 3:12? Who knows, but one thing is for sure; they didn't follow the instructions.

God so loved the people of the world that He gave His only Son to die for our sins, but that doesn't mean that everyone is going to go to Heaven. God loves us, and Jesus died for us, but that doesn't mean automatic eternal life for everyone.

Therefore, part of what that preacher said is true, Christ did die for our sins, past, present, and future, but the remainder of what he said is philosophy. Colossians 2:8 warns us not to allow anyone to take us captive by philosophy.

You will know it's philosophy because it will sound great, but you won't find it written in the Bible anywhere. It is assumed knowledge.

My experience in dealing with those who rely on philosophy rather than scripture, is that there is always a verse or two that says the exact opposite of what they are proclaiming. Therefore, they can only fool those who do not know the truth, since they never test what is said, by comparing it with scripture, due to peer pressure. Among them, the lies of those who oppose the truth, grow like cancer (2 Timothy 3:8, 2:17).

Just because Jesus died for our past, present, and future sins, it doesn't mean that we can use His blood as a license to continue in sin. If we willfully continue in sin, after we have received the knowledge of the truth, no sacrifice for sins is left.

Hebrews 10:26-30
26 For if we sin willfully after we have received the knowledge of the truth, there no longer remains a sacrifice for sins, 27 but a certain fearful expectation of judgment, and fiery indignation which will devour the adversaries. 28 Anyone who has rejected Moses' law dies without mercy on the testimony of two or three witnesses. 29 Of how much worse punishment, do you suppose, will he be thought worthy who has trampled the Son of God underfoot, counted the blood of the covenant by which he was sanctified a common thing, and insulted the Spirit of grace? 30 For we know Him who said, "Vengeance is Mine, I will repay," says the Lord. And again, "The Lord will judge His people." NKJV

Jesus is our sacrifice for sins, but as you can see, He is not a license to continue in sin. We can lose our right to the blood according to verse 29 above. We all need to know that.

Therefore, if a Christian is sick, and he has willfully continued in sins, he should repent immediately and start continuing in his faith, while asking God to forgive him, and perhaps the Lord our God will have mercy upon him.

We serve a very merciful God, Who is slow to anger, and abounding in love. If that were not true, I would have been dead a long time ago. Praise God, halleluiah! Cry out to Him, but at the same time, do not reject His Word.

Praise the Lord our God for His great patience, and abundant mercy! Let us repent of the past, and turn toward Him! He will see it, and help us in our time of need! Cry out to Him! Call on His holy name! Save us from our sins Lord Jesus! Great is our God, Who alone is worthy to be praised!

Father, in Jesus' name, have mercy on us. We did not know Your Word, and we have cast Your ways behind us. According to Your abundant mercy, and Your great compassion, please have mercy on us, and forgive us for our sins. Wash us clean again that times of refreshing may come, and that we may glorify Your name. In our ignorance we have taken our stand against You. May we turn toward You and find mercy. May we learn Your ways that we may walk in them, pleasing You in every good work. Give us what we need in order to do Your will. Amen.

Now what

The Word of God living in us brings life, and health to our body (verses 20-22 below). The person who ignores God's instructions, rejects life and health.

Proverbs 4:20-22
20 My son, give attention to my words; Incline your ear to my sayings. 21 Do not let them depart from your eyes; Keep them in the midst of your heart; 22 For they are life to those who find them, And health to all their flesh. NKJV

You might be thinking that many people are healed without turning, and that is true, since God does heal backsliders. I know people who were healed of life threatening diseases, and they will tell you that the Lord healed them. Praise the Lord God almighty!

However, what they will not tell you is that when their condition got serious, they got serious about God's ways, and turned toward Him in accordance with the truth. By simply turning away from sin, and toward God, they were healed.

They either picked up their Bible for the first time in years, or they began to read scriptures from a book like this one, or they stopped doing something that they knew was wrong, or a combination of moves in the right direction.

Think about this. The only thing that the prodigal son did was repent (change his mind), humble himself, and turn back. That was all he did, and his father had compassion on him.

Luke 15:17-21

17 "But when he came to himself, he said, 'How many of my father's hired servants have bread enough and to spare, and I perish with hunger! 18 I will arise and go to my father, and will say to him, "Father, I have sinned against heaven and before you, 19 and I am no longer worthy to be called your son. Make me like one of your hired servants."' 20 "And he arose and came to his father. But when he was still a great way off, his father saw him and had compassion, and ran and fell on his neck and kissed him. 21 And the son said to him, 'Father, I have sinned against heaven and in your sight, and am no longer worthy to be called your son.' NKJV

While he was still a great way off, his father had compassion on him (verse 20 above). Just by deciding to do what was right, and taking a few steps in the right direction, the son was received with open arms by the father. We serve a very compassionate God. Amen.

Allow me to show you that in a promise. In the passage of scripture below, if a wicked person was going to die, but he turned from whatever he was doing, he would surely live.

Ezekiel 33:10-16

10 "Therefore you, O son of man, say to the house of Israel: 'Thus you say, "If our transgressions and our sins lie upon us, and we pine away in them, how can we then live?"' 11 Say to them: 'As I live,' says the Lord God, 'I have no pleasure in the death of the wicked, but that the wicked turn from his way and live. Turn, turn from your evil ways! For why should you die, O house of Israel?' 12 "Therefore you, O son of man, say to the children of your people: 'The righteousness of the righteous man shall not deliver him in the day of his transgression; as for the wickedness of the wicked, he shall not fall because of it in the day that he turns from his wickedness; nor shall the righteous be able to live because of his righteousness in the day that he sins.'

13 When I say to the righteous that he shall surely live, but he trusts in his own righteousness and commits iniquity, none of his righteous works shall be remembered; but because of the iniquity that he has committed, he shall die. 14 Again, when I say to the wicked, 'You shall surely die,' if he turns from his sin and does what is lawful and right, 15 if the wicked restores the pledge, gives back what he has stolen, and walks in the statutes of life without committing iniquity, he shall surely live; he

shall not die. 16 None of his sins which he has committed shall be remembered against him; he has done what is lawful and right; he shall surely live. NKJV

It is turning away from sin, and turning toward God in faith that brings life. Basically, we follow those instructions, and after following those instructions, we should be careful to continue in our faith, in order that we will remain holy in God's sight (Colossians 1:21-23).

The situation we are in determines the next set of guidelines (teachings, commands, orders) that we should follow. For example, God may receive a prodigal son with open arms while he is yet a long way off, but that doesn't mean that he is where he needs to be in his faith. If he doesn't continue in his faith, after he returns, then he will soon be back in the same state he was in, which is exactly what happens to many Christians today.

I have met plenty of people who were miraculously healed of diseases by the Lord, but from those, the ones that did not turn from their ways, died a few months later, usually from that same disease. My friend, God is not healing people so that they can continue in sin, but continue in their faith.

I have seen a man in hospice care, healed of an incurable disease. Praise God, halleluiah! He got up and walked out of the hospital the next day, but he continued in the same things that he was doing before he was crippled with the disease. Therefore, he died a few months later.

Theoretically speaking, we could have a Christian who was healed of a disease in the past, end up in a position where none of the promises are working in his life because of his sins. Many Christians chase miracles all their life, and never learn how to live by faith, or how to continue in their faith. Consequently, they go from one sickness to the next until they die.

John 5:14
14 Afterward Jesus found him in the temple, and said to him, "See, you have been made well. Sin no more, lest a worse thing come upon you." NKJV

Sin will shorten the days of those whom God considers to be wicked. It has been appointed for men to die (Hebrews 9:27), but we can add to, or take away from our days, depending on how we live. When sin is fully grown, it will bring death (James 1:15). Deceitful people will not live out half their days (Psalm 50:23).

Proverbs 10:27
27 The fear of the Lord prolongs days, But the years of the wicked will be shortened. NKJV

Proverbs 9:11
11 For by me your days will be multiplied, And years of life will be added to you. NKJV

Proverbs 4:10
10 Hear, my son, and receive my sayings, And the years of your life will be many. NKJV

Get this. There will always be sickness, disease, and hardship for people who are called to be Christians, but who disobey the message (Deuteronomy 28:60-61, Hebrews 12:7-13). If man discovers a cure for AIDS, and every other disease on the planet today, there will be another disease to take its place. The only complete solution is to live by faith in Jesus Christ, and to continue in our faith.

The same is true concerning addictions. We don't force people off drugs, or alcohol, or make them live right, but we give them the tools needed to correct their situation by faith, and the ones who want to stop, will stop. Faith, and continuing in the faith, is the only permanent solution for Christians. Let the people of this world use whatever method they come up with, but faith is the cure for Christians.

How do we continue in our faith? Faith comes by hearing the Word (Romans 10:17). That's the beginning of the process of continuing in our faith, and then we put the things we hear into practice (Luke 6:46-49). In the next few chapters we will discuss things that hinder us from continuing in our faith.

One Sunday, as I was teaching in an inner city church, a homeless alcoholic wandered into the room and sat down. He had been saved years before, but he wasn't living a new life, and he wanted to know what he should do. Many in this condition simply go through the motions of being saved again, but that is not the solution.

He could not read, and so we gave him a simple CD player with a recording of the books of James, 1 Peter, and 1 John on it, and we asked him to listen to it as much as he could every day for the purpose of retaining it. We told him that it didn't matter if he could not remember any of it by the next weekend, but we wanted him to listen to the entire recording at least once a day. He agreed and left.

The following Sunday, as soon as we saw him we could tell by his face that he had followed our instructions. Not only was he cleaned up and sober, but he could not stop grinning from ear to ear. He was so full of joy, and God's grace. Praise God, halleluiah!

God had provided a place for him to bathe, and wash his clothes. Basically, God gave him the things that he needed simply because he positioned himself to receive them.

That's just a small glimpse of the power contained in the Word of God. Just by thinking it worthwhile to "retain the knowledge of God," that man was delivered from alcohol, and we never even asked him to stop drinking. We just gave him the tools he needed to live the new life in Christ, and taught him according to God's instructions, and God came through with what He promised.

Our focus was on the sins that gave him over to alcohol. Therefore, our fifteen minute discussion with him was simply to make sure that he understood what we wanted him to do, which was within his power to do, and not to try and make him do something that he could not possibly do on his own. Praise be to the Lord our God almighty, Who is worthy of all praise!

I wonder how many people are out there like I was, homeless at seventeen years old, feeling like I had to clean up before I could seek help from a church? I wonder how many people are like I was, when I was kicked out of the homeless shelter because I could not control my behavior?

I felt like a piece of trash, which needed to be picked up, and thrown into the garbage. However, all I needed was instructions straight out of the Word of God, but there wasn't anyone teaching those instructions.

I wonder how many people are like I was when I slept on top of a school building in order to keep the ants, bugs, and small animals from bothering me? Yes, the Bible does tell us not to associate with people in the situation I was in, but it also instructs us how to overcome that situation, and it doesn't take a lifetime of struggling with the same old sin, when we get the instructions right.

My grandmother talked to me until she was blue in the face, so to speak, but that didn't work. She was a very spiritual person, but she did not know what to tell me in order to make me rely on the God she trusted. I disappointed her, and I am very sorry for doing that.

I've met many spiritual people since my youth, but none of them had any instructions for me to follow, except "go to church" with us. That didn't work for me years ago, and it's not working today for millions of church-attending people. However, the instructions found in the Word of God work, and they work every time.

We can build more homeless shelters, and we probably need to in some areas, but if we would simply give God's people the tools they need in accordance with the Word of God, and tell them how to use them, God will do what He has promised.

We can feed the homeless and support programs that help people in need from now on, but if we teach them how to believe like Abraham, follow God's instructions like Noah, and to live by faith in Jesus Christ, they won't need us for very long. In fact, they won't need any of us, but the Lord God almighty as their provider. Amen.

Today new converts accept Jesus as Lord, and they are delivered from all sorts of bondage, but a few months, or years later, they are right back where they started and even worse. That's because they were never taught to continue in their faith, or how to abide in Jesus. We need to instruct them in accordance with the Word of God, and not with human wisdom, or philosophy.

Christians can be delivered by knowing Jesus and fall back to being worse than they were before they got saved. According to the following passage of scripture, we can come to know our Lord Jesus, and be entangled in the pollutions of this world, to the point of being overcome again.

2 Peter 2:20-22
20 For if, after they have escaped the pollutions of the world through the knowledge of the Lord and Savior Jesus Christ, they are again entangled in them and overcome, the latter end is worse for them than the beginning. 21 For it would have been better for them not to have known the way of righteousness, than having known it, to turn from the holy commandment delivered to them. 22 But it has happened to them according to the true proverb: "A dog returns to his own vomit," and, "a sow, having washed, to her wallowing in the mire." NKJV

Many return after making a mess of their life and go through the motions of being saved all over again, but simple repentance is the solution, and then starting over with godly instructions. Saved people don't need to be saved twice. They just need to turn, and then continue in their faith.

Father, in Jesus' name, if You should mark iniquities, who could stand? Our sins, which are many, have turned Your ears away from us. Have mercy upon us O' Lord I pray. Forgive us of our sins. We shall return to You in accordance with Your ways, that we may receive the help and guidance that we so desperately need. Therefore, we shall walk in Your ways and bring glory to Your holy name. Amen.

I want to mention that most of the newer Bibles have totally changed Romans 1:28 (above) to say something different. However, I have used this passage for many years to help people in these conditions, and so I know it works just like it is written in the New King James Bible. I'm not asking you to throw your Bible away, but you will do well to add a copy of the NKJV to your collection since it works just like they are written.

According to John 8:31-37, you shall know the truth, and the truth shall set you free from what? Knowing the truth will set you free from being a slave to sin. Also, according to John 17:17, the truth itself sanctifies us. Check it. Romans 1:28-32 above, is certainly in-line with John 8:31-37 and John 17:17, and therefore, hearing the pure Word of God to the point of retaining it can still be taught to Christians who use one of the newer Bibles, that is until they change the book of John in the newer Bibles.

I'm Alan Ballou; a servant. If I may be of service to you, please contact me.

www.HowToStopSinning.com

୫୬ଓଏ

6

Do Not Conform

ℰℭℬ

A s we have learned, we must continue in our faith, by renewing our mind with the truth now that we are saved, and baptized into Christ Jesus. The only way to completely accomplish that to the point of being transformed, is to give our life to God (verse 1 below), and to stop conforming to this world (verse 2 below).

Romans 12:1-2
1 I beseech you therefore, brethren, by the mercies of God, that you present your bodies a living sacrifice, holy, acceptable to God, which is your reasonable service. 2 And do not be conformed to this world, but be transformed by the renewing of your mind, that you may prove what is that good and acceptable and perfect will of God. NKJV

In order to successfully renew our mind with the truth to the point of being transformed, we need to stop conforming to the world around us (verse 2 above). That means that we need to stop imitating the people of this world, or in other words, we're going to stop following their ways.

That doesn't mean that we are going to stop going to work, bathing, clipping our fingernails, checking our email, or washing our clothes. No, all things are lawful (permissible), but not all things are helpful, or edify (educate).

1 Corinthians 6:12
12 All things are lawful for me, but all things are not helpful. All things are lawful for me, but I will not be brought under the power of any. NKJV

We're going to put off the things that are not helpful, and that hinder us from being all God has called us to be. Therefore, not only are we going to turn toward God in repentance, but we are going to do away with anything that hinders us from continuing in our faith, and living by faith.

How can we tell if something is not helpful, or if something has us under its power (bondage)? Any worldly thing that we cannot stop from controlling our actions, or stop from controlling our thoughts continually when we are not participating in it, controls us.

All things are lawful, but if something that we are participating in controls us, or if it is preventing us from being what God has called us to be, then it has us in bondage (verse 19 below).

2 Peter 2:19
19 While they promise them liberty, they themselves are slaves of corruption; for by whom a person is overcome, by him also he is brought into bondage. NKJV

It doesn't have to be something that is considered evil. Anything that we are overcome by, brings us into bondage (verse 19 above). That could be something like golf, tennis, TV, or advanced basket weaving, to name a few.

Why was the Apostle Paul concerned that his work for the Galatians had been in vain?

Galatians 4:8-11
8 But then, indeed, when you did not know God, you served those which by nature are not gods. 9 But now after you have known God, or rather are known by God, how is it that you turn again to the weak and beggarly elements, to which you desire again to be in bondage? 10 You observe days and months and seasons and years. 11 I am afraid for you, lest I have labored for you in vain. NKJV

They were turning back to observe special days, months, and seasons (verses 9-10 above). Basically, they returned to the things they were doing before they were saved. The Apostle Paul asked them if they wanted to be in bondage to them again (verse 9 above).

More than likely, he was referring to the special days, months, and seasons that are required by the Laws of Moses, but anything like that can enslave us to the point of using up all of our time. Think about everything you do, and why you do it. Now, what percentage of those things are because of your faith in Jesus Christ?

Faith always includes the evidence of things not seen (Hebrews 11:1). Therefore, if we are living by faith, then there will be a verse that explains why we do, what we do. If there is not a verse that tells us to do what we are doing then faith cannot possibly be the reason why we do it.

Does the Bible tell us to work? Yes, it does (2 Thessalonians 3:10). Does it tell us to take care of our body? Yes (1 Corinthians 3:16-17). Does the Bible identify places that we should stay away from (Proverbs 5:1-15), and people that we should avoid (Ephesians 5:5-7)? It most certainly does. There are many every day activities that are described in the Bible, including, "do not conform to this world."

The most noticeable difference between Christians who conform to this world and Christians who do not, is their priorities. The world system will make us participate in the things of this world to the point of being consumed by them, and if there is any time left over, then we seek God, and live up to certain parts of scripture (Ephesians 2:1-3).

That's not going to work. Worldliness will always prevent us from renewing our mind with the truth to the point of being transformed. The cares of this life choke the Word and make it unfruitful (verse 22, and 19 below), and those who are unfruitful cannot possibly abide in the vine (John 15:1-6).

Therefore, a worldly Christian may have good intentions, but by default, his worldliness will lead him into following his sinful nature. That means that worldliness will eventually lead us into being cut off, if we continue in it.

It takes faith in order to receive more grace (Romans 5:2), and it takes grace to live the Christian life. Therefore, worldliness can eventually result in having our ability to live the Christian life taken away, even to the point of becoming God's enemy (James 4:4).

Matthew 13:22
22 Now he who received seed among the thorns is he who hears the word, and the cares of this world and the deceitfulness of riches choke the word, and he becomes unfruitful. NKJV

Mark 4:18-19
18 Now these are the ones sown among thorns; they are the ones who hear the word, 19 and the cares of this world, the deceitfulness of riches, and the desires for other things entering in choke the word, and it becomes unfruitful. NKJV

In the following passage of scripture, Martha was caught up with all the preparations that she felt had to be made, but Mary was listening to the Word of God spoken by Jesus. She was putting God's Word first, and it would not be taken from her (verse 42 below).

Luke 10:38-42
38 Now it happened as they went that He entered a certain village; and a certain woman named Martha welcomed Him into her house. 39 And she had a sister called Mary, who also sat at Jesus' feet and heard His word. 40 But Martha was distracted with much serving, and she approached Him and said, "Lord, do You not care that my sister has left me to serve alone? Therefore tell her to help me." 41 And Jesus answered and said to her, "Martha, Martha, you are worried and troubled about many things. 42 But one thing is needed, and Mary has chosen

that good part, which will not be taken away from her." NKJV

I'm not saying to stop eating. However, I am saying that listening to God's Word is more important than eating. Things that "have to be done" can prevent us from being what God has called us to be. Continuing in our faith is more important than most, if not all, of our daily activities.

In fact, when the Holy Spirit places God's love in our heart, one of the things we will notice is a drastic decrease in our love for the things of this world. The amount of God's love that is in us is evident by our lack of worldliness. If the love of the Father is in us, we will not love this world (verse 15 below).

1 John 2:15-17
15 Do not love the world or the things in the world. If anyone loves the world, the love of the Father is not in him. 16 For all that is in the world — the lust of the flesh, the lust of the eyes, and the pride of life — is not of the Father but is of the world. 17 And the world is passing away, and the lust of it; but he who does the will of God abides forever. NKJV

We could easily fight against what God has placed in our heart, and begin to once again grow our love for this world, and the things of this world, especially if we do not know what has happened to us. However, to do so is considered adultery (verse 4 below).

Therefore, Christians who accept Jesus as Lord, but later reject offering their body as a living sacrifice, and continue in worldliness, end up opposing God.

James 4:4
4 Adulterers and adulteresses! Do you not know that friendship with the world is enmity with God? Whoever therefore wants to be a friend of the world makes himself an enemy of God. NKJV

We need to understand that when we were saved, God purchased us with the blood of Christ (Acts 20:28). We were bought at a price (1 Corinthians 6:20), and then transported (conveyed) into the Kingdom of Christ (verse 13 below).

Colossians 1:13
13 He has delivered us from the power of darkness and con- veyed us into the kingdom of the Son of His love, NKJV

Ephesians 2:5-6
5 even when we were dead in trespasses, made us alive to- gether with Christ (by grace you have been saved), 6 and raised us up together, and made us sit together in the heavenly places in Christ Jesus, NKJV

We were purchased, and then delivered out of the kingdom of this world, and into the Kingdom of Christ, where we were seated with Christ (verses above). Now you can see why it is considered adultery to go back to be a friend of this world, and to live as if we belong to the kingdom of this world (James 4:4 above).

Worldly Christians will never be able to live the Christian life, they will always reap corruption (Galatians 6:8), and they will always find themselves in situations where they will not understand why God doesn't answer their cry for help (Proverbs 1:22-33). For them, bad things will always happen to seemingly good people.

We need to know that if we do not listen to God's advice, He will not answer our cry for help, but we will eat the fruit of our ways (Proverbs 1:31), reaping exactly what we have sown (Galatians 6:7-9). We all need God's grace (ability, favor) in order to live the Christian life, but very few Christians position themself to receive an answer from God, when they cry for help.

One phrase that I have heard countless times over the past twenty years is, "This is what normal people do." I have now accepted as fact that I am not a normal person, and I never want to be normal if it means that I need to give up trying to live up to what is written in the Bible.

What do we need to cut out of our life in order to follow this passage of scripture wholeheartedly, and would we seem normal if we did?

2 Timothy 2:3-4
3 You therefore must endure hardship as a good soldier of Jesus Christ. 4 No one engaged in warfare entangles himself with the affairs of this life, that he may please him who enlisted him as a soldier. NKJV

Christians do not get entangled in the affairs (activities, concerns) of this life. That means that we don't allow ourself to get caught up in the dealings, and undertakings of what is going on in this world.

Worldliness hinders us from growing spiritually. The Apostle Paul told the Corinthians that they were acting like mere men (verse 3 below). He could not address them as spiritual, but as babies in Christ because they were carnal (fleshly, worldly).

1 Corinthians 3:1-3
1 And I, brethren, could not speak to you as to spiritual people but as to carnal, as to babes in Christ. 2 I fed you with milk and not with solid food; for until now you were not able to receive it, and even now you are still not able; 3 for you are still carnal. For where there are envy, strife, and divisions among you, are you not carnal and behaving like mere men? NKJV

Imagine that. They could not receive spiritual teachings because they were not ready for it yet. They were Christians, but they were still acting like everyday people of this world. They stunted their spiritual growth by the things that they participated in, and the same is true for us.

As we have learned, obedience comes from faith. Therefore, if faith says, "Stop doing this, and start doing that," then the first question we should be asking people whose faith is not producing the right results is, "Are you living by faith?" All Christians have been given faith as a gift (Ephesians 2:8), but are we living by it?

My Bible says, if we died with Christ, why subject ourselves to the ways of the world (verse 20 below)? Therefore, my wife Lucie and I have stopped participating in many things that robbed us of the time we needed, to be what God has called us to be. I strongly suggest that you do the same.

Colossians 2:20-23
20 Therefore, if you died with Christ from the basic principles of the world, why, as though living in the world, do you subject yourselves to regulations — 21 "Do not touch, do not taste, do not handle," 22 which all concern things which perish with the using — according to the commandments and doctrines of men? 23 These things indeed have an appearance of wisdom in self-imposed religion, false humility, and neglect of the body, but are of no value against the indulgence of the flesh. NKJV

There are many things that the people of this world participate in that promise better health, controlling sinful behavior, and the like. However, according to verse 23 above, none of them can stop the flesh. If they cannot stop the flesh from controlling us, then they cannot prevent sinful behavior, addictions, or the sickness and disease brought on by that type of conduct. Therefore, at best, worldly solutions are only temporary fixes, or cover-ups that mask our problems.

Some might even ask, "If we can be what God has called us to be, who cares what we participate in?" The Lord does. We cannot partake (share, contribute) in the activities of demons, without provoking the Lord to jealousy (verses 21-22 below).

1 Corinthians 10:20-22
20 Rather, that the things which the Gentiles sacrifice they sacrifice to demons and not to God, and I do not want you to have fellowship with demons. 21 You cannot drink the cup of the Lord and the cup of demons; you cannot partake of the Lord's table and of the table of demons. 22 Or do we provoke the Lord to jealousy? Are we stronger than He? NKJV

The things that the people of this world sacrifice, is not to God, but to demons (verse 20 above). In other words, they give to support someone who is preaching the wrong message (1 Timothy 4:1-2, 2 Timothy 4:3-4), or they give to support more worldliness among Christians who are trying to escape the corruption of the world. This is very obvious today.

I suggest that we take a good look at everything we participate in, and ask ourself if it is of God, or of man. Is it written in the Bible, or is it a man's doctrine (Colossians 2:22 above)? Anything can be called "Christian," but does it promote following Jesus Christ, or is it a means of worldliness in the church, which will stunt the growth of those who partake in it?

For example, are people who play Christian sports any less tangled up in the corruption of this world than those who do not? I would still rather play Christian sports, than the alternative, but are we learning to die to worldliness, or are we learning that a worldly Christian is okay with God? Think about that.

Do I mean that there is anything wrong with a game? No, but at the end of the day, someone needs to ask if our good intentions have resulted in making enemies of God rather than Christ followers (James 4:4 above). Are we learning how to abide in Jesus, or how to be a good sport?

Am I anti-sports? No, but I will stand up for Jesus Christ, and God's Word. Think about it this way. If we have been learning how to abide in Jesus, in accordance with God's Word, why is the church full of worldly Christians, who testify that we cannot stop sinning? We take the time needed to teach sports, even in the church, but we do not take the time needed to teach what is far more important than sports.

It's time to check our faith, because something is off course. Get the Word of God right first, and then we can play games, if we have time. Let us return to the Lord our God.

Is the Easter bunny of God, or man? Why is it in the church? I want you to understand that we will never have a problem finding funds for something that promotes worldliness in the church (1 Corinthians 10:20-22 above), since the devil controls the kingdoms of this world (Matthew 4:8-9). However, does that make it godly? No, it does not.

Having plenty of money for this program or that program is not evidence of a blessing. In fact, it could be evidence of the opposite. God makes all grace abound for every good work (2 Corinthians 9:8), but it's not God's work to promote worldliness in the church. No, that would be the opposite of God's work.

How about Santa and his reindeer? My point is, if we cut all worldliness out of our life, so that we can receive spiritual teachings to the point of being transformed, what would we celebrate, and how would we celebrate it? Think about that.

Some will say that there isn't anything wrong with celebrating Christmas, and maybe there wouldn't be anything wrong with it, if we celebrated Jesus Christ. Did the wise men celebrate Christmas or Jesus? The people of this world need to call it something other than Jesus' birthday, since they do not celebrate Jesus.

All things are permissible, but not all things are helpful. We need to stop conforming to this world, so that we can grow up spiritually.

Look at it this way. In the past, how much time have we spent reading our Bible in the month of December? That should reveal if Christmas is a hindrance or if it is all about Jesus. If Jesus came to live with us this December, would He want us to prepare something for Him, like Martha was doing, or listen to His Words, like Mary did?

Let's say that our reading habits haven't changed, and we are still seeking God first place in our life. Great, but let's ask ourself this question. While we are celebrating Jesus' birthday, if Jesus passed by our house, would He know that we have chosen to honor Him by celebrating His birthday? Does anything say "Happy birthday Jesus?"

If He came inside, how would He know that it was His birthday celebration, or would coming inside confirm that we are still conformed to the ways of the world around us? My friend, Jesus has already seen inside our house, and He already knows our intentions before we even set those decorations up. Imagine that.

What do we need to do differently this year, if we are going to celebrate Jesus, but not conform to the world, so that it will not hinder our spiritual growth? First of all, know that Jesus would rather that we know the Word of God, but if we decided to sacrifice for Him, He said that whatever we do for the least of His brethren, we do for Him (Matthew 25:40).

That's something that we can do for Jesus all year long, without waiting for Christmas, and it doesn't promote worldliness in the church. Why don't we celebrate Jesus once a month, by declaring a certain day of the month, "Jesus day," and give gifts to poor Christians (Galatians 6:10)? That way we can do without all of the holidays that the people of this world celebrate, and at the same time promote Jesus Christ rather than worldliness in the church.

We may not do everything right. However, we don't have to live in total opposition to the Word of God either. There is a thin line between the "it doesn't matter" attitude, and the "respect for Jesus Christ, and what He has done for us" attitude. That line is crossed when we refuse to live up to what we know is right (Philippians 3:16). Let us repent and return to the Lord our God.

The only holiday my wife and I celebrate is Thanksgiving, and we celebrate it every single day of the year. Praise God, we don't have to rush out to buy fireworks for the 4th of July, or even presents for each other in December. There is no need for us to buy new clothes for Easter Sunday anymore, but instead we can wait until our old clothes wears out. Praise God!

Celebrate whatever you want to celebrate as long as it doesn't violate scripture. However, for us, all of that pressure created by those worldly expectations is gone. Therefore, we have plenty of time to renew our mind with the truth of God's Word, which sets our priorities in order, Lord willing. If God is first, put Him first, and let everything else be second, fifth, eleventh, and so on.

One lady asked me if I was a Jehovah's Witness because I do not celebrate holidays. I had no idea that Jehovah's Witness' did not celebrate holidays before that question was asked. However, I'm just trying to follow the instructions found in the Bible. I don't want anything to keep me from receiving spiritual blessings. That's a choice, and not a religion.

I'm a Christian, who happens to believe what the Bible says, and I'm here to testify to you, that it works just like it is written, regardless of what other groups are doing. I'm simply a believer, and I'm asking you to be one also. Praise God, halleluiah! I wish that every group would follow the principles that we will cover in this book.

Some people may argue that there are plenty of things that Christians have to participate in that are not spelled out in the Bible, and that would be true. However, standing up for something that is not in God's Word, and standing up for something that is against God's Word is two different things.

The Bible doesn't specifically say to brush my teeth either, but I brush them so that I won't set my wife's hair on fire.

"Do not conform to this world, but be transformed by renewing your mind" is basically telling us that there are some things, in which the people of this world are participating in, that will prevent us from being able to renew our mind to the point of being transformed into a new person. I don't think that brushing our teeth is one of them.

However, there is something that we are doing today, that is preventing the average Christian from learning the verses we will cover in this book. I believe that some of those things may be different for certain people, but I don't think we will be so confused that we will not be able to figure out what is hindering us from renewing our mind with God's Word.

Just ask yourself, "What do I need to stop doing in order to have time to read my Bible to the point of being transformed?" However, there is a better way to tell. Read your Bible for about an hour each day, and then cut out whatever activity you do not have time to complete. That will reveal what you need to stop doing.

Now what

The Christian life is set up in such a way that if we reject knowledge, we "will" end up in destruction. Show me a household that doesn't read their Bible, and I will show you a family who will soon be in need of prayer and assistance from someone outside of that house.

The more involved we are with the things of this world, the more difficulty we will have renewing our mind. Worldly Christians cannot receive spiritual teachings (1 Corinthians 3:1-3, 2:6, Hebrews 5:11-14). Therefore, even if they read their Bible, they will never be able to retain it (Mark 4:24-25).

We will be transformed through the power already contained in the Word as it lives on the inside of us (Romans 12:1-2). However, those who reject that process, also reject God's power, and they may never come to the knowledge of the truth.

2 Timothy 3:5-7
5 having a form of godliness but denying its power. And from such people turn away! 6 For of this sort are those who creep into households and make captives of gullible women loaded down with sins, led away by various lusts, 7 always learning and never able to come to the knowledge of the truth. NKJV

If we have no intention of allowing the Word of God to change us, then we could find ourself in a situation where we would always be learning, but never able to come to the knowledge of the truth. Many Christians are in this position today, and consequently, they are blown and tossed by the doctrines of men (Ephesians 4:13-14).

Get this. If God's people experience destruction for lack of knowledge, then the power to avoid that destruction in our life is the Word of God living on the inside of us. Think about that. Whatever is robbing us of the time needed to renew our mind with the truth is certainly against us. Identify it, and reclaim the time.

Ephesians 5:15-16
15 See then that ye walk circumspectly, not as fools, but as wise, 16 Redeeming the time, because the days are evil. KJV

Father, in Jesus' name, Your mercies endure forever, and great is Your loving kindness. Forgive us for not being what You have called us to be, and forgive us for wasting our time on worldly things. Allow us to return to You in accordance with Your Word. Renew a right Spirit within us, and instill in us an overwhelming desire to know You. Amen!

Think about this. If you have been gathering with Christians, and studying the Bible for years, but you did not know the verses we have covered so far, then your life has been affected by the issues we have discussed in this book. Do something about it.

I'm Alan Ballou; a servant. My wife Lucie and I conduct small group meetings, free of charge. If we may be of service to you, please contact us.

www.HowToStopSinning.com

Alan's email alan@howtostopsinning.com

Lucie's email lucie@howtostopsinning.com

෨ා౧ൿ

7

Everything a Loss

ಶಿಲಿ

Trying to live the Christian life while trying to remain who we were before we were saved is like running a race with ankle weights on. The things that we participate in, and even the company we keep (1 Corinthians 15:33-34) can easily lead to sin and corruption, which will entangle us, and cost us even more time.

Hebrews 12:1
1 Therefore we also, since we are surrounded by so great a cloud of witnesses, let us lay aside every weight, and the sin which so easily ensnares us, and let us run with endurance the race that is set before us, NKJV

Lay aside the extra weight. Life can be difficult with extra baggage, and many of us have never experienced life without it, since there has never been a point in our life that we haven't had any.

Jesus calls us to take the road that few people travel, and it starts with entering the right gate; the narrow gate.

Matthew 7:13-14
13 "Enter by the narrow gate; for wide is the gate and broad is the way that leads to destruction, and there are many who go in by it. 14 Because narrow is the gate and difficult is the way which leads to life, and there are few who find it. NKJV

We don't just say "Jesus is Lord," and follow the crowd, but we enter the race (1 Corinthians 9:26-27). The Christian life is a race (Hebrews 12:1 above). Now that we are saved, those who enter the race go through the narrow gate, and they are getting to know Christ at all cost. For them, time is of the essence.

That may be more difficult at first on our flesh, because our flesh doesn't want us to take time for Jesus, but to do what the people of this world are doing. However, the narrow gate leads to life, but the broad gate leads to destruction.

Instead of remaining a friend of this world, God has called us into fellowship with His Son our Lord Jesus Christ.

1 Corinthians 1:9
9 God is faithful, by whom you were called into the fellowship of His Son, Jesus Christ our Lord. NKJV

Some might say that we already have fellowship with Jesus because we have been saved, but that is not necessarily true. We were seated with Christ in the Kingdom of Christ when we were saved, but to fellowship with Jesus is a choice.

1 John 1:3-7
3 That which we have seen and heard declare we unto you, that ye also may have fellowship with us: and truly our fellowship is with the Father, and with his Son Jesus Christ. 4 And these things write we unto you, that your joy may be full.

5 This then is the message which we have heard of him, and declare unto you, that God is light, and in him is no darkness at all. 6 If we say that we have fellowship with him, and walk in darkness, we lie, and do not the truth: 7 But if we walk in the light, as he is in the light, we have fellowship one with another, and the blood of Jesus Christ his Son cleanseth us from all sin. KJV

We cannot have fellowship with God, and Jesus, if we walk in darkness. Yes, we were seated with Christ, in His Kingdom, when we were saved, and God is with us because we have confessed that Jesus is Lord (1 John 4:15), but we cannot assume that we have fellowship with Jesus, or even know Who He is, until we obey His Word (1 John 2:6).

Jesus told His disciples that He would not even be their friend unless they obeyed what He commanded (verse 14 below). How are we any different?

John 15:13-14
13 Greater love hath no man than this, that a man lay down his life for his friends. 14 Ye are my friends, if ye do whatsoever I command you. KJV

Jesus knew them, since He had walked with them for years, but that didn't mean that He was going to be their friend, unless they obeyed Him. We can't use scripture against scripture, but we read scripture with scripture, without assuming anything. If we walk in darkness, we are out of fellowship.

Consider that when we were saved, we were delivered from the power of darkness, and at the same time, called out of darkness to live a holy life (1 Peter 2:9, 3:9). In other words, we have been redeemed from our former conduct (verse 18 below). Therefore, we, who are saved, do not have to live in the way that we used to live before we were saved.

1 Peter 1:14-19
14 as obedient children, not conforming yourselves to the former lusts, as in your ignorance; 15 but as He who called you is holy, you also be holy in all your conduct, 16 because it is written, "Be holy, for I am holy."

17 And if you call on the Father, who without partiality judges according to each one's work, conduct yourselves throughout the time of your stay here in fear; 18 knowing that you were not redeemed with corruptible things, like silver or gold, from your aimless conduct received by tradition from your fathers, 19 but with the precious blood of Christ, as of a lamb without blemish and without spot. NKJV

We were called to live a holy life, and we were redeemed from our old way of life, by the blood of Jesus (verses above), and we were delivered from the power of darkness (Colossians 1:13). That means that if we remain in darkness, we have chosen to live there, by our actions.

We can be forgiven, if we confess our sins (1 John 1:9), but what happens if we do not know that we should be living a new life, or even that Christians are capable of living a new life? Combine that with a crowd of people headed in the wrong direction, and we may never change our lifestyle. That describes the path that most people take; the wide gate.

It's very easy to join the crowd of people headed in the wrong direction when we do not know the truth. For them, the Christian life is just doing the best that we can do, but that's far from what we should be doing.

Actually, we are supposed to fight, in order to remain in the faith (1 Timothy 1:18-20, 2 Corinthians 10:3-5). I say remain, because when we were saved, we were given everything we needed to stop sinning, and to walk in newness of life (Romans 6:1-12).

This is evident in the life of new converts, who after accepting Jesus as Lord, have the God-given ability to say no to sin through grace (Titus 2:11-14). However, most of us do not know that we have to continue in what we were given. We must continue in what we were given, and even fight to remain in it.

Why should Christians fight to remain in the light after we are saved, rather than fall back to live in darkness? There are a few reasons.

The first one is written in 1 Peter 1:16 above. God says to "Be holy" because He is holy. He has called us out of darkness (1 Peter 2:9), and asked us to be holy in our conduct. In other words, God, Who saved us, and reconciled us to Himself, through His Son our Lord Jesus Christ, is telling us to come out of darkness, and to live like Him (Ephesians 5:1, 1 Thessalonians 4:3-4).

As we have learned, if we walk in darkness, we are out of fellowship with God (1 John 1:3-7), and by refusing to come out of darkness, we refuse to answer

His call. Consequently, He will not answer our call (Proverbs 1:22-33).

There goes our prayer life. Most Christians have no idea that how we live determines how God will answer our cry for help (1 Peter 3:10-12). That's because our view of the Christian life is not in-line with scripture.

We think that we are just waiting here to go home, but God saved us for a purpose; His purpose (2 Timothy 1:9). To reject God's purpose for saving us is the same as rejecting God's will for our life, which brings up the second reason why Christians should come out of darkness, and fight to remain in the light.

Matthew 7:21-23
21 "Not everyone who says to Me, 'Lord, Lord,' shall enter the kingdom of heaven, but he who does the will of My Father in heaven. 22 Many will say to Me in that day, 'Lord, Lord, have we not prophesied in Your name, cast out demons in Your name, and done many wonders in Your name?' 23 And then I will declare to them, 'I never knew you; depart from Me, you who practice lawlessness!' NKJV

Not everyone who calls Jesus "Lord" will be able to enter the Kingdom of Heaven, but only those who do the will of God (verse 21 above). For me, that's reason enough to come out of darkness, and fight to remain in the light, since the will of God is for us to be holy (sanctified).

The will of God is our sanctification (1 Thessalonians 4:3-5). In other words, God wants us to be holy in conduct, and He has already given us the means to do it.

Shall we say no, and join those who will never come to know Jesus in accordance with the Word of God? Let us repent and return to the Lord our God so that He will have mercy on us. Amen.

Notice that many people will declare that they have done all sorts of spiritual things, such as casting out demons, and prophesying, but they never took the time needed to become holy in conduct, through knowing Jesus. Jesus says that He will tell them, "Away from Me, I never knew you."

Therefore, how important is getting to know Jesus? Is it more important than what you are presently participating in, in your spare time? If you thought that I was being too hard on you in the last chapter, this chapter should straighten that out.

Those who do the will of the Father, come out of darkness, and live a holy life. They come to know Jesus Christ, in accordance with the Word of God. Those who do not, will not make it, according to the Word of the Lord written in Matthew 7:21-23 above, and Luke 13:23-28 below.

I thought being saved meant that we "knew Jesus" at one time too, but that isn't the case, and there aren't any verses to support that. However, there are verses that describe how to know Him. If we come to know Him in the way described in scripture, then surely we will not be among those who take the wide gate to destruction.

In order to renew our mind to the point of being transformed, we have to stop conforming to this world, which we have already discussed. Coming to know Christ includes doing that, plus putting on the new person (verse 24 below).

In the passage of scripture below, notice that the first few verses describe what not to do (verses 17-19), and the remainder describe what we should be doing in order to learn Christ (verses 20-24).

Ephesians 4:17-24
17 This I say, therefore, and testify in the Lord, that you should no longer walk as the rest of the Gentiles walk, in the futility of their mind, 18 having their understanding darkened, being alienated from the life of God, because of the ignorance that is in them, because of the blindness of their heart; 19 who, being past feeling, have given themselves over to lewdness, to work all uncleanness with greediness. 20 But you have not so learned Christ, 21 if indeed you have heard Him and have been taught by Him, as the truth is in Jesus: 22 that you put off, concerning your former conduct, the old man which grows corrupt according to the deceitful lusts, 23 and be renewed in the spirit of your mind, 24 and that you put on the new man which was created according to God, in true righteousness and holiness. NKJV

Knowing Christ means that we willingly put off our former conduct, renew our mind, and put on the new man created according to God (verses 21-24 above). If we refuse to do that, we will become ignorant, separated from the life that God has given us, and our understanding will be darkened (verse 18 above).

Imagine being separated from the life of God, and not even knowing the verses we have covered above. That's ignorance. People in that predicament, wouldn't even know that there was a problem, except that their prayers go unanswered, but most people are used to that.

We cannot ignore the verses above concerning being redeemed from our former conduct, delivered from the power of darkness, being called out of darkness, and being called to be holy. Although, it is a choice, those who make the decision to remain in darkness will regret that decision one day.

Don't assume that just because spiritual things are happening all around you, that you are answering God's call to live a holy life, or that you have come to know Jesus. Many think that because someone was healed, or someone spoke in tongues, or someone prophesied, that everything is okay. However, read Matthew 7:22 again.

Matthew 7:22
22 Many will say to me in that day, Lord, Lord, have we not prophesied in thy name? and in thy name have cast out devils?

and in thy name done many wonderful works? KJV

Spiritual things were happening, but none of those people came to know Jesus. God's gifts are irrevocable (Romans 11:29), and those who use them are not exempt from coming out of darkness. Therefore, absolutely, nothing is more important than doing the will of God, and coming to know Christ.

My friend, get this. I have asked many groups of people from different denominations, "How do we come to know Jesus," and "What is God's will?" Unfortunately, I have never received an answer in-line with what is written, even from the Bible they were using. However, they knew all about worldly things that Christians participate in.

We are not putting two and two together here. If we know all about why Christians celebrate on Halloween night, and many other worldly Christian events, but we do not know the basic building blocks of the faith, then our worldliness has prevented us from growing up spiritually.

We need God's Word living on the inside of us long before we need to be overly concerned about spiritual gifts, miracles, signs and wonders, or any worldly Christian event. Don't chase miracles, or anything else, but chase the truth, until it is living on the inside of you. God's Word is truth (John 17:17).

Therefore, do what you have the faith to do, but for those of us who know the scriptures, everything is a loss compared to knowing Christ Jesus, and we do away with worldly things, that we may gain more of Him (verse 8 below).

Philippians 3:8-9
8 Yet indeed I also count all things loss for the excellence of the knowledge of Christ Jesus my Lord, for whom I have suffered the loss of all things, and count them as rubbish, that I may gain Christ 9 and be found in Him, not having my own righteousness, which is from the law, but that which is through faith in Christ, the righteousness which is from God by faith NKJV

Everything is a loss compared to knowing Christ, and we come to know Him by putting off our old self, renewing our mind, and putting on the new man (Ephesians 4:20-24 above).

Therefore, in order to gain more of Christ, we need to lose more of who we used to be, before we were saved. That means that we need to separate ourself from the world's ways, rather than create a Christian version of everything we used to participate in.

You can choose to ignore those verses like many today, who are betting their eternal future on the Words of Jesus Christ being a lie. Imagine that. There are whole denominations today that do not believe Matthew 7:21-23 above, or Luke 13:23-28 below, which basically say the same thing. That may shock you, but these things will happen just like they are written.

Heaven and earth may pass away, but Jesus said that His Word would never pass away (verse 35 below). Do you believe Jesus?

Matthew 24:35
35 Heaven and earth shall pass away, but my words shall not pass away. KJV

Everything is a loss compared to knowing Christ. That means that there is absolutely nothing going on in your life right now, that is more important than following Ephesians 4:20-24 above; nothing.

Cancel your calendar, call in emergency vacation, turn the TV off, and ask the neighbors to cut your grass, because you have some studying to do. Change the message on your phone to say that you will return all calls after you come to know Jesus Christ our Lord, since nothing is more important.

"Many will say to me on that day, Lord, Lord, did we not" do this or that in Your name (Matthew 7:22 above)? What happened? They allowed their flesh to decide what was more important, rather than allowing the Word of God to lead them. They decided what they were going to give God, rather than follow the instructions written in scripture. Many will make that mistake according to Matthew 7:22 above.

Read the following passage of scripture again, and ask yourself if you know Jesus, or if you had taken the wide gate that leads to destruction before you started reading this book? Those who do not know Him, will not make it.

1 John 2:3-6
3 Now by this we know that we know Him, if we keep His commandments. 4 He who says, "I know Him," and does not keep His commandments, is a liar, and the truth is not in him. 5 But whoever keeps His word, truly the love of God is perfected in him. By this we know that we are in Him. 6 He who says he abides in Him ought himself also to walk just as He walked. NKJV

That passage of scripture tells us two things. We must obey Jesus' commands, and keep His Word, before we will know Him. Is that something that any of us can do before we get saved? If we could obey before we got saved, why would we need Jesus?

Yes, we got saved, and now that we are saved, we're coming to know Jesus in accordance with the Word of God, and not according to human wisdom, or philosophy. Part of the will of the Father is to believe in the Son (John 6:29), and the Son has said that those who do not know Him, will not enter the Kingdom of Heaven. Do we believe the Son?

One of the biggest mistakes that Christians make is to assume that being saved from the power of darkness, is the same as eternal salvation. Eternal salvation is not the same as when we first got saved. Jesus is the source of eternal salvation for those who obey Him (verse 9 below).

Hebrews 5:9
9 And having been perfected, He became the author of eternal salvation to all who obey Him, NKJV

That verse describes receiving eternal salvation. It's different from confessing Jesus as Lord, and believing in our heart that God raised Him from the dead (Romans 10:9-10), and that is the reason why many misinterpret Romans chapter 10:9-10.

Believing with our heart, and confessing doesn't start and stop with calling Jesus, "Lord," but it is "unto" salvation. If we had known Romans 10:6-8, we would have known that the righteousness of faith doesn't start and stop with one statement of faith, but it is a life-time commitment, or a lifestyle change.

The righteous live by faith (Romans 1:17, Galatians 2:20, Hebrews 10:37-39), and those who have the Spirit of faith, always speak in-line with what is written (2 Corinthians 4:13). We will cover that in a later chapter.

Here is another passage that is similar to Matthew 7:21-23 above.

Luke 13:23-28
23 Then one said to Him, "Lord, are there few who are saved?" And He said to them, 24 "Strive to enter through the narrow gate, for many, I say to you, will seek to enter and will not be able.

25 When once the Master of the house has risen up and shut the door, and you begin to stand outside and knock at the door, saying, 'Lord, Lord, open for us,' and He will answer and say to you, 'I do not know you, where you are from,' 26 then you will begin to say, 'We ate and drank in Your presence, and You taught in our streets.' 27 But He will say, 'I tell you I do not know you, where you are from. Depart from Me, all you workers of iniquity.'

28 There will be weeping and gnashing of teeth, when you see Abraham and Isaac and Jacob and all the prophets in the kingdom of God, and yourselves thrust out. NKJV

"Away from Me, I never knew you!" How important is getting to know Jesus, in view of those verses? Get this. According to their response, the people who will hear Jesus say "Away from Me, I never knew you" will be shocked (verse 26 above, Matthew 7:22 above).

It would be a shock if a person attended church services all his life, but never learned how to know Jesus in accordance with what is written in the Bible.

However, according to those two passages of scripture, Luke 13:23-28, and Matthew 7:21-23 above, it will happen. Therefore, make sure that you know Jesus in accordance with Ephesians 4:20-24, and 1 John 2:3-6 above.

One lady said that she didn't believe that a loving God, Who sent His Son to die for us would turn around and just kick us out in the end because we didn't do something right. I pray that He doesn't, but shall I believe what I want to believe, or the Word of God, which endures forever?

Many people live by what they feel, and not by faith. Big mistake. There is a way that seems right, but in the end, it will lead to death (Proverbs 14:12, 16:25).

Therefore, we all have a choice. We can trust Jesus, or trust our feelings. I choose Jesus, and the following verses gives me reason enough.

John 3:36
36 He who believes in the Son has everlasting life; and he who does not believe the Son shall not see life, but the wrath of God abides on him." NKJV

John 5:24
24 "Most assuredly, I say to you, he who hears My word and believes in Him who sent Me has everlasting life, and shall not come into judgment, but has passed from death into life. NKJV

Should I teach what I feel like teaching, and pray really hard that God's Word is not truth? That way I too can ignore huge passages of scripture and even teach the opposite. No, I will not! Lord willing, I shall preach the Word of Him Who reached down into the fire, and pulled me out when there was nobody else to save me. May my mouth never speak against what is written in the Word of God.

Glory be to the living God forever, and to the Lamb Who was slain, and was raised to life, so that a piece of garbage like me could lay hold of eternal life! Praise, glory, and honor belong to the Lord our God forever, and ever! Amen.

My Lord said to lean not on our own understanding (Proverbs 3:5). He also said to preach His Word, and be prepared, because a time will come when people would not put up with what is written in the Bible (2 Timothy 4:1-4). We're here! Therefore, I will keep preaching the Word of God, and if somebody wants to bet their eternal future on the verses above being false, then that's on them.

It's so easy to get caught up in feelings, and if we are not careful our feelings can be our guide, but feelings are not faith. We have to deny ourself in order to follow Jesus, and that's the part of ourself that we should be denying; our feelings.

Now what

If you are like me and believe every Word of God, then by now you know that there is no way possible to remain as you were before you were saved, and grow spiritually. You should "no longer walk as the rest of the Gentiles walk," which means that you should stop living like you used to live (Ephesians 4:17 above).

Show me someone who is willing to die to the ways of this world, renew their mind with the truth, and put on the new man, and I will show you someone who has positioned himself to receive what is promised. Glory be to God.

It is our responsibility as Christians to put off who we used to be, and put on the new person created to be like God in true righteousness and holiness (Colossians 3:10, Ephesians 4:22-24 above).

We are debtors (verse 12 below). In other words, we owe our very life to God, but if we continue to live according to the flesh, we will die (verse 13 below).

Romans 8:12-13
12 Therefore, brethren, we are debtors — not to the flesh, to live according to the flesh. 13 For if you live according to the flesh you will die; but if by the Spirit you put to death the deeds of the body, you will live. NKJV

Therefore, participate in whatever you want to participate in without violating scripture, but whatever you are doing that is keeping you from knowing Jesus, in accordance with His Word, is against your very soul (verse 11 below).

1 Peter 2:11-12
11 Beloved, I beg you as sojourners and pilgrims, abstain from fleshly lusts which war against the soul, 12 having your conduct honorable among the Gentiles, that when they speak against you as evildoers, they may, by your good works which they observe, glorify God in the day of visitation. NKJV

Withdraw (abstain) from fleshly (worldly) lusts (desires), which war against your soul (verse 11 above). Get this. The desires we have within us that make us want to fit in with the people of this world are trying to kill us. Imagine that. However, if we submit to God's ways, and resist the devil, he will flee from us (James 4:7).

James 4:7
7 Submit yourselves therefore to God. Resist the devil, and he will flee from you. KJV

We are supposed to be separated from the life of God when we do not die to self (Ephesians 4:18 above). We are supposed to have a darkened understanding when we live like everybody else in this world (Ephesians 4:17), just as we are supposed to have a depraved mind if we do not continue in our faith (Romans 1:28).

Those things are supposed to happen because it is written that they will happen to those who do not submit to God's ways. At that point in time, we are taught to blame everything on the devil, but the course of action we should be taking is to repent, and then submit to God's ways.

We shouldn't be shocked if we become blind to God's ways, and given over to lewdness (filthiness), if we refuse to die to self, renew our mind with the truth, and put on the new man (Ephesians 4:17-24), because it is written that it will happen. That's not something that we can pray away.

In the following verses, Jesus explains how He expects His disciples (Christians) to live in this world, and the consequences for those who reject His teachings. Allow the following verses to paint a picture in your mind.

Matthew 16:24-25
24 Then Jesus said to His disciples, "If anyone desires to come after Me, let him deny himself, and take up his cross, and follow Me. 25 For whoever desires to save his life will lose it, but whoever loses his life for My sake will find it. NKJV

Matthew 10:37-39
37 He who loves father or mother more than Me is not worthy of Me. And he who loves son or daughter more than Me is not worthy of Me. 38 And he who does not take his cross and follow after Me is not worthy of Me. 39 He who finds his life will lose it, and he who loses his life for My sake will find it. NKJV

John 12:25-26
25 He who loves his life will lose it, and he who hates his life in this world will keep it for eternal life. 26 If anyone serves Me, let him follow Me; and where I am, there My servant will be also. If anyone serves Me, him My Father will honor. NKJV

Does Jesus expect those who follow Him to change their way of life here on earth? Yes sir, He does, and those changes would be very noticeable to the people around us. If we start doing those things, the people of this world will start telling us that "normal people don't do that."

However, those who find their life will lose it (Matthew 16:25 above). Those who love their earthly family more than Jesus are not worthy of Him (Matthew 10:37 above), but those who serve Jesus, even to the point of hating their life will keep it for eternal life (John 12:25). We need to know that.

In what way do Christians who "do not" lose their life for the Lord, end up losing their life later? Could denying ourself now be the cure for all sorts of ailments that rob Christians of their way of life in their later years, such as Alzheimer's disease, Parkinson's disease, dementia, strokes, heart disease, cancer, diabetes, and the like? Like it or not, that fits the description, and so does any type of life-hindering disability, or lingering illness.

If we refuse to die to self, putting the old man to death, then we will "never" be totally free from sin (Romans 6:1-7). We can be forgiven, if we confess our sins (1 John 1:9), but we still reap what we sow.

How much destruction would it take to change you? That's how much is on the way (Hebrews 12:4-13). Think about that. I've had enough.

I asked an elderly gentleman, who was seeking to be healed by the Lord, if he was in the process of putting off his old self, and renewing his mind with the truth? He answered by saying, "Well, I go to church every Sunday." He had no idea what I was talking about, even though he had been a Christian for a very long time.

How do you discreetly ask a lifelong Christian if the reason he has a lingering illness, is because he has not lost his life for the Lord? You can't, because he won't understand it.

This man had lived what I would call the perfect worldly Christian life. He went to church, paid his tithes, took care of his earthly family, and he had recently settled into his retirement home. Why wouldn't God answer his cry for help?

How long would it take to explain what we have covered so far? Most people just want us to say a prayer and go, because "they have things to do!"

This man had everything ready, set, go! He was ready to enjoy his retirement. He found his life, except he hadn't lived by faith in Jesus Christ. Consequently, what was predicted to happen by Jesus Christ according to His Word, did happen. A few months after retirement, he lost his life to cancer.

How do you tell the perfect Christian, in the world's eyes, to repent and turn toward God? Does the Bible tell us to "go to church" once a week, and everything will be fine?" No, it doesn't. Is there a verse that says to sing as loud as we can every Sunday morning and we will be healed? Nope. Do the instructions tell us to read our Bible every now and then, and God is going to see to it that we will have the things that we worry about? No, that is not what it says.

In fact, we can do those things and not even come to know Jesus, or come out of darkness, or renew our mind with the truth, or stop conforming to this world. It says "If we find our life, we will lose our life, but if we lose our life for the Lord, we will find life." In order to lose our life for the Lord, we need to get our instructions from the Lord. We need to find out what He wants us to do.

Father, in Jesus' name, we have lived in opposition to Your Word and Your ways. According to Your great mercy, forgive us our sins. We want to know You in accordance with Your Word. We want to follow Your ways. Help us Lord to be what You have called us to be. Restore us to Your favor. Watch over us and lead us in the way everlasting. You alone are worthy of all the praise, glory, and honor, forever and ever. Amen.

I'm Alan Ballou; a servant. If I may be of service to you, please contact me.

ഇൻൻ

8

Doers of the Word

෮උ෪

Faith without deeds is a dead faith, and a dead faith cannot save us (James 2:14), since the goal, or the outcome of our faith is the salvation of our souls (verse 9 below).

1 Peter 1:9
9 Receiving the end of your faith, even the salvation of your souls. KJV

Therefore, we're going to be doers of the Word, rather than just hearers. In other words, as we hear the Word, we are going to put it into practice.

James 1:22-24
22 But be doers of the word, and not hearers only, deceiving yourselves. 23 For if anyone is a hearer of the word and not a doer, he is like a man observing his natural face in a mirror; 24 for he observes himself, goes away, and immediately forgets what kind of man he was. NKJV

There is great value in hearing the Word, especially if that is where a person is in their faith. If you have been a Christian for less than four years, or if you are starting over, then you need to be reading the Word of God, out loud, on a daily basis.

I have seen many lives changed just by either reading fifteen chapters a day, or listening to the pure Word of God being read from the New King James Bible. Hearing the pure Word of God on a daily basis will heal and deliver people with addictions, mental problems, as well as anger issues, and the like, if they believe what they hear (1 Thessalonians 2:13).

However, at some point during our walk of faith, we need to become doers of the Word. Hearing it will bring supernatural results, but hearing alone is not enough, especially for long-time Christians.

Trouble will come to test us, in order to see if we will remain in the faith (Matthew 13:20-21). Those who become doers of the Word will bear the right type of fruit (Matthew 13:23, Mark 4:20). Those who are not doers of the Word, will not stand in the faith.

I'm not trying to get you to do anything besides what is already written in your Bible. Many people try to make this out to be something new, but it's not. It's just new to them, and it works just like it is written.

Read the following passage of scripture, and take notice of the two homes. One will soon face destruction, and the other will still be standing after the storm. What is the difference between the two?

Luke 6:46-49
46 "But why do you call Me 'Lord, Lord,' and not do the things which I say? 47 Whoever comes to Me, and hears My sayings and does them, I will show you whom he is like: 48 He is like a man building a house, who dug deep and laid the foundation on the rock. And when the flood arose, the stream beat vehemently against that house, and could not shake it, for it was founded on the rock. 49 But he who heard and did nothing is like a man who built a house on the earth without a foundation, against which the stream beat vehemently; and immediately it fell. And the ruin of that house was great." NKJV

Both houses heard Jesus' Word, but only one practiced what He taught. The trouble came upon both. Christians are not necessarily protected from trouble, but from calamity without remedy (Proverbs 1:22-33, Acts 14:22, Psalm 34:19, 1 Peter 1:6-7).

The stream is beating against both houses according to the scriptures above, and both need God to rescue them from the trouble. Both may cry out to God for help, but only one remains standing; the one with the doers living in it.

The people in the other home may cry out, over and over, but there is no answer. They may even have everyone praying for them, and comforting them in some fashion, but there is no direct answer from God.

I don't mean this in a bad way, but the church is full of people who always live in some form of total destruction, even though they are screaming how blessed they are. Why? God has promised that the house that heard His Words, but did not put it into practice would be in ruins (Luke 6:46-49).

There is no prayer that can be used to avoid the ruin that comes on those who reject God's Word. We can repent for not following the teachings and be heard, but there is no way around obedience. We reap what we sow.

Therefore, show me a family who hears the Word, but does not put it into practice, and I will show you a family who will soon go through hard times without being rescued from the destruction (Luke 6:46-49 above). Even if they are partially delivered, the storms keep coming, until they repent and turn, or they are living in ruins.

They will begin to say things like, "I can't win for losing." "When it rains, it pours." "If I didn't have bad luck, I wouldn't have any luck at all." However, no one asks if they are hearing the Word of God, but refusing to put it into practice.

The future is very predictable when we use the Word of God as a ruler. Drastic changes are needed to prevent destruction, but who will listen to godly advice, when someone full of worldly wisdom is waiting to answer questions with the best the world has to offer (Luke 16:15, 1 Corinthians 3:18-20)? Get your answers from the scriptures.

Sometimes we think that because we have been attending some type of religious service for many years, God will keep us from calamity without remedy, but that isn't what is promised. In fact, if we sit and listen to the Word of God being preached, but never do what it says, that's a guarantee that total destruction is on the way (verse 49 above). It's just a matter of time.

Some people quote false teachers in saying that "God will not put on you more than you can bear." That's not written in any Bible that you need to be reading.

Some might dare to say that they won't listen to the Word of God if they will be punished for not putting it into practice, and so it is today (2 Timothy 4:3-4). However, these are the ones who will surely hear, "Away from Me, I never knew you," on the last day (Matthew 7:21-23, Luke 13:22-28).

It is the Word of God that sanctifies (John 17:17, 8:31-38). Therefore, can we avoid the Word, and do the will of God, at the same time? No, we cannot. However, there are people who will change churches, if they have to listen to the verses we have covered so far.

Even today there are huge crowds developing where people are gathering in order to get away from the verses we will cover in this book, and that is what is predicted to happen (2 Timothy 4:3-4). Don't follow the crowd.

If you have never heard the verses we have covered so far, then you are probably gathering in a house of cards. It may be the biggest, and the prettiest place you have ever seen, but in a house of God, God's Word is proclaimed to God's people (2 Timothy 4:1-4). We cannot avoid God's Word, and be sanctified by the truth (John 17:17).

Therefore, if you want to make sure that you are in God's house, close your eyes, and listen with your faith. We walk by faith, and not by sight (2 Corinthians 5:7). God's people willingly offer their body as a living sacrifice, stop conforming to this world, and renew their mind with the truth (Romans 12:1-2).

Offering our body as a living sacrifice, means that we no longer own our body, but now we allow Jesus to tell us what to do.

2 Corinthians 5:14-17
14 For the love of Christ compels us, because we judge thus: that if One died for all, then all died; 15 and He died for all, that those who live should live no longer for themselves, but for Him who died for them and rose again. 16 Therefore, from now

on, we regard no one according to the flesh. Even though we have known Christ according to the flesh, yet now we know Him thus no longer. 17 Therefore, if anyone is in Christ, he is a new creation; old things have passed away; behold, all things have become new. NKJV

One died for all that those who live, should no longer live for themself, but for Him Who died for them (verse 14-15 above). We regard no one according to the flesh (16 above). Old things have passed away (verse 17 above).

What would you need to cut out of your life in order to live like that? That is the direction that God is expecting you to head in. The old is gone when we decide to die to the old and live for Jesus, then we will be a new creation.

If the old man is not gone then we are not yet a new creation. Many today interpret verse 17 as if it does not come after verse 15 above, and consequently, they do not mix faith with this passage of scripture. They proclaim to be a new creation, but they never deny themself and live for Jesus.

Get this. All who belong to Christ "have" killed their sinful nature. That's past tense (have). That's a new creation. The old is gone; dead, done away with (Romans 6:6 below).

Galatians 5:24
24 And those who are Christ's have crucified the flesh with its passions and desires. NKJV

Don't try to keep twenty percent of the old you alive because it has a way of growing again (2 Peter 2:20-22). I've already tried to live with one foot in the world. Big mistake. Thank You, Jesus! May the Lord have mercy on all of us.

We don't see many people concerned about their sinful nature today because Galatians 5:24 is ignored for the most part, and 2 Corinthians 5:17 is interpreted outside of the context it is in. Consequently, today it is obvious that church gatherings are changing more and more, to meet the expectations of the people of this world, which means that we can expect more destruction in the future.

However, those who hear the Word of God and keep it are blessed.

Luke 11:28
28 But He said, "More than that, blessed are those who hear the word of God and keep it!" NKJV

There is a reason why most Christians do not believe that we can stop sinning, and it isn't because we are full of the Word of God. No, somebody taught us that Christians cannot stop sinning, and we believed it. Instead of hearing the Word and believing it, we believed a lie, that doesn't bring about blessings, but curses.

Nobody asked questions, because human traditions, that have been passed down to us, make us listen without questioning. One of the newer Bibles has even changed a verse in the New Testament to say that we cannot question authority.

That's okay because 1 Thessalonians 5:21 is still in it, which basically tells us to test everything we receive as truth to make sure that it is written in the Bible, and in the context we are hearing it (verse 21 below).

1 Thessalonians 5:21
21 Prove all things; hold fast that which is good. KJV

Everything is suspect until tested. Always read what comes before a verse, and after it. Look for any instructions contained in a promise, or even in the same chapter. Check to see who the promise is referring to, and ask yourself if you have the same type of faith as the people to whom the promise is made.

If we get the instructions wrong, the results will be wrong. However, even after "not" receiving what is promised, time and time again, most never check to see if they have the right instructions. Imagine trying to be a doer of the Word of God, but following worldly instructions, or philosophy. It happens.

Therefore, test everything, and only hold on to the good. The wisdom of men and worldly traditions, can rob God's Word of the effect it should have on a person (Matthew 15:6, 1 Corinthians 1:17).

Do not accept anything that is beyond what is written in the Bible, or even think beyond what is written (1 Corinthians 4:6, Proverbs 30:5-6 below). Anything that is beyond what is written is an addition to what is written.

1 Corinthians 4:6
6 Now these things, brethren, I have figuratively transferred to myself and Apollos for your sakes, that you may learn in us not to think beyond what is written, that none of you may be puffed up on behalf of one against the other. NKJV

Proverbs 30:5-6
5 Every word of God is pure; He is a shield to those who put their trust in Him. 6 Do not add to His words, Lest He rebuke you, and you be found a liar. NKJV

If it is "not" written in the Bible, you don't need it for this life and godliness (2 Peter 1:3-4). It's just that simple. It may even be true, but if it is not written, you don't need it. On the other hand, if it is written, be careful not to reject it (Mark 4:24-25), or speak against it (1 Timothy 6:20-21).

Now what

Here is yet another reason for destruction in the life of well-meaning Christian people. The lack of knowledge can bring a lifetime of hurt.

We owe our life to the Lord Jesus Christ, and He wants us to live for Him. In order to do that, we have to offer our body to Him as a living sacrifice. In order to do that, we have to renew our mind with the truth to the point of being transformed. In order to do that, we have to stop conforming to the world around us, and in order to do that we have to die to self.

When we are in the process of doing these things, we live the life that God has laid out for us. He answers our prayers. He provides the things we need. He delivers us from trouble, and so on, but it is when we step away from this process that destruction, and great ruin is guaranteed.

Show me a long-time, well-meaning Christian, who stops continuing in his faith, remains a friend of this world, or refuses to die to self, and I will show you someone who will desperately need your prayers on a continual basis. Without godly instructions, in accordance with the Word of God, he will never understand what is happening to him, or how to solve the problem.

You might say that there is nothing wrong with praying for one another, and that is true. However, how much destruction could we avoid if we would simply be doers of the Word?

The real problem is that we don't want to die to "self," but instead, all we want out of the Christian life is to be saved to the point of making it to Heaven. Therefore, all we are interested in is the bare minimum, and we suffer the consequences of that decision.

For example, we suffer when we do not grow spiritually because of our worldliness, which we covered in a previous chapter. We suffer when we do not continue in our faith, and end up being given over to a depraved mind, which we have covered.

We suffer when we refuse to deny ourself. Our feelings will prevent us from living by faith, and lead us down paths that make God's promises seem untrue, because they are not materializing. We suffer when we refuse to put the old man to death, and now we know that those who refuse to become doers of the Word of God will soon live in ruins.

All we really want is for God to take our problems away. However, our problems identify the solution. Die to sin, and live for righteousness. If we were living by faith, we would be looking for the promises that solve our problems, and we would mix faith with them, in order to receive our hope.

We're still living in sin because we haven't died to it. We haven't died to sin because we refuse to die with Christ, and we are shocked when sin brings about our destruction. We ask for prayer, but nobody looks for the violated spiritual principles.

Consequently, we may be comforted for a while, but the problem is never resolved, until we repent, and return to the Lord our God, in accordance with His ways. Put the things we have covered so far into practice, and watch your life change for the better. It works!

Look at this question again. How can we who died to sin, live any longer in it (verse 2 below)? That's the question that the Bible is asking us, and the answer is that we haven't died to sin yet. That's why we are still living in it, and if we never die to our old self, we will never be freed from sin (verses 6-7 below).

Romans 6:1-7
1 What shall we say then? Shall we continue in sin that grace may abound? 2 Certainly not! How shall we who died to sin live any longer in it? 3 Or do you not know that as many of us as were baptized into Christ Jesus were baptized into His death? 4 Therefore we were buried with Him through baptism into death, that just as Christ was raised from the dead by the glory of the Father, even so we also should walk in newness of life. 5 For if we have been united together in the likeness of His death, certainly we also shall be in the likeness of His resurrection, 6 knowing this, that our old man was crucified with Him, that the body of sin might be done away with, that we should no longer be slaves of sin. 7 For he who has died has been freed from sin. NKJV

He who has died has been freed from sin (verse 7 above). We were baptized into Christ's death (verse 3 above). In other words, we agreed to die with Him through our baptism, in order that the body of sin might be done away with (verse 6 above).

Imagine that. Through your baptism, you agreed to die with Christ. That means that you agreed to put the old person (the old you) to death. Count it all a loss, and start over.

We have already agreed to do the things we have covered in the past few chapters through our baptism. However, we have broken our promise, and we wonder why we are in destruction. The trouble has come in order to change our character; what we do, and what we say (Romans 5:3-5). God is helping us make good on our promise, since He is not willing that any should perish (verse 9 below).

2 Peter 3:9
9 The Lord is not slack concerning His promise, as some count slackness, but is longsuffering toward us, not willing that any should perish but that all should come to repentance. NKJV

Father, in Jesus' name, have mercy upon us. Forgive us for the sins that we have committed against You, and wash us clean with the blood of Christ that we may now serve You with a clear conscience. Instill in us an overwhelming desire to know You in accordance with the instructions found in Your Word. Forgive us for grieving Your Holy Spirit, and now fill us with Your Spirit, that we may walk in Your ways, and bring glory to Your holy name. In the name of Jesus Christ we pray. Amen!

Read the passage of scripture below, and know where we are headed if we continue the course. How can we be angry and sin not according to verse 26 below, if we have not been transformed into a new creation? We can't.

We probably won't be able to do any of those things effectively, until we put off the old man, and that's my point. It's difficult to be a doer of the Word until after we believe like Abraham, learn to use God's promises, mix faith with what we hear, continue in our faith, die to self, stop conforming to the world around us, and come out of darkness.

Therefore, everything we have learned up to this point we should be putting into practice, because it will have an effect on the next chapter, and so on. We should have the ability to follow the list of things to do below, if we continue in our faith. It may not happen overnight, but it will happen for those who are determined to be doers of the Word.

Ephesians 4:25-32
25 Wherefore putting away lying, speak every man truth with his neighbour: for we are members one of another. 26 Be ye angry, and sin not: let not the sun go down upon your wrath: 27 Neither give place to the devil. 28 Let him that stole steal no more: but rather let him labour, working with his hands the thing which is good, that he may have to give to him that needeth. 29 Let no corrupt communication proceed out of your mouth, but that which is good to the use of edifying, that it may minister grace unto the hearers. 30 And grieve not the holy Spirit of God, whereby ye are sealed unto the day of redemption. 31 Let all bitterness, and wrath, and anger, and clamour, and evil speaking, be put away from you, with all malice: 32 And be ye kind one to another, tenderhearted, forgiving one another, even as God for Christ's sake hath forgiven you. KJV

Notice that we can eventually put away anger according to verse 31 above, and Colossians 3:8, if we continue in our faith. Like I said, it doesn't happen overnight, but God gives us the grace needed to live the Christian life, assuming we are doing what we are supposed to be doing at any given time.

Put the things we have discussed so far into practice, and you will be ready for spiritual things by the time we get to the end of this book, Lord willing. God will help those who practice the truth. May the Lord bless you!

I'm Alan Ballou; a servant. My wife Lucie and I conduct group seminars, free of charge. If we may be of service to you, please contact us.

www.HowToStopSinning.com

ℰℭ

9

Share in His Holiness

ಬಂಡ

By now, you can probably tell that we can avoid some serious destruction in our life, just by knowing what Christians should be doing at any given time during our walk of faith.

Never blame the devil for any destruction that is due us because of our lack of knowledge, or our unwillingness to follow God's instructions found in His Word (Jude 1:8-10). God has no problem whatsoever with protecting us from the devil if we would do what we are supposed to be doing as Christians (1 John 5:18, 2 Thessalonians 3:3-4 below).

2 Thessalonians 3:3-4
3 But the Lord is faithful, who will establish you and guard you from the evil one. 4 And we have confidence in the Lord concerning you, both that you do and will do the things we command you. NKJV

The wicked one cannot even touch those who do not sin (verse 18 below). Therefore, wouldn't it be better to focus on our sin problem, rather than slandering the devil?

1 John 5:18
18 We know that whoever is born of God does not sin; but he who has been born of God keeps himself, and the wicked one does not touch him. NKJV

Hypothetically speaking, let's say that a person rejected the doctrine of abiding in Jesus, and spoke against God's promises concerning dying to sin, putting off the old man, and being transformed into a new person, and then he blamed all of his troubles on the devil. How do you think God should respond to that?

What if He responded in the same way that He responded toward Israel in the desert according to Numbers 14:26-35? Would He give those, who blame everything on the devil, what they so confidently proclaim? Imagine that.

Yes, the devil is an adversary, but some of us know more about the devil than we know about the doctrine of Jesus Christ.

All of the devil's fiery darts can be extinguished by faith (Ephesians 6:16); every last one of them. Let that sink in. Therefore, learn how to continue, and remain in the faith first (2 Corinthians 13:5, 1 Timothy 1:18-19).

Ephesians 6:16
16 above all, taking the shield of faith with which you will be able to quench all the fiery darts of the wicked one. NKJV

Our fight is a fight of faith. Therefore, our focus should be on remaining in the faith, rather than worrying about what the devil is up to, since remaining in the faith shields us from him.

1 Timothy 1:18-19
18 This charge I commit to you, son Timothy, according to the prophecies previously made concerning you, that by them you may wage the good warfare, 19 having faith and a good conscience, which some having rejected, concerning the faith have suffered shipwreck, NKJV

1 Timothy 6:11-12
11 But you, O man of God, flee these things and pursue righteousness, godliness, faith, love, patience, gentleness. 12 Fight the good fight of faith, lay hold on eternal life, to which you were also called and have confessed the good confession in the presence of many witnesses. NKJV

The devil has to seek someone to devour. That someone will be the one who does not have the Lord's protection, and does not know how to resist him by remaining in the faith.

1 Peter 5:8-9
8 Be sober, be vigilant; because your adversary the devil walks about like a roaring lion, seeking whom he may devour. 9 Resist him, steadfast in the faith, knowing that the same sufferings are experienced by your brotherhood in the world. NKJV

I want to teach you how to remain in the faith, so that the Lord will guard you. A part of remaining in the faith is to stop slandering the devil (Jude 1:8-11). That's not good, and we overcome evil with good (Romans 12:21). In other words, we do not return evil for evil, but with blessing, in order that we will be blessed.

1 Peter 3:8-9
8 Finally, all of you be of one mind, having compassion for one another; love as brothers, be tenderhearted, be courteous; 9 not returning evil for evil or reviling for reviling, but on the contrary blessing, knowing that you were called to this, that you may inherit a blessing. NKJV

If you asked me to name one characteristic of the people with the worst ill-nesses, or the worst diseases that I have ever worked with, I would say that they were always talking about the devil, and rarely about Jesus. In fact, they didn't even know the doctrine of Jesus Christ, but they seemed to know everything there was to know about what the devil was doing; well beyond what is written in the Bible.

One lady, seeking to be healed, told me that she could no longer pray out loud because the devil would know what she was praying, and somehow ruin her prayers. Is there a verse that says "Don't pray out loud?"

Is there a verse that says that the devil can ruin our prayers, or does God's instructions say to cast all of our cares on Him (1 Peter 5:7)? Never say things such as that unless you have a verse that instructs you to do so. When someone tells you "this is what we need to do," ask them to show it to you in black, white, and red. Then believe it.

If you accept and believe something that is against God's Word, then it can become real to you. However, we are supposed to cast anything out of our mind that is against the knowledge of God (2 Corinthians 10:3-5). That's why we should always ask "where is that written," so that we can accept it as truth, and follow it too. Test everything (1 Thessalonians 5:21)!

Get this. Each man's own words become his oracle (Jeremiah 23:36). There-fore, if the Bible doesn't say that the devil is doing this or that, then you should not say it, unless you want the devil to be able to do whatever it is that you are proclaiming.

Instead you should say, "Greater is the Lord Who is in me, than he that is in the world!" That would be speaking faith over your life. "The Lord is my helper!" "Whom shall I fear?"

1 John 4:4
4 You are of God, little children, and have overcome them, be-cause He who is in you is greater than he who is in the world. NKJV

Even if Christ is not living in you yet, you will be proclaiming that He is, as though that is the direction you are headed in; calling things that are not, as though they were (Romans 4:17).

Hebrews 13:6
6 So we may boldly say: "The Lord is my helper; I will not fear. What can man do to me?" NKJV

You may be shaking with fear, but you can still speak faith over your life, since you have not rejected God's Word. I'm assuming that you started this book at the beginning, and that you have at least repented of the things we have covered so far, if you had been living in violation of them.

We overcome the devil in the same way as the people of old; by the blood of Jesus, and the words that we proclaim (Romans 10:6-8).

Revelation 12:11

11 And they overcame him by the blood of the Lamb and by the word of their testimony, and they did not love their lives to the death. NKJV

This doesn't mean that we can avoid the instructions, and just speak words of faith like some are in the habit of doing. No, we're going to live by faith, and then speak our faith. It takes mixing faith with what is promised in order to make it materialize, which we have already covered (Hebrews 4:2).

Therefore, the devil is not our problem. Not living by faith is our problem. Living by faith in the Lord will deliver us from any kind of trouble, and that is what we will focus on in this book.

Many people learn to quote verses long before they learn how to live by faith. I have met some very sick people who could quote many good-sounding promises from the Bible, but they do not know the conditions associated with those promises.

Therefore, they never associate their sickness with their lack of living by faith. Those who cast aside God's instructions, have no right to proclaim His promises (Psalm 50:16-17 below).

Psalm 50:16-17

16 But unto the wicked God saith, What hast thou to do to declare my statutes, or that thou shouldest take my covenant in thy mouth? 17 Seeing thou hatest instruction, and castest my words behind thee. KJV

I'm not saying that we have to be perfect before we speak faith over our life, but repenting of dead works is an elementary teaching (Hebrews 6:1). In other words, quoting faith-building verses over our life, will not take away the destruction due us for living in opposition to God's ways.

Father, in Jesus' name, according to Your great compassion, have mercy on us. Forgive us for our ignorance. We do not know the things that we should know by now, and we do not live up to what we have already attained. Forgive us, and restore us to the joy of Your salvation. Save us Lord from the destruction that we have brought on ourself. In the name of Jesus Christ we pray. Amen.

Our God is able to deliver us, and our God is merciful, and He is with us! Amen. Praise God, halleluiah! However, there are a few things that we need to know, and things that we should do before the trouble comes.

First, we should make the Lord our refuge. A refuge is a place that provides protection in times of danger.

The Lord is able to deliver us from traps set by the wicked (verse 3 below), from destruction, and pestilences (verse 6 below), from terror (verse 5 below), from plagues (verse 10 below), from trouble (verse 15 below), and from the reward of the wicked (verse 8 below).

Psalm 91:1-16

1 He who dwells in the secret place of the Most High Shall abide under the shadow of the Almighty. 2 I will say of the Lord, "He is my refuge and my fortress; My God, in Him I will trust." 3 Surely He shall deliver you from the snare of the fowler And from the perilous pestilence. 4 He shall cover you with His feathers, And under His wings you shall take refuge; His truth shall be your shield and buckler.

5 You shall not be afraid of the terror by night, Nor of the arrow that flies by day, 6 Nor of the pestilence that walks in darkness, Nor of the destruction that lays waste at noonday. 7 A thousand may fall at your side, And ten thousand at your right hand; But it shall not come near you. 8 Only with your eyes shall you look, And see the reward of the wicked. 9 Because you have made the Lord, who is my refuge, Even the Most High, your dwelling place,

10 No evil shall befall you, Nor shall any plague come near your dwelling; 11 For He shall give His angels charge over you, To keep you in all your ways. 12 In their hands they shall bear you up, Lest you dash your foot against a stone. 13 You shall tread upon the lion and the cobra, The young lion and the serpent you shall trample underfoot. 14 "Because he has set his love upon Me, therefore I will deliver him; I will set him on high, because he has known My name. 15 He shall call upon Me, and I will answer him; I will be with him in trouble; I will deliver him and honor him. 16 With long life I will satisfy him, And show him My salvation." NKJV

Many people proclaim Psalm 91 over someone, or in certain situations, but if we wanted to place our faith in this passage of scripture, in order to receive what is promised, we have to pay close attention to verses 4, 9 and 14, before disaster strikes.

Those are the verses that contain the instructions. As we have learned, in order to make a promise materialize, we must mix faith with the written evidence. Therefore, we are looking for any instructions found with the promise, in order to follow them; doing our part.

Many people quote promises without ever mentioning the instructions, or the conditions. They are either living in ignorance, blind, deceived, or they are purposely distorting the truth in order to draw disciples after themself in keeping with Acts 20:29-32.

His truth is our shield (verse 4 above). David said, "By the Word of Your lips, I have kept away from the paths of the destroyer" (Psalm 17:4). The Word of God is truth (John 17:17), and it directs us in paths far from the destroyer. In other words, if we follow God's teachings, they will keep us away from the destroyer.

If you have begun practicing the teachings that we have covered so far, then I am confident that you have already noticed changes in your life for the better. It may be small changes, such as being able to sleep through the night, or being able to work without that little pain that always bothers you, but still those changes were a result of you taking a few steps toward doing what is right. Praise be to the Lord God almighty, Who is worthy of praise, glory, and honor, forever.

On the other hand, some of us like walking on the edge, with one foot in the world. Repent of that, since what is lame, may become dislocated (Hebrews 12:12-13).

Because we make the Lord our dwelling place (verse 9 above), and because we love the Lord (verse 14 above), we will receive what is promised in Psalm 91. Jesus said that the people who love Him keep His Word, but those who do not love Him do not keep His Word.

John 14:23-24
23 Jesus answered and said to him, "If anyone loves Me, he will keep My word; and My Father will love him, and We will come to him and make Our home with him. 24 He who does not love Me does not keep My words; and the word which you hear is not Mine but the Father's who sent Me. NKJV

That is a part of the doctrine of Jesus Christ, and those who shun the doctrine of Jesus, do not have God (2 John 1:9-11). By now you should know that I'm going to tell you to take Jesus at His Word. Believe that passage of scripture as if Jesus, Himself was proclaiming it to you, because He is.

After we keep Jesus' Word, He will come to us, and make His home with us (verse 23 above). Then the scripture will be fulfilled which says, "Greater is He that is in me, than he that is in the world" (1 John 4:4)!

As you can see, there is something that we can do that will provide the refuge that we need, and make Psalm 91 a reality in our life. The question is, are we willing to do it?

Do you love Jesus? If you do not keep His Word, then He doesn't think that you love Him. All of a sudden, Jesus' instructions about denying yourself, taking up your cross, and following Him, become more of a priority, don't they? Now you can see how ignoring one part of the message can have a direct effect on a different part.

To worship is to acknowledge the worth of something. Idolatry is to worship something, or value something above, or more than God. Therefore, the question we need to ask ourself is, how much do we acknowledge man-made things in comparison to God, or our Lord Jesus Christ?

If we celebrate the birth of Jesus, do we acknowledge Him more than our Christmas lights? If we have made an idol out of the Easter bunny, then the Lord would tell us to let it be our refuge according to Isaiah 57:13. Imagine that.

Sometimes we have no idea that the way we live determines what we are receiving, and that's called blindness (Ephesians 4:17-19). Blindness is for those who do not come to know Jesus in accordance with the Word of God. That's a promise just like any other promise in the Bible. O' Lord have mercy on us.

Now we will pay more attention to Jesus' instructions, such as forgiving everyone, loving one another, and seeking God's Kingdom, and His righteousness first place in our life because we need Him for a refuge. However, it is difficult to teach these things to people who are in the middle of destruction, when all their life they have believed false doctrines.

Repent of the past, and start over, being careful to follow the instructions. Get the instructions right, and the results will be right. I'm not saying that we have to be everything we were called to be in one day, but we do need to repent, turn, and simply take a few steps in the right direction. The Lord our God will see it! However, afterwards, we need to be careful to continue in our faith (Colossians 1:21-23), and live up to what we have attained (Philippians 3:16).

As I have mentioned, if we do not answer the Lord's call, He will not answer our call. If we disregard (disdain, scorn) His advice, and ignore His correction (rebuke), He will not answer us, but we will reap what we have sown. What will the Lord do when we call if we have not answered His call, according to the following verses?

Proverbs 1:24-33
24 Because I have called and you refused, I have stretched out my hand and no one regarded, 25 Because you disdained all my counsel, And would have none of my rebuke, 26 I also will laugh at your calamity; I will mock when your terror comes, 27 When your terror comes like a storm, And your destruction comes like a whirlwind, When distress and anguish come upon you. 28 "Then they will call on me, but I will not answer; They will seek me diligently, but they will not find me.

29 Because they hated knowledge And did not choose the fear of the Lord, 30 They would have none of my counsel And despised my every rebuke. 31 Therefore they shall eat the fruit of their own way, And be filled to the full with their own fancies.

32 For the turning away of the simple will slay them, And the complacency of fools will destroy them; 33 But whoever listens to me will dwell safely, And will be secure, without fear of evil."
NKJV

Father, in Jesus' name, it is because of Your mercies that we are not consumed, for they are new every morning. They are everlasting. If You punished us according to our transgressions, who would stand? Who would still be alive? Have mercy on us Lord according to Your loving kindness, as You have many times before, and forgive our sins in the name of Jesus Christ. Open our eyes that we may see Your Word, and open our ears that we may hear You speak. Lead us in the way everlasting. We love You, and we thank You for Your kindness toward us. You alone are worthy of our praise. Amen.

Verse 33 above says, "Whoever listens to Me will dwell safely, and be secure, without fear of harm." That's the kind of protection we need.

God loves us and takes no pleasure in our death (Ezekiel 18:32). Therefore, He doesn't allow us to continue on a path of destruction, without discipline.

Discipline (chastening) is correction that leads toward obedience, and God disciplines us so that we will share in His holiness (Hebrews 12:10).

Hebrews 12:4-8
4 You have not yet resisted to bloodshed, striving against sin.
5 And you have forgotten the exhortation which speaks to you as to sons: "My son, do not despise the chastening of the Lord, Nor be discouraged when you are rebuked by Him; 6 For whom the Lord loves He chastens, And scourges every son whom He receives." 7 If you endure chastening, God deals with you as with sons; for what son is there whom a father does not chasten? 8 But if you are without chastening, of which all have become partakers, then you are illegitimate and not sons.
NKJV

If we can live like the people of this world, and not receive God's discipline for our sins, then we are not saved (verse 8 above). God disciplines (chastens) everyone whom He accepts as a son (verses 6-7 above). Those who do not receive discipline for their sins, are not true sons (verse 8 above).

Many Christians, who are under the Lord's discipline, are told that it is the devil that is on their back. Never assume that it is the devil, but even if it is, the solution is still the same; submit to God's way, and resist the devil (James 4:7), by remaining in the faith (Ephesians 6:16, 1 Peter 5:9).

In disciplining us, God is trying to change our conduct. Those who accept Jesus as Lord and continue living like they used to live, "for themself," will discover what the wrath of God is like. However, by simply repenting of our sins we can avoid much heartache.

Just as God will give us over, because we are not continuing in our faith (Romans 1:28-32, 11:20-24), the wrath of God comes on the "sons" of disobedience (verse 6 below).

Colossians 3:5-10
5 Therefore put to death your members which are on the earth: fornication, uncleanness, passion, evil desire, and covetousness, which is idolatry. 6 Because of these things the wrath of God is coming upon the sons of disobedience, 7 in which you yourselves once walked when you lived in them. 8 But now you yourselves are to put off all these: anger, wrath, malice, blasphemy, filthy language out of your mouth. 9 Do not lie to one another, since you have put off the old man with his deeds, 10 and have put on the new man who is renewed in knowledge according to the image of Him who created him NKJV

That's God's wrath, and not "the devil is on our back," so to speak, like many proclaim, since they do not believe that God will discipline us. What they do not realize is that judgment for those who are going to Heaven, begins here on earth.

1 Peter 4:17
17 For the time has come for judgment to begin at the house of God; and if it begins with us first, what will be the end of those who do not obey the gospel of God? NKJV

Judgment begins for Christians right now ("the time has come," verse 17 above). We are judged when we do not obey the Gospel, but that is much better than what those who have no intention of obeying the Gospel will receive in the end (2 Thessalonians 1:8-9).

If we are among those who are going to Heaven, we are receiving discipline for our sins here on earth. Therefore, we could take two identical people, except for their eternal future, who are involved in the same sin, and they will have two totally different outcomes. One may get away without receiving punishment for now (Romans 2:5), but the other will receive what he is due here on earth.

We are judged by the Lord now, so that we will not be condemned with the world later (verse 32 above). It is the Lord Who judges His people (Hebrews 10:30). Therefore, we can't look at the person who doesn't experience discipline for their sins, and say that they are blessed (Acts 14:22). No, on the contrary, they are on slippery ground (Psalm 73:1-19).

I have some great news. If we judge ourselves, we will not be judged.

1 Corinthians 11:30-32
30 For this reason many are weak and sick among you, and many sleep. 31 For if we would judge ourselves, we would not be judged. 32 But when we are judged, we are chastened by the Lord, that we may not be condemned with the world. NKJV

In this book, I have tried to explain what living by faith is like. You don't have to believe me, but if you have accepted and believed the verses that we have covered, then you have already been judging yourself, using the Word of God as a ruler (Hebrews 4:12). That is how you should live from now on.

In other words, as you continue in your faith, which includes hearing the pure Word of God, you are going to allow what you hear to judge your way of life instead of hardening your heart against it. In doing this, you will judge yourself, and escape being judged by the Lord.

John 5:24
24 Verily, verily, I say unto you, He that heareth my word, and believeth on him that sent me, hath everlasting life, and shall not come into condemnation; but is passed from death unto life. KJV

John 8:51
51 Verily, verily, I say unto you, If a man keep my saying, he shall never see death. KJV

Before the Lord judges us, He gives us time to repent. He shows no partiality and therefore, He gives everyone time to repent, since if we were struck by lightning a few minutes after we committed a sin, none of us would be alive today. Therefore, God's kindness toward us is meant to lead us to repentance.

Romans 2:5-8
5 But in accordance with your hardness and your impenitent heart you are treasuring up for yourself wrath in the day of wrath and revelation of the righteous judgment of God, 6 who "will render to each one according to his deeds": 7 eternal life to those who by patient continuance in doing good seek for glory, honor, and immortality; 8 but to those who are self-seeking and do not obey the truth, but obey unrighteousness — indignation and wrath NKJV

By simply judging ourselves, using the Word of God as a ruler (Hebrews 4:12), and repenting of any violations, we will return to where we were before we sinned, and avoid being judged by the Lord. We need to know that, since that is another reason why we need the Word of God living on the inside of us.

Many Christians do not know this and believe that the problems that eventually arise due to the Lord's discipline, are simply the devil attacking them. This is because their view of the Lord is not in-line with what is actually written in the Bible.

If a person has been given over, as we have discussed in an earlier chapter, then he will have a depraved mind. If he refuses to stop conforming to this world, he will experience wrath, and if he hears the Word of God, but does not put it into practice, he will experience destruction. All of these things can make it seem like he is under some type of demonic attack, but simple repentance, and turning toward God in accordance with His Word will deliver him.

Read the following passage of scripture as an example, and notice that even though major things were about to happen, simple repentance was the solution.

Revelation 2:18-23
18 'These things says the Son of God, who has eyes like a flame of fire, and His feet like fine brass: 19 "I know your works, love, service, faith, and your patience; and as for your works, the last are more than the first. 20 Nevertheless I have a few things against you, because you allow that woman Jezebel, who calls herself a prophetess, to teach and seduce My servants to commit sexual immorality and eat things sacrificed to idols. 21 And I gave her time to repent of her sexual immorality, and she did not repent. 22 Indeed I will cast her into a sickbed, and those who commit adultery with her into great tribulation, unless they repent of their deeds. 23 I will kill her children with death, and all the churches shall know that I am He who searches the minds and hearts. And I will give to each one of you according to your works. NKJV

The Lord gave this woman time to repent, or to judge herself so that she would not be judged, but she did not (verse 21 above). Therefore, He was going to cast her into a sickbed, and those who have sinned with her into great tribulation (verse 22 above), even to the point of destroying the children with death (verse 23 above).

If this woman asked the church to pray for her and her children, all of us would rush over to lay hands on her, and none of us would ask the hard questions. "Are you committing sins that lead to death, and consequently, need to repent of something before we pray for you?"

I don't mean to shock you, but we have hidden the truth from people for so long, that now our view of the Lord is more in-line with someone who works at the Red Cross once a disaster strikes. We live as if there is nothing we can do about calamity, and as if the Lord can only help us after it is over.

However, the truth is our shield (Psalm 91:4), which will keep us far from the path of the destroyer (Psalm 17:4), and through living by the truth (faith), we will quench all of the fiery darts of the enemy (Ephesians 6:16). Therefore, ignoring the truth is the same as not having a hiding place in times of trouble.

Psalm 91:4
4 He shall cover you with His feathers, And under His wings you shall take refuge; His truth shall be your shield and buckler. NKJV

The Word of God is truth (John 17:17), and the power of God is already in the Word of God. The power to save (Romans 1:16-17), the power to provide (Matthew 6:33, 2 Peter 1:3-4), the power to deliver (John 8:31-37, Romans 1:28-32), and the power to heal are already contained in the Word of God (Psalm 107:17-22, John 6:63, Romans 8:11).

Psalm 107:17-22
17 Fools, because of their transgression, And because of their iniquities, were afflicted. 18 Their soul abhorred all manner of food, And they drew near to the gates of death. 19 Then they cried out to the Lord in their trouble, And He saved them out of their distresses. 20 He sent His word and healed them, And delivered them from their destructions. 21 Oh, that men would give thanks to the Lord for His goodness, And for His wonderful works to the children of men! 22 Let them sacrifice the sacrifices of thanksgiving, And declare His works with rejoicing. NKJV

Proverbs 4:20-22
20 My son, give attention to my words; Incline your ear to my sayings. 21 Do not let them depart from your eyes; Keep them in the midst of your heart; 22 For they are life to those who find them, And health to all their flesh. NKJV

That same Word of God works all by itself on the inside of those who believe it (verse 13 below). However, if we do not believe, we cannot receive (James 1:5-7).

1 Thessalonians 2:13
13 For this reason we also thank God without ceasing, because when you received the word of God which you heard from us, you welcomed it not as the word of men, but as it is in truth, the word of God, which also effectively works in you who believe. NKJV

God's power, which is in God's Word, is meant to work to change us from the inside out. That same Word living on the inside of us is also Spirit, and He gives life to our body (Romans 8:11).

John 6:63
63 It is the Spirit who gives life; the flesh profits nothing. The words that I speak to you are spirit, and they are life. NKJV

Say it again, "Greater is He that is in me, than he that is in the world!" It is that same Word, by which we are "born again" (verse 23 below); changed into new people.

1 Peter 1:22-25
22 Since you have purified your souls in obeying the truth through the Spirit in sincere love of the brethren, love one another fervently with a pure heart, 23 having been born again, not of corruptible seed but incorruptible, through the word of God which lives and abides forever, 24 because "All flesh is as grass, And all the glory of man as the flower of the grass. The grass withers, And its flower falls away, 25 But the word of the Lord endures forever." Now this is the word which by the gospel was preached to you. NKJV

Now what

Is it the devil or is it the Lord's discipline? Do we need to repent of something, or do we need prayer? That can be a tough question to answer, but one thing is for certain. We are not supposed to slander the devil.

Who would know for sure if someone is caught up in sexual sins, like the woman mentioned in Revelation 2:18-23 above? She would, but what if she had no knowledge of the Lord's discipline, and came to you for prayer? Are Christians instructed to pray for everyone?

1 John 5:16-17
16 If anyone sees his brother sinning a sin which does not lead to death, he will ask, and He will give him life for those who commit sin not leading to death. There is sin leading to death. I do not say that he should pray about that. 17 All unrighteousness is sin, and there is sin not leading to death. NKJV

It would seem like we should pray for all Christians no matter what, but that is not exactly the truth according to 1 John 5:16-17 above. When it comes to sins that lead to death, repentance is the solution, but it may take godly advice to reach that point.

I have met plenty of Christians who believed that if anything went wrong, it was because of the devil. That's what they were taught, and so that is what they believed. Knowing the truth changes that attitude.

All of us are supposed to be allowing the Word of God to judge our attitudes and thoughts (Hebrews 4:12), but what if we do not know what the Word says?

Destruction awaits (Hosea 4:6).

The Lord judges His people (Hebrews 10:30). However, before He judges us, He gives us time to repent, and even judge ourself in the same way that we judge others (Matthew 7:1-2). "Forgive us our sins, as we forgive those who sin against us" (Luke 11:4). That should sound familiar. Think about that.

As I have mentioned, after we repent and experience more grace, then we need to be careful to remain on the path, fighting the good fight of faith. We will remain in the faith by continually hearing the pure Word of God, and allowing it to judge our attitudes and thoughts.

If for whatever reason we decide to leave that path, and not allow the Word to judge us, we will experience discipline again, and those who hate the Lord's correction will die.

Proverbs 15:9-10
9 The way of the wicked is an abomination to the Lord, But He loves him who follows righteousness. 10 Harsh discipline is for him who forsakes the way, And he who hates correction will die. NKJV

Most of us think of the hospital as the last place that a Christian should be questioned about their faith, but I beg to differ. When a Christian is sick, there are questions that need to be answered about their faith, before we start blaming the devil, because simple repentance could very well be the solution, which I believe it is in most cases.

The Lord uses affliction (illness, disease, weakness) in order to turn us, and by simply turning, we will be delivered from all affliction of this sort.

Psalm 34:19
19 Many are the afflictions of the righteous, But the Lord delivers him out of them all. NKJV

Psalm 119:67
67 Before I was afflicted I went astray, But now I keep Your word. NKJV

The first thing that happens to a Christian, who has forsaken (abandoned) the path is severe discipline, after being given time to repent. If they hate correction, they will die (Proverbs 15:10 above). Therefore, one of the worst things that a Christian can do is to close their ears to the Word of God, and refuse to hear instruction, regardless if they are in a hospital bed or not.

From time to time, we may need to be reminded of the instructions found in the Bible. What should sick people do?

James 5:13-16
13 Is anyone among you suffering? Let him pray. Is anyone

cheerful? Let him sing psalms. 14 Is anyone among you sick? Let him call for the elders of the church, and let them pray over him, anointing him with oil in the name of the Lord. 15 And the prayer of faith will save the sick, and the Lord will raise him up. And if he has committed sins, he will be forgiven. 16 Confess your trespasses to one another, and pray for one another, that you may be healed. The effective, fervent prayer of a righteous man avails much. NKJV

What do the people of this world do when they get sick? They call one or two people who are good at gossiping, and then pray that they will do what they do best; spread the news. Then they wait to see how many people show up.

When Christians get sick, we are supposed to call the elders (verse 14 above). An elder will know about sins that lead to death, since he himself, should be free from them (verse 20 below). Therefore, if our sickness is caused by our sins, we can confess our sins to him in order that we will be healed (verse 16 above).

1 Timothy 5:19-22
19 Do not receive an accusation against an elder except from two or three witnesses. 20 Those who are sinning rebuke in the presence of all, that the rest also may fear. 21 I charge you before God and the Lord Jesus Christ and the elect angels that you observe these things without prejudice, doing nothing with partiality. 22 Do not lay hands on anyone hastily, nor share in other people's sins; keep yourself pure. NKJV

I know that there are many today who call themselves elders, apostles, prophets, and whatever else without even being close to qualifying for those positions. They will reap what they sow. However, that does not excuse us from following our instructions.

Therefore, call an elder if you need one, and there shouldn't be anything wrong with looking for one who meets the requirements in accordance with the verses above. You can ask questions, just as they can. There isn't a position in the church that is above questioning, with the exception of Jesus Christ.

Notice in verse 22 above that we don't rush to lay hands on anyone. No, because in many cases, healing has to be ministered. I believe that everyone can be healed. However, attend any healing seminar you want, and eighty percent or more of the people, who come up for prayer, will not receive anything unless questions are asked to see where they are in the faith, and what they need to do in order to continue in it.

We're going to have to ask questions, and then instruct people according to where they happen to be in the faith. Most of the time, repenting of sin, and turning toward God in accordance with His Word, will cure any problem, even in the comfort of a person's home.

Are we continuing in our faith? Have we stopped conforming to the world around us? Are we obeying Jesus? Are we living up to what we have obtained, being doers of what we have learned (Philippians 3:16)? Are we reading our Bible, seeking God's Kingdom and His righteousness? Turn and live!

If any of that describes you, turn and live. I expect people to be healed just by following the instructions in this book and by believing the verses. Praise God. If I was ministering to someone face to face, I would ask about the things we have covered in order to see where they are in the faith, and what they needed to do in order to continue.

God does not have a problem protecting us from the devil (2 Thessalonians 3:3, 1 John 5:18). His Word keeps us safe, and it frees us from being slaves to sin (John 8:31-37). We can make the Lord our refuge through loving Him, and all who love Him obey His teachings.

We should fight the good fight of faith, which involves holding to the teachings, and with the shield of faith, we can extinguish all of the devil's fiery darts. However, in order to do that without understanding all of it, we must take God at His Word (Proverbs 3:5).

Father, in Jesus' name. We need You. We can't do anything without You. Have mercy on us and forgive us for our sins. Forgive us for slander. Forgive us for not knowing You in accordance with Your Word. Restore us Lord. Make us do what You want us to do, and show us Your salvation. You alone are worthy of praise, glory, and honor, forever, and ever. Amen.

May the Lord bless you and give you everything needed to do His will. May He cause in you what is pleasing to Him. I'm Alan Ballou; a servant. If I may be of service to you free of charge, please contact me.

www.HowToStopSinning.com

Alan's email alan@howtostopsinning.com

Lucie's email lucie@howtostopsinning.com

&)CR

10

Against the Faith

Our words have had an effect on our body all of our life. That may be a shock to you, but spiritual principles work whether we know them or not, and many of us suffer needlessly as we violate them.

Good days, and bad days in the past, and in our future are not just set up by what we do, but also by the words we speak. Now that we have learned what to do in order to remain in the faith, we will learn how our words affect our faith.

1 Peter 3:10-12
10 For "He who would love life And see good days, Let him refrain his tongue from evil, And his lips from speaking deceit. 11 Let him turn away from evil and do good; Let him seek peace and pursue it. 12 For the eyes of the Lord are on the righteous, And His ears are open to their prayers; But the face of the Lord is against those who do evil." NKJV

If you could control your days in the future, would you plan good days, or days where everything falls apart? Think about that. If you could control who you are, would you be who you are right now? Learn these principles and change your life forever.

Simple words can change us for the better or for the worse. They can bring life and death; blessings as well as curses. They can give us the ability to control our life, or take control away from us. The words that we speak have the power of death and life.

Proverbs 18:21
21 Death and life are in the power of the tongue, And those who love it will eat its fruit. NKJV

Proverbs 12:18
18 There is one who speaks like the piercings of a sword, But the tongue of the wise promotes health. NKJV

Proverbs 12:14
14 A man will be satisfied with good by the fruit of his mouth,

And the recompense of a man's hands will be rendered to him. NKJV

Imagine how powerful that can be. Did your words take you where you are right now, or the things that you have participated in, which we covered in previous chapters? Most of us never consider our words as having that much power.

In this chapter, we will mainly focus on the doctrines that are associated with the things we say, but the Bible is loaded with spiritual principles. In this book, we're just covering the ones that deal with stopping sin from ruining our life, and healing as a result of that.

In the last days there will be dangerous times. The people of this world have always dealt treacherously with one another, but in the following passage of scripture, we see that even people who have a form of godliness will live like the people of this world.

2 Timothy 3:1-5
1 But know this, that in the last days perilous times will come:
2 For men will be lovers of themselves, lovers of money, boasters, proud, blasphemers, disobedient to parents, unthankful, unholy, 3 unloving, unforgiving, slanderers, without self-control, brutal, despisers of good, 4 traitors, headstrong, haughty, lovers of pleasure rather than lovers of God, 5 having a form of godliness but denying its power. And from such people turn away! NKJV

Lawlessness will abound. In other words, even among church-attending people, many will not hold to any doctrine of faith, or any law, but each will follow his own desires.

Matthew 24:10-13
10 And then many will be offended, will betray one another, and will hate one another. 11 Then many false prophets will rise up and deceive many. 12 And because lawlessness will abound, the love of many will grow cold. 13 But he who endures to the end shall be saved. NKJV

Because lawlessness will abound, the love of many people will grow cold (verse 12 above). Now you can see where we are headed, if we are not already there.

As I have already mentioned, it is also predicted that in the last days, people will turn away from what is actually written in their Bible, and turn toward teachers who will teach them what they want to hear.

2 Timothy 4:3-4
3 For the time will come when they will not endure sound doc-

trine; but after their own lusts shall they heap to themselves
teachers, having itching ears; 4 And they shall turn away their
ears from the truth, and shall be turned unto fables. KJV

That describes the direction that we as a people are headed, and we may
already be at that point in certain areas of this country. However, what does all
this have to do with sin and healing, and what do we need to do to make sure that
we are not caught up in these things?

Basically, what would it take for church-attending people to act just like the
people of this world, dealing deceitfully with each other, and hating one another
(Matthew 24:10-13 above)? In order for church-attending people to deal treacherously with one another, as it is predicted to happen in the last days, we would
have to lose all self-control.

That is exactly what would happen if the church at large stopped speaking
what is written in their Bible and started speaking things that sound good, and seem
right, since those who speak against the faith, can stray (fall away) from the faith.

1 Timothy 6:20-21
20 O Timothy! Guard what was committed to your trust, avoiding the profane and idle babblings and contradictions of what
is falsely called knowledge — 21 by professing it some have
strayed concerning the faith. NKJV

By simply speaking against the faith we can fall away from it. Many Christians don't realize that, and since fewer and fewer of us are in the process of
renewing our mind with the truth, speaking against the faith is very common.
Consequently, many fall away from the faith without even realizing it.

Foolish talk, idle babbling (godless, useless talk), and quoting things that
are not written, will lead to more of the same, and by participating in it, many
have fallen away.

2 Timothy 2:16-18
16 But shun profane and idle babblings, for they will increase
to more ungodliness. 17 And their message will spread like
cancer. Hymenaeus and Philetus are of this sort, 18 who have
strayed concerning the truth, saying that the resurrection is
already past; and they overthrow the faith of some. NKJV

Notice that just by teaching that the resurrection had already past, they strayed
from the faith, and overthrew the faith of others who believed what they taught
(verses 17-18 above). That's how easy it is to stray from the faith.

The righteousness that is "by faith," includes speaking in-line with the faith
(Romans 10:6-8). That means that we should be very careful never to speak against
what is actually written in the Bible.

If we stray from the faith, we are not remaining in it, and as we have learned, it is remaining in the faith that shields us from the devil (1 Peter 5:8-9, Ephesians 6:16). The Word of God keeps us away from the path of the destroyer (Psalm 17:4). This is another reason why we should never blame the devil for our problems.

Those who accept and believe something that is false cannot possibly be on the right path, and consequently, they cannot resist the devil by standing in the faith (1 Peter 5:9), or extinguish his fiery darts with their shield of faith (Ephesians 6:16). As I have mentioned before, our sins give us over (1 John 5:18).

Resisting the devil begins by submitting to God's ways (James 4:7-8), and God's ways include never speaking against the faith, in order to be right with God through the "righteousness of faith" (Romans 10:6-8).

If we do not submit to God, how can we resist the devil? We can't. God's power of protection works through faith (1 Peter 1:5 below), and faith always includes the evidence of things not seen (Hebrews 11:1), but if we continually speak against the faith, we will not remain in it.

1 Peter 1:5
5 who are kept by the power of God through faith for salvation ready to be revealed in the last time. NKJV

The only safe path is to always speak in accordance with what is written in the Bible, no matter what. Therefore, if the evidence, which is the Word of God, doesn't say it, then we don't need to quote it as truth.

We don't even need to say "amen" to something that we are not sure is written in the Bible, since amen means "let it be so for me." Saying "amen" to something we hear is like saying it ourself.

Therefore, even though something sounds good, and seems right, we still need to test it, because sounding good, and seeming right doesn't necessarily amount to godliness. As I have said before, when someone teaches you something, ask them to show it to you, word for word. Once you see it written in the Word, then say amen.

Spiritual principles have no boundaries, and they work whether we know them or not. Therefore, the sooner we know them the better off we will be.

There is no substitute for the Word of God living on the inside of us. It is able to build us up and give us an inheritance (verse 32 below). However, the need for more money, and more followers has made many well-meaning people teach what sounds good, and hide what doesn't keep the crowd going. The love of money is the root of all kinds of evil (1 Timothy 6:10).

Those who do not abide in the doctrine of Christ, do not have God (2 John 1:9), and those without God, willingly support the doctrine of demons (1 Corinthians 10:20, 1 Timothy 4:1-2). Therefore, the money is sitting there, ready and waiting on someone to tell the crowd what they want to hear.

However, once the listeners fall away from the faith, or reject different parts of the Word of God, then the verses we have covered will not abide (remain) in them (John 5:38, Mark 4:24-25). This is already happening today. All we have covered so far, are elementary teachings that any long-time Christian should know, but most of us do not know these things.

I'm not saying that to put you down, but simply to make you aware that these things are already taking place today. The Word is not being taught like it is written in keeping with 2 Timothy 4:3-4 above, and it is being taken from those who speak against the faith, even though they may have known the scriptures at some point in their life.

Father, in Jesus' name, You know everything about us. You know where we are in the faith, and what we need to continue in the faith that You have given us. Open our eyes so that we can see where we are standing, and open our ears in order that we can hear Your Word. Make it live on the inside of us. Sanctify us with Your truth. Forgive us for rejecting it in the past, and now fill us, that we may walk in Your ways, and bring glory to Your holy name; in the name of Jesus Christ. Amen.

The Apostle Paul warned the Ephesians for three years that after he left, fellow Christians from among them would begin to speak perverse things in order to draw away disciples after themself (verses 30-32 below).

Acts 20:30-32
30 Also from among yourselves men will rise up, speaking perverse things, to draw away the disciples after themselves. 31 Therefore watch, and remember that for three years I did not cease to warn everyone night and day with tears. 32 "So now, brethren, I commend you to God and to the word of His grace, which is able to build you up and give you an inheritance among all those who are sanctified. NKJV

Find a place where the doctrine of Jesus Christ is never mentioned, and the truth is suppressed, and you will be in a place where there will be an obvious lack of self-control in the life of the people. Suppressing the truth, and false doctrines will always set up bad days in the future of those who support that type of message (1 Peter 3:10-12).

We cannot reject the scriptures and not reject God. In the beginning was the Word, and the Word was with God, and the Word (He) was God. He was with God from the beginning, and all things were made through Him (John 1:1-3). Those who belong to God, hear their Father's Word (John 8:47).

I know that the majority of Christians today are not going to change, since it is written that most of us will take the wrong path (the wide gate of destruction), and people will become worse in the last days (2 Timothy 3:1-5 above). Therefore, as 2 Timothy 4:3-4 begins to take precedence, the church buildings across this country will fill up with more people who have no self-control. It's just a matter of time.

The tongue controls the body, just as a rudder controls a ship. If the rudder is out of control, then the aftereffect will be a ship that's out of control.

James 3:3-6
3 Indeed, we put bits in horses' mouths that they may obey us, and we turn their whole body. 4 Look also at ships: although they are so large and are driven by fierce winds, they are turned by a very small rudder wherever the pilot desires. 5 Even so the tongue is a little member and boasts great things. See how great a forest a little fire kindles! 6 And the tongue is a fire, a world of iniquity. The tongue is so set among our members that it defiles the whole body, and sets on fire the course of nature; and it is set on fire by hell. NKJV

Simple words can set the whole course of our life on fire (verse 6 above), and when we reach that place of destruction in our life, we ask the church to pray for us, which is good. However, most of us never learn the spiritual principles that we have violated, which placed us in the predicament we are in. Therefore, it happens over and over again.

We can't pray spiritual principles away. Therefore, the problem is never solved, and consequently, it is very possible to have a church full of people who live in lack, sickness, and disabilities without remedy.

If left unchecked, attending church can become just a meeting place where people, who willingly live in such conditions, only come to find comfort without advice, which means that they will continue living in those situations. In this way, church can become a hopeless support group, rather than a place to be cleansed through the washing with water by the Word of God (Ephesians 5:26).

After 2 Timothy 4:3-4 takes precedence, they will not put up with hearing sound doctrines (the solutions), but only want to hear something that makes them feel better, and receive your sympathy. That's almost like watching a man drown while he is screaming "Don't throw that life preserver, but just listen to me, and watch me drown."

However, the tongue works both ways. Not only can it set our life on fire, but it can also bring us blessings, good days, and by our words we can control our whole body.

James 3:2
2 For we all stumble in many things. If anyone does not stumble in word, he is a perfect man, able also to bridle the whole body. NKJV

If we never stumble in word (what we say), we would be perfect in God's eyes and have the ability to control (bridle) our whole body. That's right, our words cause us to either gain or lose self-control. Imagine that.

In order to mix faith with that promise, we would have to always speak in-line with what is written in the Bible; never being at fault in what we say (verse 2 above). That would require us to test everything we quote right now to make sure that it is written in the Bible, and test everything we hear before we accept it as truth in the future.

The evidence is in the results. In other words, if we have been speaking in accordance with what is actually written in our Bible, then we will have the ability to control our body. Therefore, the aftereffect of living by faith in what God has promised, according to James chapter three is that all Christians would gain control over their body. Think about that.

If all Christians learned how to control their body, in keeping with those verses, who would have an addiction, except non-Christians? Who would be caught up in sexual sins? Who would be stealing from their employer?

Church should be a place where people go to gain self-control, but in the last days, it will be a place where people without self-control gather. That is already happening today.

If you had self-control, what would you change about yourself? How would you change over the next twelve months if you gained more and more self-control?

May the Lord open our eyes, and enable us to see. May He provide us with the grace (ability) needed to do His will, in the name of Jesus Christ. Amen.

God's idea of being perfect is to always speak the right words (verse 2 above), and our body follows our words (James 3:2-12). Christians, who have the Spirit of faith, always speak in-line with the faith. We believe, and therefore we speak.

2 Corinthians 4:13
13 And since we have the same spirit of faith, according to what is written, "I believed and therefore I spoke," we also believe and therefore speak NKJV

Those who have the Spirit of faith, believe what is written in their Bible, and then speak it like it is written. As Christians we should already be speaking with the Spirit of faith, being careful to speak in-line with what is written, and rejecting what isn't (Romans 10:6-8, 2 Corinthians 10:3-5, 1 Thessalonians 5:21).

Why? In order to be righteous by faith, or in other words, right in God's eyes through faith, we have to be careful "not" to speak against the faith, even in our heart. That is according to the Word of the Lord, written in Romans 10:6-8 below.

Romans 10:6-8
6 But the righteousness of faith speaks in this way, "Do not

say in your heart, 'Who will ascend into heaven?'" (that is, to bring Christ down from above) 7 or, "'Who will descend into the abyss?'" (that is, to bring Christ up from the dead). 8 But what does it say? "The word is near you, in your mouth and in your heart" (that is, the word of faith which we preach) NKJV

According to those verses, the righteousness that is by faith, involves saying certain things that are in-line with the faith (verse 8 above), and not saying things that contradict (verses 6-7 above). In other words, we should "speak" our faith, and avoid saying things that do not line-up with what is written in the Bible.

That is what those verses are telling us to do, and they are very much a part of the Gospel message that every Christian should already be practicing (Romans 1:16-17, 4:13). As I have mentioned, if we knew this, we would be very careful with our words, which would make us slow to speak (James 1:19).

According to Romans 1:16-17 below, an explanation of the "righteousness of God, which is by faith" should be included in the message that we call the Gospel.

Romans 1:16-17
16 For I am not ashamed of the gospel of Christ, for it is the power of God to salvation for everyone who believes, for the Jew first and also for the Greek. 17 For in it the righteousness of God is revealed from faith to faith; as it is written, "The just shall live by faith." NKJV

In verse 16 above, this passage of scripture starts by explaining that the Gospel itself, is the power of God unto salvation for everyone who believes it. In other words, the Word of God itself already contains the power unto salvation for those who believe it.

Verse 17 declares that "in it," meaning in the Gospel itself, an explanation of the righteousness of God is revealed (made known), which is from faith to faith. That means it starts with faith, the faith we were given when we were saved (Romans 12:3, Ephesians 2:8), and it continues in faith until the end, since the "just shall live by faith" (verse 17 above, Galatians 2:20, 3:10-12, Hebrews 10:38, 2 Corinthians 5:7).

Therefore, the Gospel message itself, should contain an explanation of the righteousness of God, which is by faith. That means that if you have not heard the righteousness of God explained, then you have not heard a complete Gospel message. Don't panic, but let us return to the Lord our God, that He may have mercy on us, and help us in our time of need.

Father, in Jesus' name, have mercy on us. We have rejected the Spirit of faith, and refused to learn righteousness in accordance with Your Word, and we have made up our own way. Through Your mercies we have not been consumed because Your compassions fail not. Forgive us and restore us that we may experience the joy of Your salvation, and bring glory to Your holy name; in the name of Jesus Christ we pray. Amen.

The promises given to Abraham were through the righteousness of faith.

Romans 4:13
13 For the promise that he would be the heir of the world was not to Abraham or to his seed through the law, but through the righteousness of faith. NKJV

Those who are righteous by faith, speak with the Spirit of faith. Those who are not righteous by faith, speak whatever sounds good, and seems right, but in doing so, they fall away from what is actually written in their Bible (1 Timothy 6:20-21 above), and open the door for deceiving spirits, the doctrine of demons, and myths (1 Timothy 4:1-2).

As I have already mentioned, this is obvious today since so many Christians speak in direct opposition to what their Bible says. In some cases, Kingdom teachings have been removed from their mind altogether, and in other cases they never learned what was actually written in the New Testament to begin with (Mark 4:24-25, Matthew 13:18-21). Let us repent and return to the Lord our God.

Never regard anyone, or try to identify people by their length of service, or their education, or the number of followers they may have (2 Corinthians 5:16). Jesus didn't do that, and neither should we (Mark 12:14).

If they do not teach righteousness as a part of the Gospel message, and they cannot explain it in accordance with what is written in the Bible, they are still baby Christians according to Hebrews 5:13-14 below, regardless of their worldly stature.

Hebrews 5:13-14
13 For everyone who partakes only of milk is unskilled in the word of righteousness, for he is a babe.14 But solid food belongs to those who are of full age, that is, those who by reason of use have their senses exercised to discern both good and evil. NKJV

What happened? We have drifted away from what is actually written in our Bible, and we now use the world's standards right inside of the church.

Hebrews 2:1
1 Therefore we must give the more earnest heed to the things we have heard, lest we drift away. NKJV

We need to pay close attention to what we are reading. That may mean changing our schedule in order to put God-time first place in our life, rather than after we have done everything else that we have planned for our day. Let us return to the Lord our God so that He will heal us (Hosea 6:1)!

Father, in Jesus' name, You alone are worthy of praise, glory, and honor. Our desire is to return to You, in accordance with Your ways, written in Your Word. Forgive us for speaking against the faith, and now restore us, and enable us to speak with the Spirit of faith, that we may gain control over our body, and purify ourselves through Your Word, in the mighty name of Jesus Christ. Amen.

Now what

We cannot speak against the faith and remain in the faith. Those who speak against the faith, do not have the verses that they speak against living in them, and consequently, they cannot be righteous by faith (Romans 10:6-8).

Wicked people receive grace, but do not learn righteousness (verse 10 below). We were all wicked at one time, and so I am not saying that I am any better than anyone else, but we must learn righteousness, unless we only received grace as a license for sinning.

Isaiah 26:10
10 Let grace be shown to the wicked, Yet he will not learn righteousness; In the land of uprightness he will deal unjustly, And will not behold the majesty of the Lord. NKJV

God's righteousness is a part of what Christians are supposed to be seeking first place in their life in order that God will give us the things we worry about (Matthew 6:33). If we are seeking God's righteousness through faith, then we are practicing speaking in-line with the faith, with the end result of gaining control over our body.

I know that most church-attending people will ignore this because it is written that it will happen, and we are already in the last days. However, it does not have to happen to you.

If you desire to be what God has called you to be, then you need to refuse to speak against what is written in the Bible, and start speaking words of faith over your life. That's actually very simple to do, but it will take time and practice to accomplish it.

You see, what is mostly in our heart comes out of our mouth (Matthew 12:34). That means that we can't just change our words overnight. We have to change what is mostly in our heart first.

In order to change our heart, we need to read the Bible out loud, and especially the New Testament over and over, and by doing so we will replace what is in our heart with truth over time. Maturity comes by reason of use (Hebrews 5:14 above), and not by simply being a Christian over a long period of time, or by having a title.

What is mostly in our heart, comes out of our mouth (verse 34 below). That could be football, golf, the latest gossip, or what is in the news.

There is nothing wrong with some things, but a little bit of truth, and a large amount of junk means that we will still be speaking trash. However, only speaking in-line with the faith, gives us the ability to control our body.

If we are in the process of renewing our mind with the truth, which is our reasonable service toward God (Romans 12:1-2), then we are in the process of changing into a "good tree," which will produce "good fruit" (verses 33-35 below).

Matthew 12:33-37
33 "Either make the tree good and its fruit good, or else make the tree bad and its fruit bad; for a tree is known by its fruit. 34 Brood of vipers! How can you, being evil, speak good things? For out of the abundance of the heart the mouth speaks. 35 A good man out of the good treasure of his heart brings forth good things, and an evil man out of the evil treasure brings forth evil things. 36 But I say to you that for every idle word men may speak, they will give account of it in the day of judgment. 37 For by your words you will be justified, and by your words you will be condemned." NKJV

We have to make the tree good before the fruit will be good (verse 33 above). Many of us get that backwards. We get saved and pushed right out the door to go serve rotten fruit. We mean well, and God's love may be in us, but are we speaking with the Spirit of faith?

It is written, "Then we will be able to test and approve what God's will is" (Romans 12:2). How can we know what God wants us to do until after we stop conforming to this world, and are transformed by the renewing of our mind? We can't, and before that period of time, we mostly serve in the flesh.

Therefore, refusing to conform to this world, and renewing your mind with the truth is much more important than serving. According to Luke 10:38-42, Martha was busy serving while Mary was listening to Jesus' Words, which was considered to be much better, and the Word would not be taken from her. Therefore, renew your mind with the truth, before you get too busy serving, even in the church.

We can't speak according to what is written until what is written is living on the inside of us, unless of course we are reading the Bible Word for Word. Until then, out of the abundance of the heart our mouth will speak, or what is mostly in our heart will come out of our mouth (verse 34 above). What comes out of our mouth will control our life (1 Peter 3:10, James 3:2-12).

If the Word is not living on the inside of us, and someone asks us to explain something beyond our understanding, what are we going to do? Like most people, we're going to fill in the blanks with what we think, especially if we hold some type of position in the church.

We're supposed to know, and so that pressure will make us speak, but we cannot speak with the Spirit of faith beyond the Word of God that is living on the inside of us. Therefore we speak with the spirit of error.

1 John 4:5-6
5 They are of the world. Therefore they speak as of the world, and the world hears them. 6 We are of God. He who knows God hears us; he who is not of God does not hear us. By this we know the spirit of truth and the spirit of error. NKJV

Well-meaning people, who do not have the Word living in them, speak from the viewpoint of this world, which is the spirit of error (verse 6 above). Even if they have a few verses living in them, people with the spirit of error fill in the blanks with what they think, or with philosophy (Colossians 2:8). That's never a good idea.

Understand this. What is highly valued among men is detestable in God's sight (Luke 16:15), and the wisdom of this world is foolishness in God's sight (1 Corinthians 3:19). Therefore, if you want to know what not to do spiritually, then ask someone who doesn't have spiritual principles living in them, but is full of human wisdom, and follows the ways of this world.

The people of this world, and worldly Christians can't possibly speak with the Spirit of faith, since they cannot receive spiritual things (1 Corinthians 3:1-3, 2:13-14). Therefore, speak what you know to be true, and never take a guess.

It is not a good for us to worship God on Sunday morning without ever changing our heart. True worshipers worship God in spirit, and in truth (John 4:23-24). Therefore, we need to get our heart in-line with our mouth.

Matthew 15:8-9
8 "These people draw near to Me with their mouth, And honor Me with their lips, But their heart is far from Me. 9 And in vain they worship Me, Teaching as doctrines the commandments of men." NKJV

We always hear that God inhabits the praises of His people, but we never hear that the Lord has said to take away the noise of our songs, until righteousness flows like a river (Amos 5:22-23). We should always consider the goodness and the sternness of God (Romans 11:22), so that we won't be lopsided in our faith.

The doctrines of men only serve to rob the cross of Christ of its power.

1 Corinthians 1:17
17 For Christ did not send me to baptize, but to preach the gospel, not with wisdom of words, lest the cross of Christ should be made of no effect. NKJV

If they will not hear the Word, they do not belong to God (John 8:47). Therefore, the only way to fill the house with those who belong to God is to preach the Word continually (2 Timothy 4:1-2). As they say "amen" to the Word being preached, they will proclaim the Word of Him Who is true, and consequently, change their life, through the righteousness of faith.

One of the biggest mistakes we are making today is changing the message, or hiding the message to suit the listener. God enables a person to come to Him (John 6:44), and if God has not enabled them to come, then they will not accept Jesus' Words anyway (John 6:60-69). Therefore, we don't change the message, but we ask God to enable the hearer.

Father, in Jesus' name, enable us and our families to come to You. Enable us to hear Your Word that we may receive it, and that Your Word may live on the inside of us to change us from the inside out. May we always speak in accordance with Your Word. In the mighty name of Jesus Christ we pray. Amen.

I'm Alan Ballou; a servant. If I may be of service to you free of charge, please contact me.

www.HowToStopSinning.com

Alan's email alan@howtostopsinning.com

Lucie's email lucie@howtostopsinning.com

&)(&

CHRISTIANS, WHO HAVE THE SPIRIT OF FAITH, ALWAYS SPEAK IN-LINE WITH THE FAITH. WE BELIEVE, AND THEREFORE WE SPEAK.

Alan Ballou

11

Have What You Say

𝕭𝕺𝕮𝕭

What would you say if everything you said came true? If every word you are going to speak today was going to come true, what would you say? Immediately, most people would start off saying something like they are going to win the lottery. Whatever you come up with at this point, is fine, but go ahead and say a few words.

Now, if you said something like, "I will win the lottery today," then you would need to check your odds of winning with the lottery people. However, there is something to consider. If you are a true Christian, and winning the lottery would make you less of a Christ follower, then don't worry about winning, since God will not allow you to be tempted beyond what you can bear (1 Corinthians 10:13). Sorry.

If you "do not" live by faith, then forget about receiving whatever it is you said, if it is a promise in the Word of God (verse 22 below). Concerning promises found in the Word of God, we have to mix faith with everything we hear in order to make it materialize (Hebrews 4:2).

For example, if we have not forgiven someone, we cannot possibly be remaining in the faith, since Jesus requires us to forgive people in order to be forgiven (Matthew 6:14-16, verses 25-26 below). Therefore, if we are relying on a promise in the Word of God that requires faith, but we are not remaining in the faith, we can forget about receiving it.

If you "do" live by faith, and what you would say is a promise written in the Word of God, then from everything you would say, take away anything that you do not actually believe in your heart will happen for you. Faith is something that is believed in the heart, and then spoken (verse 23 below, Romans 10:6-10).

Whatever remains is what "can" happen. Abiding in Jesus is a condition of asking whatever we want (John 15:7). Therefore, if we do not remain in the faith, we are not in the position to ask for just anything.

Now, is there anything left that you would say that can come true? For most of us, there won't be much left. However, we can learn to use spiritual principles to our advantage, as we have discovered in previous chapters. Once we learn how to position ourself in order to receive what we say, then we can use our faith to receive it. Praise God.

I don't teach the so-called "name it, claim it" gospel. However, just as speaking against the faith can cause us to fall away from the faith altogether, speaking in-line with the faith can make big things happen, for those who live by faith. We can actually position ourself to have what we say (verse 24 below).

Mark 11:22-26
22 So Jesus answered and said to them, "Have faith in God. 23 For assuredly, I say to you, whoever says to this mountain, 'Be removed and be cast into the sea,' and does not doubt in his heart, but believes that those things he says will be done, he will have whatever he says. 24 Therefore I say to you, whatever things you ask when you pray, believe that you receive them, and you will have them. 25 "And whenever you stand praying, if you have anything against anyone, forgive him, that your Father in heaven may also forgive you your trespasses. 26 But if you do not forgive, neither will your Father in heaven forgive your trespasses." NKJV

From everything you know about the Christian life right now, what do you honestly believe in your heart will happen for you? Check and make sure that what you believe is actually written like you believe it, and that you have the type of faith needed to receive it, and then speak it! That's not the "name it, claim it" gospel, but that is in-line with what is written in the Bible.

For example, if you have been seeking God's Kingdom and God's righteousness, first place in your life, but you are living without daily necessities (Matthew 6:25-34), then speak your faith and say, "My God is going to supply the things that I worry about, in the name of Jesus Christ. Amen! It's just that simple.

It does not matter if you are living in the middle of the desert under a cactus plant. If you have been following the instructions, and you believe it in your heart, speak it, and watch God fulfill His promise.

However, if you have allowed your circumstances to be a part of the requirements, then you would need to add that to the equation. We're supposed to live by faith, and not by what we can see (sight), but that may take a little practice (2 Corinthians 5:7).

For example if you have been seeking God's Kingdom and His righteousness first place in your life, and you are ready to speak your faith, but you also think that you will have to be under a bigger cactus plant before God will actually deliver the water you so desperately need, then you need to find a bigger plant before you die of thirst. By adding the bigger cactus plant to your belief, you added it to your faith.

If we are not careful, we can add all kinds of things to our faith, even though they have nothing to do with the written promise. Faith works either way, as long as we are remaining in the faith, but sometimes we create our own predicaments.

For example, I know several people who always said, "Every time I eat pork, I get a headache," and sure enough every time they ate pork, their head started hurting soon thereafter. Through their words, they were pronouncing what they believed in their heart, and in doing so, they were building their own future.

We could use this principle in reverse, but the question is whether or not we can believe it in our heart. For example, we can start saying, "I love my wife as Christ loves the church," on a daily basis (Ephesians 5:25). That's certainly in-line with the will of God, and if we can believe that in our heart, it will soon change our body.

However, we have to look at our words as a whole. For example, there are many people who speak against their spouse during the day at work. That shows the direction they are headed in, since words control the body, and even if they do not leave their spouse, their words will eventually lead them into participating in things such as porn, as a replacement.

Even if you casually agree with people who speak against their spouse, you have somewhat participated in, or supported the conversation. Therefore, whatever amount of that conversation you believe in your heart is what you are building through your words.

Even if you start saying that you love your spouse as Christ loves the church, you would simply have to add that to the pile you have already created. Here again, you can probably see that everything you do, participate in, and speak with your mouth has an effect on your life, whether directly or indirectly.

You may not have a spouse, but this works in every area of life; healing, provisions, deliverance, employment, etc. Therefore, replace the word spouse in my example with whatever it is that you are talking about on a daily basis, and you will be able to see where your body is headed.

If you learn the principles we have covered, you will actually be able to listen to people speak and know what is in their future, if they do not change their course. Not only that, but you will be able to speak your future, by speaking in the direction you want your body to take. Philippians 4:13 will probably become one of your favorite verses.

Philippians 4:13
13 I can do all things through Christ which strengtheneth me. KJV

However, it's difficult to change directions, especially for people who have no knowledge of this, and it would be a challenge for someone who has spent weeks, months, and years, declaring something that they believe in their heart, to change overnight. Nevertheless, thank God that it's not impossible to change.

Know that all of our words, including our careless words count (Matthew 12:33-34). The words we spoke Monday through Saturday, and all the while we were getting ready on Sunday morning, up until the time we hit that smile switch, as we were getting out of the car at church, count. Let us return to the Lord our God in accordance with His ways, giving Him what He has required of us.

Father, in Jesus' name, we need a new start with a clean slate. Forgive us I pray, and wash us clean with the blood of Jesus. May the words of our mouth, and the meditations of our heart be acceptable, and pleasing in Your sight. You alone are our Rock and Redeemer. And You alone are worthy of praise. Amen.

Now can you see what a difference reading the Word of God out loud every day, and believing it in your heart would make. You can actually position yourself to receive what you say, and not only that, but you will be able to recognize where the people around you are headed, by their words. You will become slow to speak, and quick to listen (James 1:19).

Some people would be quick to say, "God isn't going to allow us to just say anything and it come true." That's practically true, but usually when I hear someone say that, they really don't know what God will allow us to do.

Nevertheless, they have spoken their faith, and therefore, they are not going to be able to just say anything and it come true, because that is what they proclaim. If that sounds like you, simply repent and turn.

Our faith can move mountains, or it can place mountains in the way. Take Matthew 7:1-2 as an example.

Matthew 7:1-2
1 "Judge not, that you be not judged. 2 For with what judgment you judge, you will be judged; and with the measure you use, it will be measured back to you. NKJV

Faith says that in the same way that we judge others, we will be judged. Therefore, our mouth can either place the bar on the ground, or we can make it so high that the jolly green giant can't get over it, and here is the part we may not realize. The promise doesn't give a time frame.

In other words, what if we committed a sin today, but nine months from now, we judge someone doing the same thing we did. Would that count?

King David slept with Bathsheba, Uriah's wife, and she became pregnant (2 Samuel 11:1-5). Afterwards, he arranged for Uriah to meet an untimely death in battle (2 Samuel 11:6-26). More than nine months later, after the child was born, the Lord sent Nathan the prophet to confront David about his sin (2 Samuel 12).

The Lord waited nine months to settle accounts with David. Think about that. Nine months later, after we have probably forgotten about the things we have done, we could pronounce judgment on someone else for doing the same thing we have done, and end up receiving the same judgment we pronounce. Oh

Lord, have mercy upon us.

Our faith can build a mountain that we don't want to climb. Think before you speak! Ask yourself, "have I ever done the same thing?" Mercy triumphs over judgment (James 2:13). May the Lord have mercy on us.

There are plenty of Christians who do not believe that we can have what we say. I can see how that would happen, because I used to be in the same boat. Many of us learn Mark 11:23, and off we go! We start speaking this and that, and we keep speaking it until we run out of breath.

However, you may be like me. I didn't know anything about the spiritual principles we are discussing when I first started trying to speak faith over my life, nor any of the conditions. I just knew a few of the promises, and when that didn't work out for me, I got angry, but that was my fault. It's called "lack of knowledge."

Let me tell you this. It's never a good idea to be angry with God. It's far better to find a hole to hide in, and tape your mouth shut with duct tape, until you get over it. Praise God, the Lord had mercy on me, and if you were like I was, I will pray that the Lord will have mercy on you also.

Father, in the name of Jesus Christ, if it was not for Your great mercy, we would not be here. We are absolutely nothing without You. Forgive us for our ignorance. We learned three verses and set out to change the world, and then we pouted when things didn't go our way. Forgive us for our great transgressions. Save us from our sins, and place an overwhelming desire in our heart to know You. Give us the grace needed to draw near to You in accordance with Your Word. Make us into the people You have called us to be, in the name of Jesus Christ. Amen. Praise the Lord God almighty, Who is worthy of praise!

Now, faith can remove mountains also.

Matthew 17:20-21
20 So Jesus said to them, "Because of your unbelief; for assuredly, I say to you, if you have faith as a mustard seed, you will say to this mountain, 'Move from here to there,' and it will move; and nothing will be impossible for you. 21 However, this kind does not go out except by prayer and fasting." NKJV

Faith can remove mountains, but here again, what are the instructions, and requirements associated with that promise? First, we would need a good understanding of what faith is (Hebrews chapter 11), which we have covered in this book. Next, we must do away with any and all unbelief.

Is the unbelief mentioned in the passage of scripture above associated with being able to cast the demon out, or is it unbelief associated with the things of

God? I believe it is the latter, since the disciples seemed suppressed that they could not cast the demon out of the boy (Matthew 17:18). In other words, they were used to casting out demons, but this one was different.

It is not just speaking, and believing that what we are saying will come true, but there are conditions that must be met. What if the disciples words over the past few weeks were the reason why the demon didn't come out? The thing is, we really don't know, but whatever it is, it is a form of unbelief. We must believe God, and take Him at His Word as Abraham did.

Jesus said that "This kind does not go out except by prayer and fasting" (verse 21 above). Obviously, the disciples didn't know that, and yet it seemed like they had been casting out demons for some time before this incident.

The Bible tells us that there are things that we do not know right now (1 Corinthians 13:9), and that we should not go beyond what is written (1 Corinthians 4:6). Therefore, there will always be things that we do not know, this side of glory.

Here is what to keep in mind. There will always be conditions to every promise, and sometimes you will have to search an entire book of the Bible, or even read the same parable from a different book in the Bible, before you will understand it.

Do your homework first. Remain in the faith, ask God for wisdom in dealing with whatever it is that you are going through, and then speak to whatever mountain you may have in your way. Always remain humble before God, because the problem is always on our side. He has already given us everything we need (2 Peter 1:3-4).

There are many other things to consider. For example, God will not allow someone, even with great faith, to speak against what He has already decreed. No one can speak, and make what God has decreed void (verse 37 below).

Lamentations 3:37
37 Who is he who speaks and it comes to pass, When the Lord has not commanded it? NKJV

For example, God has said that He will never flood the entire earth again according to the Word of the Lord written in Genesis 9:15. Therefore, even if we had great faith, and declared that the earth will be covered with water, it's not going to happen, since God has already declared that it would not happen again.

We can apply this to everything that God has decreed (ruled, commanded). For example, God has said that we need to forgive in order to be forgiven, and that is what must happen. Therefore, if we are praying for a person who is experiencing the Lord's discipline because they have not forgiven someone, then our prayers may work temporarily, but they will need to forgive others before they are totally delivered.

If our prayer doesn't work, this would be the time to examine our faith, and the faith of the person we are praying for. It's never God's Word that fails (Isaiah

55:11). It endures forever (1 Peter 1:25). Praise God, halleluiah!

God shows no partiality (Acts 10:34, Romans 2:11). Therefore, He will treat each individual the same, based on what they do and say. If we are righteous by faith, then we will receive what is due a person who is righteous by faith. If we do not believe as Abraham believed, then we cannot possibly be blessed with him, since only those of faith are blessed with him (Galatians 3:7-9).

In the same way, if we fall away from the faith, or if we do not continue in our faith, we can expect God to react accordingly. In other words, we cannot speak or pray our way out of following spiritual principles.

We cannot say, "I will not continue in my faith, but I will remain holy in God's sight," since God has already decreed the opposite (Colossians 1:21-23). The person who does not continue in their faith, will be cut off (Colossians 1:21-23, John 15:1-6, Romans 11:20-23). That would be a good time for repentance.

We can't just "name it, claim it," but we can speak in-line with what God has already decreed, and declare it, "if we have the faith to receive it." Therefore, learn the principles, and put them into practice as you read this book from the beginning. Lord willing, then your faith will be ready for the things we will cover in each chapter.

Many Christians get caught up in the excitement of proclaiming empty promises, or great swelling words of emptiness (2 Peter 2:18, Ephesians 5:6). In other words, they get pleasure out of hearing promises that do not apply to them, since they are not in the position to receive what is promised.

For example, every promise in Romans chapter five is promised to people who have been justified by faith (Romans 5:1), and have access by faith into grace (Romans 5:2). These things are discussed in Romans chapter four. Therefore, Romans five was written in such a way as to assume that the reader accepted Romans four.

Now you can see what happens to people who quote promises written in Romans five, but do not have the faith of Abraham described in Romans four. They wait in vain. Actually, almost every book (letter) in the New Testament is written in this way. Therefore, before you pull a promise out of a particular chapter, it is best to know the whole letter.

Many people quote promises today to unsuspecting people, who have no idea that they are not in a position to receive what is promised. They do it in order to build their crowds in keeping with Acts 20:29-31, and 2 Timothy 4:3-4. They mention promise after promise without ever mentioning any of the conditions, and consequently, they deceive the listeners.

Who is Romans chapter eight written to according to the following verse?

Romans 8:4
4 That the righteousness of the law might be fulfilled in us, who walk not after the flesh, but after the Spirit. KJV

The word "us" in the passage above is referring to Christians, who do not walk in the flesh, but after the Spirit, and the Apostle Paul describes the difference between these two people in the verses that follow (Romans 8:5-8). However, no one ever mentions the conditions when they quote promises from that chapter.

Get this. If God has said that a person who does certain things will be sick, then they will be sick (Revelation 2:20-23). They may enjoy a moment of peace through someone else's faith, who intercedes on their behalf, but if they do not turn, they will be sick, point, blank, period.

In the same way, if God has said that the person who finds their life will lose it, then that is what will happen, unless they turn (John 12:25-26, Matthew 16:24-25). Many of us can help someone for a few minutes, but by teaching them to live by faith, we will help them for a lifetime. Praise be to the Lord God almighty.

If we find ourself in similar situations, we need to repent of the past, start over with the right instructions, and look for opportunities to show mercy and love. Showing others mercy will triumph over judgment due us (James 2:13), and love covers a multitude of sins (1 Peter 4:8, Proverbs 10:12). Also, righteous acts will produce love (Hosea 10:12).

Following those spiritual principles will reduce, or even cover over what is due us if we find ourself in a predicament. It doesn't enable us to continue heading in the wrong direction, but we can avoid the judgment due us, since we reap what we have sown (Galatians 6:7-10). We need to know that.

Do you see how important it is to know what God's Word says for yourself? There are many things written in the Bible that the average Christian does not know, which can be used to deliver us from predicaments, and to help fellow Christians. Take John 15:7 as an example.

John 15:7
7 If you abide in Me, and My words abide in you, you will ask what you desire, and it shall be done for you. NKJV

This verse is evidence that we can position ourself, to be able to ask for "anything." I say position ourself because it comes with two conditions. First we have to "abide in Jesus," which we have already covered, and second we would have to make His Word remain (abide) on the inside of us.

We have already learned that in order to make the Word remain on the inside of us, we need to read it over and over, being very careful not to speak against it, and live up to what we have attained (Philippians 3:16). Whoever has will be given more.

Mark 4:24-25
24 Then He said to them, "Take heed what you hear. With the same measure you use, it will be measured to you; and to you who hear, more will be given. 25 For whoever has, to him more

will be given; but whoever does not have, even what he has will be taken away from him." NKJV

We covered abiding in Jesus in chapter four. Those who abide in Jesus obey His commands (John 15:10). He commanded us to love one another, and to believe in His name (1 John 3:23, John 15:12, 17). Know that for yourself.

Therefore, if we make the Word remain in us, and obey Jesus' commands, we will certainly be able to receive what is promised in John 15:7 above, assuming that we are living by faith, believe it in our heart, and speak it with our mouth.

What is the difference between that and the "name it, claim it" gospel? The "name it, claim it" gospel never mentions the conditions. Therefore, those who are not living by faith, and have fallen away from the faith, are not even in the right ball park. No problem, just ask the Lord to forgive you, and turn toward Him in accordance with His Word.

Let's put all of this together with a real life example. Faith (the evidence of things not seen) says that all food is made clean if it is received with thanksgiving, and sanctified (made holy) through prayer.

1 Timothy 4:1-5
1 Now the Spirit expressly says that in latter times some will depart from the faith, giving heed to deceiving spirits and doctrines of demons, 2 speaking lies in hypocrisy, having their own conscience seared with a hot iron, 3 forbidding to marry, and commanding to abstain from foods which God created to be received with thanksgiving by those who believe and know the truth. 4 For every creature of God is good, and nothing is to be refused if it is received with thanksgiving; 5 for it is sanctified by the word of God and prayer. NKJV

First of all, do you believe in your heart that all food can be made clean according to the Word of God above? In other words, do you have the faith of Abraham? If not, then don't eat it! Grow your own food.

There will be much discussion about food in the last days, as it is already happening today (verse 3 above). However, those who do not believe, will not receive what is promised in the passage of scripture above.

If you believe every Word of God, as Abraham believed, then check to make sure that the instructions you have received are right. If you are following something that is not written in the Bible, such as the doctrines of demons taught by men who do not teach in accordance with the faith (verses 1-2 above), then you will not have the right results. Always double-check the instructions.

We have to mix faith with those verses. Therefore, if my wife and I have the pleasure of dining with you one of these days, and I am asked to pray, I will say something very similar to the following. Father in Jesus' name, we thank You for this food, and we ask that You bless this food, and make it clean. Amen. That's in-line with verses 4 and 5 above.

Just after praying that, I will speak directly to the mountain (the food) and say, "Food be blessed and be clean in the name of Jesus Christ. Amen. That is an example of speaking with the Spirit of faith. Add what you want to add to that if you would like, but that is what is required for those who believe the truth.

Next, instead of agreeing with people who speak in opposition to the faith, I would always be careful to speak with the Spirit of faith on a daily basis. For example, if I am having a casual conversation with someone about food, and they say "Pork is going to raise your blood pressure," then I will say, "My God is able to bless it and make it clean in accordance with His Word." Never eat pork if you don't have the faith to eat it!

We have to keep in mind that our words are working for good, or for evil 24/7, and 365 days a year. In this way, we will overcome the devil with the words of our mouth, and the blood of Jesus (Romans 12:11). Praise God, halleluiah!

Do you see how to speak faith over your life? Take any one of these steps out, and you will not receive the expected results. Now you can probably see why some people are waiting in vain on promises to materialize.

One day a bishop tried to explain to me why we needed to pray for the cooks, and the dish washers, and the people who folded the napkins, and on and on. Praise God for that, if you have time, do it. However, after learning this, a good friend of ours, who used to pray for everything, and everyone involved before eating, said that now he can eat his food before it gets cold. Praise God.

Anytime someone challenges you, I personally would go back to the scriptures and read the instructions again to see if something was missed, since we are to warn one another (Colossians 3:16). However, did God say that I need to pray for the cook before I eat the food? I may need to pray for the cook after I taste the food, but least we offend anyone, let's go ahead and pray for whomever we are expected to pray for and use the microwave when we finish, if need be.

Think about every single word you have spoken over the past twelve months because those are the words that have placed you where you are today. Now, ask yourself if you need to speak those same words again, or should you learn to say something different?

As you can see, there are huge advantages for those who learn the Word of God, and speak it like it is written. However, those who continue rejecting what is written, could reach a point where they lose all sensitivity, and even take a stand against God's Word if their blindness is left unchecked. (Ephesians 4:17-19). That describes a scoffer.

Proverbs 9:8-9
8 Do not correct a scoffer, lest he hate you; Rebuke a wise man, and he will love you. 9 Give instruction to a wise man,

and he will be still wiser; Teach a just man, and he will increase in learning. NKJV

Scoffers show contempt (hatred, scorn) toward the Word of God. They reject it, and they are full of explanations as to why it is okay to do so.

They don't believe the Word of God as it is written, and follow their own desires (2 Peter 3:3-7). For those who are defiled and unbelieving, nothing is pure (Titus 1:15-16). There is nothing you can do for a scoffer, except pray that God will grant him repentance (2 Timothy 2:24-26).

Recognize that for your own good, since if you correct him, he will use emotion, and whatever else that is not written in the Bible to combat you (Proverbs 9:8-9). Therefore, leave him alone and move on (Revelation 22:11), and do whatever leads to peace (Colossians 3:15).

1 Corinthians 11:19
19 For there must also be factions among you, that those who are approved may be recognized among you. NKJV

Differences "must" arise, but if the Word of God is not the authority, you are wasting your time. If they do not hold to the teachings found in their own Bible, but willingly speak in direct opposition to them, they will have no problem rejecting your words, even if you have the verses to back them up.

Now what

Think about every word you have used, and every conversation you have participated in over the past week, month, or year. Combine that with what you actually believe in your heart right now.

If you are like me, when I first thought about these things, I was overwhelmed thinking about every careless word I had spoken in the past (Matthew 12:37). I did not realize that casual words played such a huge role in determining the outcome of our days (1 Peter 3:10-12).

The Word of God, living on the inside of us, changes all of that. The Holy Spirit brings verses to our remembrance as we go throughout our day (John 14:26). These are verses that we can then apply to whatever situation that we are in.

We need help living the Christian life, through the Holy Spirit, but we also have to do our part, which is to stop conforming to this world, and to renew our mind with the truth, to the point of being transformed into a new person.

It's time to get busy, if you want to position yourself to make your words come true. If not, you can easily say something that you don't mean, and it can cost you years of what I call "down time."

Just by saying certain things in your heart, you could be defiled, or made unclean, which means that you will be useless for God's work (Matthew 15:16-20). The Word of God cleanses us (Ephesians 5:26), and the more we stop sinning, the more God will use us for great things (2 Timothy 2:20-21).

I'm expecting great things to happen for you, Lord willing, if you have believed the verses we have covered. Glory be to God. The verses will cleanse you, and just by turning, the Lord will see and have mercy on you. Yes, I am expecting great things for you. Praise be to the Lord our God forever, and ever. Amen.

An example of saying the wrong thing, at the wrong time, would be Israel in the desert. I have mentioned that the people of Israel complained in the desert after believing that they would not be able to take the land in which the Lord had instructed them to take through Moses. Here is what they said while complaining against Moses and Aaron.

Numbers 14:1-3
1 So all the congregation lifted up their voices and cried, and the people wept that night. 2 And all the children of Israel complained against Moses and Aaron, and the whole congregation said to them, "If only we had died in the land of Egypt! Or if only we had died in this wilderness! 3 Why has the Lord brought us to this land to fall by the sword, that our wives and children should become victims? Would it not be better for us to return to Egypt?" NKJV

The people complained against Moses and Aaron, and made statements that they would soon regret. The Lord heard their complaints, and gave them what they said should have happened to them while they were complaining.

Numbers 14:26-29
26 And the Lord spoke to Moses and Aaron, saying, 27 "How long shall I bear with this evil congregation who complain against Me? I have heard the complaints which the children of Israel make against Me. 28 Say to them, 'As I live,' says the Lord, 'just as you have spoken in My hearing, so I will do to you: 29 The carcasses of you who have complained against Me shall fall in this wilderness, all of you who were numbered, according to your entire number, from twenty years old and above. NKJV

The children under twenty years of age, whom they said would be taken captive in their complaints, were the ones that the Lord allowed to enter the promised land, after those who had complained against Him had died in the desert, with the exception of Joshua and Caleb (Numbers 14:30-31).

Israel spent forty years wandering around in the desert, until the last person who had complained had died in the wilderness as punishment for their sin (Numbers 14:32-34), and we are supposed to learn from their mistakes (1 Corinthians 10:1-11).

The moral of that story is, "Think before you speak (James 1:19)!" If you really do not want what you are saying to happen to you, then do not speak it. Do everything without complaining, or arguing (verse 14 below).

Philippians 2:14-16
14 Do all things without complaining and disputing, 15 that you may become blameless and harmless, children of God without fault in the midst of a crooked and perverse generation, among whom you shine as lights in the world, 16 holding fast the word of life, so that I may rejoice in the day of Christ that I have not run in vain or labored in vain. NKJV

Instead of proclaiming a future that you do not want, start proclaiming God's Word over your life! With long life He satisfies me and shows me His salvation (Psalm 91:16)! Amen!

The Lord is my helper (Hebrews 13:6)! I can do all things through Christ, Who gives me the strength to be able to do them (Philippians 4:13)! The Lord is my Shepherd, I shall not be in want (Psalm 23)! The Lord delivers me from trials (2 Peter 2:9), and shows me His way out of temptations (1 Corinthians 10:13)! The Lord delivers me from all my troubles (1 Peter 5:10). Amen!

I always try to say "Praise God," anytime I don't know what to say, or whenever I'm thinking something that I don't want to speak. Now, sometimes when I say praise God, some people will ask me what was I going to say, or they will say, "I know what you were thinking, go ahead and say it." Of course that defeats the purpose, and so I'm now working on changing to a new phrase, or a combination of godly phrases.

My point is, think before you speak, and there is absolutely nothing wrong with saying "praise God," while you are thinking, so that people won't look at you as if you did not understand the question.

Think of your words as if they are molding your future, and changing your days for good. The wrong time to have a long conversation, is when you are tired or sleepy, because that is when you will not be able to think before you speak.

James 1:19-20
19 So then, my beloved brethren, let every man be swift to hear, slow to speak, slow to wrath; 20 for the wrath of man does not produce the righteousness of God. NKJV

Sometimes I find myself in conversations that I don't need to be in, and you may feel the same way. Out of the blue, someone will begin to speak against the government, or their spouse, or their place of employment. I don't want to participate in those types of conversations, since they could lead me to accidentally say something that I really don't want to say.

I really don't want to complain about anything, so I try to avoid people who do. However, I used to be a complainer myself.

I was walking in town one day and came across a retired coworker, whom I had not seen in a while. She seemed to be very peaceful, but when she asked about how things were going at work, I started complaining non-stop for about ten minutes, without even realizing it. She held her hand out as if to say "take a breath," and when I stopped talking she said, "Do something about it."

That was one of those life-changing moments for me. It's easy to find things to complain about, and it is so easy to get caught up in it to the point of being out of control. I didn't even realize that I was complaining, but I received her message loud and clear. She didn't want to hear it.

Our instructions are to stop complaining (Philippians 2:14 above), and to cast all of our cares on God, Who cares for us.

Philippians 4:6-7
6 Be anxious for nothing, but in everything by prayer and supplication, with thanksgiving, let your requests be made known to God; 7 and the peace of God, which surpasses all understanding, will guard your hearts and minds through Christ Jesus. NKJV

1 Peter 5:6-11
6 Therefore humble yourselves under the mighty hand of God, that He may exalt you in due time, 7 casting all your care upon Him, for He cares for you. 8 Be sober, be vigilant; because your adversary the devil walks about like a roaring lion, seeking whom he may devour. 9 Resist him, steadfast in the faith, knowing that the same sufferings are experienced by your brotherhood in the world. 10 But may the God of all grace, who called us to His eternal glory by Christ Jesus, after you have suffered a while, perfect, establish, strengthen, and settle you. 11 To Him be the glory and the dominion forever and ever. Amen. NKJV

God takes good care of us (verse 7 above). Amen! We should tell Him what is going on around us, and let Him deal with it. He has promised that after we suffer a while, He will perfect, establish, strengthen, and settle us (verse 10 above). Praise God, halleluiah!

His peace will guard our heart and mind (Philippians 4:7 above). We don't have to put our two cents in conversations that violate the Word of God anymore. We have to learn how to cast our anxiety on Him, Who cares for us.

He cares for us! That means that He will fix it. He does the maintenance, the upkeep, the repairs, overhauls, and whatever else we need. He will do it, as long as we do our part, which is to be willing to suffer through (1 Peter 5:10 above), cast our cares on Him, and to stop complaining. Praise, honor, and glory be to the Lord our God forever, and ever. Amen.

We serve a merciful God! Cry out to Him and ask for mercy. Tell Him that you didn't know His ways, and ask for forgiveness. He already knows that we don't know the things we should know (Hosea 4:6, 1 Corinthians 8:2), but He gives more grace to those who are humble (James 4:6, 1 Peter 5:5).

Father, in Jesus' name, we love You. Forgive us our sins. Thank You for listening to us, even though we have not listened to You at times. Have mercy upon us. In Your loving kindness You have watched over us, and it is because of Your mercies we have not been consumed. We thank You Father in the name of our Lord Jesus Christ for taking good care of us. Be with us now in times of suffering to deliver us according to Your Word. Remind us of Your ways that we may remain on the paths that You have marked out for us. Our hope is in You, and we will wait on Your mercies, which are new every morning. Weeping may endure for a night, but joy cometh in the morning! You alone are worthy of praise, glory, and honor, forever and ever. Amen.

I don't expect you to remember everything we cover in this book, but please do whatever you have to do in order to learn the verses. Force yourself to learn them. Read them over and over out loud, until they are living on the inside of you. Use this book as a reference if you would like, but there is no substitute for the pure Word of God. Praise God, halleluiah! Peace be with you. Amen.

I'm Alan Ballou; a servant. If I may be of service to you please contact me.

www.HowToStopSinning.com

Alan's email alan@howtostopsinning.com

Lucie's email lucie@howtostopsinning.com

൫൝

The world cannot hate you, but it hates Me because I testify of it that its works are evil. John 7:7 NKJV

Jesus Christ

12

The Round Table

౭ాౘ

Everybody is different, and because of that, we can't assume we are all on the same page, so to speak, unless we have all renewed our mind with the truth to the point of being transformed.

Until that point in time, we have to give each other room to grow. One person soaks up all the Word he can get, and the next has to work things into his life, a little at a time, but both are still a work in progress, as long as they are continuing in their faith (Colossians 1:21-23).

If we ever reach a point where we stop continuing in our faith, which includes hearing the Word of God (Romans 10:17), and fighting to remain in the faith, that would be the point of great concern.

John 5:24
24 "Most assuredly, I say to you, he who hears My word and believes in Him who sent Me has everlasting life, and shall not come into judgment, but has passed from death into life. NKJV

Reaching a point in life where we refuse to hear the Word is evidence of backsliding. Those who hear the Word and believe, have everlasting life (verse 24 above). Those who do not want to hear what the Bible says, cannot possibly be continuing in their faith.

As I have mentioned many times, those who belong to God, hear His Word (verse 47 below). That in itself can be used as evidence of belonging to God.

John 8:47
47 He who is of God hears God's words; therefore you do not hear, because you are not of God." NKJV

If someone claims to be a Christian, but they refuse to hear what the Bible says, and they are not experiencing discipline, hardship, or affliction in their life on account of their sin, then they are probably not a true Christian (Hebrews 12:8-13). It could be that God is giving them time to repent, as He does for everyone (Romans 2:5), but keep in mind that tares (children of the enemy) grow amongst the wheat (Matthew 13:25).

Tares will use peer pressure, philosophy, worldly wisdom, or whatever else to deceive you (1 Peter 4:3-5, Matthew 24:24). The only thing that you can be sure that they will not do, is teach you to do the will of God, which is to be holy in conduct (1 Thessalonians 4:1-5). They will never teach you to obey the Gospel.

Christians receive discipline for their sins here on earth, in order that we will not be condemned with the world (1 Corinthians 11:32). Therefore, any true Christ follower, who stops up his ears to the Word of God, will eventually experience discipline.

The tares are planted alongside the wheat, and our instructions are to allow them to grow with us (Matthew 13:28-30), but we don't have to make it easy on them. One major difference between the tares and the wheat is that the tares will be weeded out of the Kingdom of Christ, in the end (verses 40-43 below).

Matthew 13:40-43
40 Therefore as the tares are gathered and burned in the fire, so it will be at the end of this age. 41 The Son of Man will send out His angels, and they will gather out of His kingdom all things that offend, and those who practice lawlessness, 42 and will cast them into the furnace of fire. There will be wailing and gnashing of teeth. 43 Then the righteous will shine forth as the sun in the kingdom of their Father. He who has ears to hear, let him hear! NKJV

These are actual people in the church, alongside of you and me. However, they "practice lawlessness," which is sin according to 1 John 3:4, and they are there to help you practice it too.

We have made it very easy for them here in these last days since we no longer follow teachings such as 1 Corinthians 5:9-11, or 2 Thessalonians 3:6, 14, or Ephesians 5:5-7, or 2 Timothy 3:1-5, or 1 Corinthians 15:33-34, or Romans 16:17-18. I wonder if God has changed His mind about His Word, as we have? May the Lord have mercy on us.

Anyway, I'm not overly concerned about any of them reading a book on how to stop sinning, and being healed, since they promote sin. They also have their own set of signs and wonders, through Satan's power (Matthew 24:24). The difference will be that their signs and wonders will be used to take people away from the truth, which is a part of God's plan, so that those who do not love the truth, will be condemned (2 Thessalonians 2:9-12). Check the verses.

They are planted by the devil, and so I am expecting them to try and keep you from being what God has called you to be, by turning you away from the truth (Matthew 13:38-39). That's why they are there.

Any Christian who turns away from the truth, for whatever reason, is in danger of losing their very soul (verses 19-20 below). Know that for yourself, because tares will certainly speak against those verses as if they are not true.

James 5:19-20
19 Brethren, if anyone among you wanders from the truth, and someone turns him back, 20 let him know that he who turns a sinner from the error of his way will save a soul from death and cover a multitude of sins. NKJV

Therefore, the truth should never be hidden if we intend on helping Christians with life issues. If sin is the issue, and it always is, since it is connected to every part of the Christian life (healing, deliverance, provisions), then the verses concerning sin, should be mentioned as part of the solution.

Tares will not allow that, because they will not hear God's Word (John 8:47 above). Everyone has sinned and has fallen short of the glory of God (Romans 3:23), and so, a tare may not be identified by their sin, but they will not hear the Word of God like it is written in the New King James Bible, or the King James Bible, or any Bible that doesn't water down the truth.

Therefore, don't hide the truth just because someone, who calls himself a Christian, doesn't want to hear it. Those who refuse to hear it, do not belong to God anyway. We put up with anything for the sake of the Gospel, with the exception of hiding the truth itself, and every Christian should already know that (1 Corinthians 9:12).

Holding on to the teachings is indeed a part of the Gospel message according to 2 Thessalonians 2:13-15, and 1 Corinthians 15:1-2 (below).

1 Corinthians 15:1-2
1 Moreover, brethren, I declare to you the gospel which I preached to you, which also you received and in which you stand, 2 by which also you are saved, if you hold fast that word which I preached to you — unless you believed in vain. NKJV

Those who do not hold to the teachings, believe in vain (verse 2 above). We are saved "if" we hold fast to the Word that was preached, according to the verses above.

John 8:31-32
31 Then Jesus said to those Jews who believed Him, "If you abide in My word, you are My disciples indeed. 32 And you shall know the truth, and the truth shall make you free." NKJV

Disciples of Jesus Christ abide (remain) in His Word, to the point of knowing the truth (verses 31-32 above). That's a characteristic of a disciple of Jesus, and that is also in-line with Romans 1:28, except in some of the newer Bibles. The same is true in the verses below.

1 John 2:24-25
24 Therefore let that abide in you which you heard from the

beginning. If what you heard from the beginning abides in you, you also will abide in the Son and in the Father. 25 And this is the promise that He has promised us — eternal life. NKJV

Therefore, a Christian who hears the truth, and receives it, even though he may not be living up to it, is a work in progress. A Christian who rejects the Word of God, avoids it, and doesn't want to hear it, is either a tare, not a true believer yet, or he is very close to affliction, and even death (Proverbs 15:9-10).

There are two things that every Christian needs to hold on to, no matter what, and that is our faith in Jesus Christ (verse 18 below), and the Word of God, which is truth (verse 17 below).

Acts 26:18
18 to open their eyes, in order to turn them from darkness to light, and from the power of Satan to God, that they may receive forgiveness of sins and an inheritance among those who are sanctified by faith in Me.' NKJV

John 17:17
17 Sanctify them by Your truth. Your word is truth. NKJV

We have to have faith in Jesus Christ, and we have to believe the truth. Take those two things out of any gathering for Christians, and you have opened the door for lawlessness.

To be sanctified is to be made holy. If we take the tools of sanctification out of our gatherings, what are we left with that can change anyone's conduct for the better?

No, we're not going to beat people over the head with the Bible, but we're not going to stop speaking it either. However, we should gently instruct those who oppose the truth (2 Timothy 4:24-26); teaching and warning (admonishing) everyone (Colossians 3:16).

2 Timothy 2:24-26
24 And a servant of the Lord must not quarrel but be gentle to all, able to teach, patient, 25 in humility correcting those who are in opposition, if God perhaps will grant them repentance, so that they may know the truth, 26 and that they may come to their senses and escape the snare of the devil, having been taken captive by him to do his will. NKJV

We correct those in opposition (verse 25 above) without quarreling, or arguing (verse 24 above, Philippians 2:14). We don't argue, and we don't quarrel, but like I said, we never stop speaking it. Those who have everlasting life will hear God's Word (John 5:24 above). Those who do not believe Jesus will not have His Word living in them (John 5:38).

For those who do hear God's Word, it will work on the inside of those who believe it (verse 13 below).

1 Thessalonians 2:13
13 For this reason we also thank God without ceasing, because when you received the word of God which you heard from us, you welcomed it not as the word of men, but as it is in truth, the word of God, which also effectively works in you who believe. NKJV

All believers need is the pure Word of God living on the inside of them in order for it to change them from the inside out. You shall know the truth, and the "truth" itself shall set you free, from being a slave to sin (John 8:31-37).

The truth is what changes people (John 8:31-37, 17:17, 1 Peter 1:22-25). If you cannot help those who have wandered away from the truth to turn (repent), and believe the truth, then you cannot help them at all (James 5:19-20). You may be able to make them feel better, but that's only temporary.

Hypothetically speaking, you've just entered a round table discussion with other Christians regarding how to help people with obvious sin problems such as addictions, and behavioral issues. As you listen, you notice that some people speak as if their feelings are their guide. Some follow worldly experiences, but very few mention what is written in their Bible.

Those who speak with their feelings are controlled by their feelings. Words control the body, and so unbeknownst to them, their words have placed their feelings in control, well above their faith. Think about that.

Those who speak from worldly experiences can't wait to tell how they did this or that. "I drank three glasses of milk, and then ate a chocolate covered donut, all while standing on my head, and I haven't had an addiction since." Their experience, mixed with a spiritual twist, becomes their testimony, and many follow that type of distortion (Acts 20:29-32).

That may be a bizarre example, but my point is that those who practice old wives' tales, and the like, believe that they are on the right path because what they did seemed to work, and not because they followed what is written in their Bible. However, for Christians, the question isn't if old wives' tales work, since God doesn't want us to follow them, but to live by faith in His Word instead. God wants us to depend on Him.

1 Timothy 4:6-7
6 If you instruct the brethren in these things, you will be a good minister of Jesus Christ, nourished in the words of faith and of the good doctrine which you have carefully followed. 7 But reject profane and old wives' fables, and exercise yourself toward godliness. NKJV

Old wives' tales and fables (myths) have no place in the church, and should be rejected (verse 7 above). Nevertheless, it is predicted that in the last days people will turn to myths instead of what is written in their Bible (2 Timothy 4:3-4), and, as I have mentioned, myths, and other signs that seem to work will only serve to draw people further away from the truth (2 Thessalonians 2:9-12). Check those verses because that is already happening today.

God has no problem whatsoever with producing results, and all things are possible for those who believe. The magicians of Egypt produced some of the same signs that God produced through Moses (Exodus 7:22, 8:18), and that may be the case today with old wives' tales, but the Lord our God is a jealous God.

Therefore, we should be careful to seek what we need from Him. Everything that will be perfect for us comes from our Father in Heaven (verse 17 below).

James 1:16-17
16 Do not be deceived, my beloved brethren. 17 Every good gift and every perfect gift is from above, and comes down from the Father of lights, with whom there is no variation or shadow of turning. NKJV

There is a reason why those who practiced magic burned their books according to Acts 19:19. Those who practice sorcery (witchcraft, magic) will not be able to enter the pearly gates of Heaven (Revelation 22:14-15).

All of these things, that are used to draw Christians away from the truth, are probably introduced by tares, or Christians who have been deceived. Some gathering places even have alternative medicines right inside the church. Imagine that. Let us repent and return to the Lord our God.

You may be in one of these situations today, or even in one I haven't mentioned. However, if you belong to God, repent and turn, and He will see it.

Father, in Jesus' name, if it wasn't for Your loving kindness, where would we be? We didn't know what we were doing, but we were led away by those who have rejected Your Word. Have mercy on us, O' Lord. Forgive us for the sins that we have committed against You, and wash us clean with the blood of Christ. Give us more grace that we may live the life that You have laid out for us, and choose all Your ways; in the name of Jesus Christ. Amen.

Now it's your turn to speak in the round table discussion, and you have decided to speak with the Spirit of faith. You boldly proclaim, "God's Word says that we can gain control over our body if we always speak the right words," and then you quote the verse below to back up your statement.

James 3:2
2 For we all stumble in many things. If anyone does not stum-

ble in word, he is a perfect man, able also to bridle the whole body. NKJV

Immediately, the feelings-based people say, "It's not what you said, but how you said it." In a tone that shows their disapproval, worldly Christians ask, "How is that supposed to work?" Scoffers slap the table with an open hand and with a raised voice say, "We don't want to know what your Bible says, but what do you say?"

Our words control our body. Therefore, scoffers, who don't want to hear what is written, won't hear what is written. It's just that simple. Their own words have positioned their body to where they hate hearing God's correction through His Word, and if left unchecked, death will soon follow, assuming they are true Christians. If not, then they store up wrath for the day of God's wrath (Romans 2:5).

Those who speak from worldly experiences will not understand faith because they have rejected it, since we have to obey the precepts before we will have a good understanding (Psalm 111:10, 119:98-105). The old wives' tales, and myths have placed them in bondage (given them over) to more of the same, and consequently, that is what they will seek unless they repent (Romans 6:16-17, 2 Peter 2:19, Acts 17:21).

The whole Christian life is lived by faith from start to finish (Romans 1:16-17). We were given the faith to come to the Lord as a gift (Ephesians 2:8, Romans 12:3), and we are expected to continue in our faith in order to remain holy in God's sight (Colossians 1:21-23).

God has no pleasure in those who draw back, or shrink back from living by faith. The end result of that course is perdition; the destruction of the soul.

Hebrews 10:36-39
36 For you have need of endurance, so that after you have done the will of God, you may receive the promise: 37 "For yet a little while, And He who is coming will come and will not tarry. 38 Now the just shall live by faith; But if anyone draws back, My soul has no pleasure in him." 39 But we are not of those who draw back to perdition, but of those who believe to the saving of the soul. NKJV

Once we have done the will of God, we will receive what is promised (verse 36 above). Now that we are saved, we have to do the will of God. Due to accepting false doctrines, many do not believe that we "have to do something" after we are saved, but Jesus Christ, in Whom we trust, makes this perfectly clear.

Matthew 7:21
21 "Not everyone who says to Me, 'Lord, Lord,' shall enter the kingdom of heaven, but he who does the will of My Father in heaven. NKJV

Yes, we do "have to do" the will of the Father, and only after doing the will of the Father will we receive what is promised (Hebrews 10:36 above). The will of the Father is our sanctification (1 Thessalonians 4:3-5), and He will see to it, if we continue in our faith (1 Thessalonians 5:23-24).

Therefore, why wouldn't we want to warn people who have wandered from the truth in keeping with Colossians 3:16, and James 5:19-20? We would, unless we have accepted false doctrines also, and have come to believe that it is okay to walk away from the Word of God after we accept Jesus Christ as our Lord and Savior.

Colossians 3:16
16 Let the word of Christ dwell in you richly in all wisdom, teaching and admonishing one another in psalms and hymns and spiritual songs, singing with grace in your hearts to the Lord. NKJV

Christians should teach and warn (admonish) one another. Take another look at 1 Corinthians 15:1-2 below.

1 Corinthians 15:1-2
1 Moreover, brethren, I declare unto you the gospel which I preached unto you, which also ye have received, and wherein ye stand; 2 By which also ye are saved, if ye keep in memory what I preached unto you, unless ye have believed in vain. KJV

Do those verses imply that we can walk away from the truth after being saved, and remain "saved?" By the Gospel we are "saved, if" we hold on to the Word that was preached. The word "if," which comes right after the word "saved" above, makes the word "saved" conditional. Read it again out loud a few times, if you cannot see it.

Eternal salvation is for those who obey Jesus (Hebrews 5:9). Tares will never teach you that verse because they do not want you to know the truth.

Disciples of Jesus Christ, hold to His teachings, or abide in His Word (John 8:31-32). Those who do not, fall away (John 6:60-69), but those who hear His Words and follow Him cannot be snatched out of His hands (John 10:26-28). We need to know that.

People who live their life based on how they feel, will always focus on how something makes them feel, since that is where their mouth leads them. What really matters to them is how you make them feel when you speak, which will lead you to avoid the truth, if your desire is to please people.

1 Thessalonians 2:4
4 But as we have been approved by God to be entrusted with the gospel, even so we speak, not as pleasing men, but God who tests our hearts. NKJV

Galatians 1:10
10 For do I now persuade men, or God? Or do I seek to please men? For if I still pleased men, I would not be a bondservant of Christ. NKJV

However, you cannot speak to please people, and be a servant of the Lord (Galatians 1:10 above). I know the saying is that "we can catch more flies with honey," but that is exactly what is caught; people who will not put up with sound doctrine in keeping with 2 Timothy 4:3-4.

Therefore, guess what happens when the scriptures are only mentioned after the house is full of people who were caught with honey? Their feelings make them leave, showing their disapproval. They came because of the honey, and just as soon as it dries up, the church across the street will enjoy their membership.

Therefore, stop catching flies, and start feeding sheep. Those approved by God to preach the Gospel, do not speak to please people (1 Thessalonians 2:4 above). The house may only fill with a few sinners, but a few sinners who want to change will be far better on the last day than a house full of sinners seeking honey, and tares.

Get this. People didn't like Jesus because of the things He said, but He said them anyway. Read the following verse and ask yourself if it describes the Jesus you know?

John 7:7
7 The world cannot hate you, but it hates Me because I testify of it that its works are evil. NKJV

There is a way that will "seem right" to us, but in the end, it leads to death (Proverbs 14:12, 16:25). We have to deny ourselves in order to follow Jesus (Matthew 16:24-25). Consequently, we can't follow what we naturally think is right, but we accept, believe, and follow the truth (Galatians 5:17).

Therefore, at some point during the time that Jesus met with sinners, He mentioned changing directions. He didn't hide the truth from people, like the unrighteous do today (Romans 1:18).

Contrary to popular belief, we don't love someone into the Kingdom of Heaven. Let that sink in. We love our neighbor as we love ourselves, but we preach the Gospel of the Kingdom, in season, out of season, when they are ready, and when they are not (2 Timothy 4:1-2, Matthew 4:23, 9:35).

We have to take the path that is written in the Bible; the one that few want to hear about (Matthew 7:13-14); the narrow gate.

Quite often people mention that Jesus ate with sinners, as if to say that He tolerated their behavior, but few mention that He called sinners to repentance.

Mark 2:16-17
16 And when the scribes and Pharisees saw Him eating with

the tax collectors and sinners, they said to His disciples, "How is it that He eats and drinks with tax collectors and sinners?" 17 When Jesus heard it, He said to them, "Those who are well have no need of a physician, but those who are sick. I did not come to call the righteous, but sinners, to repentance." NKJV

Jesus didn't just hang out with sinners for the sake of hanging out. No, He called them to repentance. In other words, if we were at the table with Jesus, then at some point He would make us regret how we had been living in the past, to the point of making us change course. That's repentance in a nutshell, so to speak.

Godly sorrow leads to repentance, but worldly sorrow leads to death (2 Corinthians 7:10). After hearing the Word of God, we will either want to get right with God, or we will hate the messenger, and look for any reason we can find that will discredit the message.

2 Corinthians 7:10
10 For godly sorrow produces repentance leading to salvation, not to be regretted; but the sorrow of the world produces death. NKJV

Repenting of the past, and accepting God's Word as it is written is the only safe path. We may not be all that God has called us to be yet, and we may not live up to the things that we know are true.

However, one thing is for sure. We cannot reject God's Word, and take our stand alongside the people of this world. A friend of the world, makes himself God's enemy (James 4:4, Romans 8:6-7). However, if we can reach a brother, or a sister who has wandered away from the truth, we will save their soul from death (James 5:19-20).

Father, in Jesus' name, help us and, be with us. Teach us through Your Holy Spirit, and enable us to speak Your Word with boldness, even in the face of suffering. Protect us, and save us from the things that we cannot see. Lead us through the power of Your Holy Spirit, and bring to our remembrance those things which are written in Your Word. In the name of Jesus Christ we pray. Amen.

Jesus did not turn everyone He met and neither will we. The ones who believed in Him, repented of the past, but the ones who did not turn, hated Him, and the same is true today. However, there is great value in taking a stand for what is right in the face of suffering.

That's called suffering for righteousness' sake. Those who are treated unfairly for righteousness' sake are blessed, and have a great reward in Heaven (Matthew 5:10-13). Praise God, halleluiah!

Matthew 5:10-13
**10 Blessed are those who are persecuted for righteousness'
sake, For theirs is the kingdom of heaven. 11 "Blessed are you
when they revile and persecute you, and say all kinds of evil
against you falsely for My sake. 12 Rejoice and be exceedingly
glad, for great is your reward in heaven, for so they persecuted
the prophets who were before you. 13 "You are the salt of the
earth; but if the salt loses its flavor, how shall it be seasoned?
It is then good for nothing but to be thrown out and trampled
underfoot by men. NKJV**

Know that if you take a stand for what is right, you will be persecuted;
treated unfairly. In fact, everyone who desires to live a godly life will be treated
unfairly (2 Timothy 3:12), even by people inside the church who are not free in
Christ (verse 29 below).

However, those who treat you unfairly for righteousness' sake, will not be
heirs (verse 30 below). Therefore, if you have treated people unfairly for mentioning the verses we have covered in this book, repent of that, ASAP.

Galatians 4:28-31
**28 Now we, brethren, as Isaac was, are children of promise.
29 But, as he who was born according to the flesh then persecuted him who was born according to the Spirit, even so it is
now. 30 Nevertheless what does the Scripture say? "Cast out
the bondwoman and her son, for the son of the bondwoman
shall not be heir with the son of the freewoman." 31 So then,
brethren, we are not children of the bondwoman but of the free.
NKJV**

Therefore, as you decide to speak with the Spirit of faith, those who oppose
the truth will speak against what you are saying in order to stop you. Unrighteous
people always suppress the truth (Romans 1:18), but they will not be heirs with
those who accept and believe the Word of God.

In order to be credited righteousness, we have to believe God as Abraham
believed Him (Romans 4:20-24). Therefore, know that those who oppose the
truth cannot possibly be righteous.

Yes, they may even be Christians too, but perhaps they have lost their salt
(verse 13 above), and have taken their stand with unbelievers. Salt that loses its
flavor is good for nothing (Matthew 5:13 above). They need to repent, and turn
to follow God in accordance with His Word.

Colossians 4:6
**6 Let your speech always be with grace, seasoned with salt,
that you may know how you ought to answer each one. NKJV**

Our conversation should be full of grace, but it should also be seasoned with salt. We don't hide our salt shaker just because nobody wants it, but we gently instruct those who oppose the truth, without arguing (2 Timothy 4:24-26). The Lord's servant must not argue.

I will admit, that this takes a bit of practice. For many years, I argued with people who opposed the truth for one reason or another.

Father in Jesus' name, have mercy on all of us who have taken a stand for Your Word, but have not done it in accordance with Your Word. Amen.

My grandmother used to tell me "Two wrongs don't make one right," and then she would give me that look. She had a way with words, but that saying puzzled me for a long time. I knew she could count, but I really didn't understand what she was saying, and I was too afraid to ask.

Keep in mind that the people you are dealing with cannot see the verses they have rejected, but those who belong to God will hear His Words that you speak (John 8:47). They may not turn right away, but the spoken Word will cut like a knife, and you will help to save the souls of those who have wandered from the truth, and have sided with the unrighteous (Hebrews 4:12, Ephesians 6:17, James 5:19-20).

Now what

I'm not asking you to interrupt a meeting with scripture, or to be rude toward those who do not believe. Knowledge puffs up, but love edifies; teaches or instructs with a desire toward improving those who hear (1 Corinthians 8:1).

Therefore, I'm not asking you to puff up, but when it is your turn to speak, I'm asking you to take a stand for the Word of God, and boldly proclaim what is written, in love (Acts 9:29, Ephesians 6:20). Contrary to popular belief, it is okay to speak the truth, in love.

Ephesians 4:15
15 but, speaking the truth in love, may grow up in all things into Him who is the head — Christ — NKJV

Love is patient, and love is kind, but love also "delights in the truth" (1 Corinthians 13:6). In fact, we don't love anyone whom we hide the truth from. That's called deception, or dishonesty. The truth is the only thing that sets people free from being a slave to sin (John 8:31-37).

When it is your turn to speak, then what can possibly be wrong with quoting the Word of God in an organization which is founded on God's Word? However, be prepared, since as you speak with the Spirit of faith, those with the spirit of error, and scoffers will not keep silent. Even if you patiently hear them out, they will interrupt you, which is a form of persecution (to be treated unfairly).

All of our life we have been taught that we cannot stop sinning, but if we spoke with the Spirit of faith, we would not be able to say that, since God's Word says the exact opposite. God says that if we would obey His doctrine from the heart, we would be set free from sin.

Romans 6:17-18
17 But God be thanked that though you were slaves of sin, yet you obeyed from the heart that form of doctrine to which you were delivered. 18 And having been set free from sin, you became slaves of righteousness. NKJV

Imagine mentioning that passage of scripture when it was your turn to speak. As soon as you did, a scoffer, or an unbeliever would quickly say, "If we say that we have no sin, we deceive ourselves, and the truth is not in us."

This is what I call using the truth, against the truth. Both verses are true, but the second one is quoted in such a way, as to make the first one seem false.

Can we say that Christians can indeed be set free from sin according to verse 18 above? Yes, we can, but if we speak against it, we can fall away from the faith, and those verses will be taken from us (1 Timothy 6:20-21, Mark 4:24-25).

Therefore, the people who quote verses like 1 John 1:8, out of context, cannot see, or hear Romans 6:17-18 above. You would have to have them read that verse out loud, before that stronghold was broken in their mind (2 Corinthians 10:3-5).

Yes, the Bible does say that if we say "We have no sin, we deceive ourselves and the truth is not in us" according to 1 John 1:8. It also says that if we say "we have not sinned," we make God out to be a liar, and God's Word is not in us according to 1 John 1:10. However, neither of those verses state that we cannot stop sinning.

I'm sure that you have heard those verses used as evidence to say that Christians cannot stop sinning, but do you ever hear anyone quote the very next verse that states why the letter of 1 John was written in the first place?

1 John 2:1
1 My little children, these things I write to you, so that you may not sin. NKJV

One of the reasons the book of 1 John was written was so that we would stop sinning. That happens to be the very next verse following the verse that so many use to say that we cannot stop sinning. If John meant that we cannot stop sinning, why did he write so that we would stop?

When we read from 1 John 1:8 down to 1 John 2:1, it becomes evident that John is not telling us that we cannot stop sinning. He is telling us that we have sinned, and even if we stop sinning completely, we still "have sinned" in the past. All of us have. Therefore, none of us are "without sin."

If people are "not" using 1 John 1:10 as an excuse to continue in sin, why do they speak against the very next verse? That should be proof enough that a verse can be taken from those who reject it. It's like it is not even there. They can't see 1 John 2:1 (above) because they speak against it in their interpretation of the two verses that come before it.

Faith comes by hearing (Romans 10:17). That's why I ask you to read the verses out loud. Sometimes I have people read them over and over until the stronghold in their mind is broken (2 Corinthians 10:3-5).

Sometimes it is very noticeable because they can't read the verse correctly at first. Other times they can read it correctly, but they cannot hear what they are saying.

Scoffers never see it. We could have a scoffer read 1 John 2:1 above, over and over, and then ask him what is one of the reasons why John wrote the letter of 1 John, and he will not answer, "So that we would not sin" because he literally cannot see it. That's why it is called blindness.

If you can see what I am saying, never speak against the verses again so that they will remain in you. If you have been one to use the book of 1 John as an excuse to continue in sin, then simply repent, and start over. However, get away from the crowd that has a form of godliness, but denies its power. People who continue to speak against the faith will eventually become scoffers.

Our body goes where our tongue takes it (James 3:2-12). Who among us can stop sinning if we have been declaring for the past twenty years that we cannot stop sinning? We need to change our heart first to make it believe in-line with what is actually written in the Bible.

If we spoke with the Spirit of faith, we would say that Christians can indeed stop sinning, and we would also declare that we "should" stop sinning, according to the following passage of scripture, which is in the same book of First John.

1 John 3:8-9
8 He who sins is of the devil, for the devil has sinned from the beginning. For this purpose the Son of God was manifested, that He might destroy the works of the devil. 9 Whoever has been born of God does not sin, for His seed remains in him; and he cannot sin, because he has been born of God. NKJV

According to those verses, it should be odd to find someone who declares that they have been born of God, yet they continue in sins that lead to death. Even if nobody at the round table has lived up to those verses, we shouldn't reject it.

No Christian should be ashamed of God's Word. If we are a work in progress, then praise God, but if we refuse to hear God's Word, we aren't making any progress.

Luke 9:26
26 For whosoever shall be ashamed of me and of my words, of

him shall the Son of man be ashamed, when he shall come in his own glory, and in his Father's, and of the holy angels. KJV

Tares practice lawlessness (Matthew 13:41), which is sin, and a bad tree cannot speak good things (Matthew 12:34). We are not tares, and therefore, as we have opportunity, and when it is our turn to speak, we boldly proclaim God's Word.

We can't reject God, and receive the help we need to live the Christian life from Him, and if we are not speaking truth, then we cannot help those who have wandered away from the truth (James 5:19-20).

The tree has to be made good before the fruit will be good (Matthew 12:33-37). However, we cannot change the tree until we change the heart, and we cannot change the heart if we refuse to put the Word of God in it. We can't reject the only thing that will make the fruit good, and then sit around in a circle and ask, "What are we going to do about this sin problem?"

That's ridiculous, but that is what the tares, and the scoffers, and the unbelievers will eventually make church-attending people do; hide the Word of God. I know that it will happen because it is written that it will happen in the last days, and I can already see it happening, but don't allow it to happen to you.

Most of us think that we can change the world, just by hanging out with the people of this world, but the reality is, we never will. God has to enable a person to come to Christ (John 6:44), and then we need to be sanctified by the truth (John 17:17) as we continue in our faith (Colossians 1:21-23).

1 Corinthians 15:33-34
33 Do not be deceived: "Evil company corrupts good habits."
34 Awake to righteousness, and do not sin; for some do not have the knowledge of God. I speak this to your shame. NKJV

Evil (bad) company will only change our habits, and not theirs. The quickest way for Christians to become a friend of the world, is to never allow our conversation to be seasoned with salt, so that we can fit in with people of this world. However, when the truth is spoken, they will either repent, or hate the messenger (2 Corinthians 7:10, John 7:7).

If you have been ashamed of God's Word, or hidden it because you haven't lived up to it yet, repent of that ASAP. God will have mercy on those who repent and turn.

It doesn't matter if you have been trying to stop sinning for the past fifty years, God says to "Reckon (consider) yourself as dead to sin, and alive to God." Store God's Word in your heart so that it will come out of your mouth, and help to guide your body where you want it to go.

Romans 6:11
11 Likewise you also, reckon yourselves to be dead indeed to sin, but alive to God in Christ Jesus our Lord. NKJV

Our body will never be dead to sin if our mouth keeps saying that we cannot stop sinning. Our words control our body, and not the other way around. Words have the power to not only change who we are, but our actions as well, and those who learn to control sin in their life, also open the door for blessings.

Jeremiah 5:25
25 Your iniquities have turned these things away, And your sins have withheld good from you. NKJV

Sin (iniquities) has withheld the good that God has planned for us. It's time to remove whatever it is that is keeping our blessing at bay.

I'm not asking you to say that you have no sin, or to say that you have not sinned. I have many sins. In fact, I've probably committed every sin in the book, and that may be why the Lord has allowed me to speak to you (1 Timothy 1:16).

However, I am asking you to believe that Christians can stop sinning in accordance with God's Word, and then I'm asking you to speak in-line with what is written so that you will not fall away from the faith.

Our body will go in the direction set by our mouth. Guess what that means for Christians who speak against God's Word and say that we will never be able to stop sinning? They will never be able to stop.

However, guess what that means for Christians who reckon themselves as dead to sin, and alive to God (Romans 6:11)? They are on the road to becoming dead to sin, and alive to God. Praise God, halleluiah!

Their tongue is repositioning their body to a better place. They are gaining self-control, and soon they will be able to control their destiny. Glory be to God.

Allow your Bible to tell you what to think and believe (Hebrews 4:12, 2 Corinthians 10:3-5). Don't worry about those who reject it. There will always be plenty of them on the sidelines as you go by saying, "Hey, stop in here."

God is able! The problem is on our side; what we believe, don't believe, and the false doctrines we have accepted as truth, that we need to trash. Be determined to be a believer who believes like Abraham believed, and put your faith into action like Noah did.

Repent of the past, and start over today! Those who have been forgiven much, simply love much (Luke 7:47).

Father, in Jesus' name, forgive us for not living by faith in the past. Forgive us for speaking against Your Word, and even joining hands with those who take their stand against what You have said. Have mercy upon us and give us the grace needed to do Your will. Renew our salt that we may boldly proclaim Your Word, and acknowledge You in all of our ways. Direct our paths by the power of Your Holy Spirit, and forgive us for grieving Your Spirit.

In Your great mercy, make us alive again, and give us what we need in order to continue in the faith You have given us. Amen! Thank You, Jesus!

I'm Alan Ballou; a servant. If you have any questions, please contact me.

My wife Lucie and I hold seminars wherever we are welcomed with small and large groups, and even from house to house. We do not charge anyone, but serve all who call on us for help.

www.HowToStopSinning.com

Alan's email alan@howtostopsinning.com

Lucie's email lucie@howtostopsinning.com

ಐ)ಲ

If a brother wanders from the truth and someone turns him back, he will save his soul from death, and cover a multitude of sins (James 5:19-20).

There is no such thing as a godly man who doesn't take the time needed to be God like. Draw near to God (James 4:8).

Just about anything can be used for good, or to promote evil. If you have a twitter account, and would like to receive godly reminders, with the verses included, please consider joining me. @AlanBallou

SUFFERING FOR DOING GOOD IS VERY MUCH A PART
OF THE CHRISTIAN WAY OF LIFE.

Alan Ballou

13

The Willingness to Suffer

෨ඁ෪

Suffering is very much a part of the Christian life, but most Christians have no knowledge of it. This day and age, it's all about a pot of gold at the end of the rainbow, and everybody is chasing after it. However, we are called to suffer.

Philippians 1:29
29 For to you it has been granted on behalf of Christ, not only to believe in Him, but also to suffer for His sake NKJV

1 Peter 2:19-21
19 For this is commendable, if because of conscience toward God one endures grief, suffering wrongfully. 20 For what credit is it if, when you are beaten for your faults, you take it patiently? But when you do good and suffer, if you take it patiently, this is commendable before God. 21 For to this you were called, because Christ also suffered for us, leaving us an example, that you should follow His steps: NKJV

Jesus didn't just come and die for our sins, but He left us an example to follow (verse 21 above). If we are seeking to live a godly life, but don't realize that, then we might be shocked by it, and not have the correct response to it.

If we do good and suffer patiently it is commendable before God (verse 20 above). However, there is no credit for returning evil for evil.

When persecutions arise, as we discussed in the previous chapter, that's when we will know that we have entered the race, and that we are headed in the right direction. Don't faint.

Hebrews 12:1-3
1 Therefore we also, since we are surrounded by so great a cloud of witnesses, let us lay aside every weight, and the sin which so easily ensnares us, and let us run with endurance the race that is set before us, 2 looking unto Jesus, the author and finisher of our faith, who for the joy that was set before Him endured the cross, despising the shame, and has sat down at

**the right hand of the throne of God. 3 For consider Him who
endured such hostility from sinners against Himself, lest you
become weary and discouraged in your souls. NKJV**

When persecutions arise because we are doing what is right, we need to look
to Jesus, and call on Him so that we don't faint in our mind; become discouraged
and give up (verse 3 above). I watched my mother go through much suffering
in the wrong way, and it had a damaging effect on her life. May the Lord have
mercy on her.

It's coming. Everyone who will be able to enter the Kingdom of God will
go through tribulations (verse 22 below), and we need to understand what is
happening so that we do not lose heart.

Acts 14:22
**22 strengthening the souls of the disciples, exhorting them to
continue in the faith, and saying, "We must through many tribulations enter the kingdom of God." NKJV**

According to the verse above, going through tribulation is not optional for
Christians. The good news is that the Lord will deliver us out of every tribulation. Praise be to the Lord God almighty. Great is His faithfulness, and His love
endures forever!

Psalm 34:19
**19 Many are the afflictions of the righteous, But the Lord deliv-
ers him out of them all. NKJV**

Christians are called to suffer in order that we would inherit a blessing. Those
who suffer as Christ did will share in His glory (verse 17 below).

Romans 8:14-17
**14 For as many as are led by the Spirit of God, these are sons
of God. 15 For you did not receive the spirit of bondage again
to fear, but you received the Spirit of adoption by whom we cry
out, "Abba, Father." 16 The Spirit Himself bears witness with
our spirit that we are children of God, 17 and if children, then
heirs — heirs of God and joint heirs with Christ, if indeed we
suffer with Him, that we may also be glorified together. NKJV**

By now, you are probably wondering how all of this relates to sin, and
healing. Well, those who are willing to suffer for righteousness (doing what is
right), at the hands of others, may cease from sin (stop sinning).

1 Peter 4:1-5
**1 Therefore, since Christ suffered for us in the flesh, arm
yourselves also with the same mind, for he who has suffered in**

**the flesh has ceased from sin, 2 that he no longer should live
the rest of his time in the flesh for the lusts of men, but for the
will of God. 3 For we have spent enough of our past lifetime in
doing the will of the Gentiles — when we walked in lewdness,
lusts, drunkenness, revelries, drinking parties, and abominable
idolatries. 4 In regard to these, they think it strange that you do
not run with them in the same flood of dissipation, speaking
evil of you. 5 They will give an account to Him who is ready to
judge the living and the dead. NKJV**

Does that say "cease from sin" in verse 1 above? That means to stop completely; finished with it, done. Praise God, halleluiah! However, are we willing to suffer at the hands of others, including other Christians (Galatians 4:29), in order to receive what is promised? Follow the instructions, and receive it!

If you are willing to suffer in your body (flesh), like Jesus did, without being swayed by the pressure and the assaults of men (Mark 12:14), you can be done with sin here on earth, and live the rest of your life for the will of God (verses 1 and 2 above).

People will think that you are strange, and they will speak evil of you (verse 4 above), but they will have to give an account for that (verse 5 above). Those who willingly suffer for righteousness, are truly the blessed of God (1 Peter 3:14).

**1 Peter 3:14-17
14 But even if you should suffer for righteousness' sake, you
are blessed. "And do not be afraid of their threats, nor be troubled." 15 But sanctify the Lord God in your hearts, and always
be ready to give a defense to everyone who asks you a reason
for the hope that is in you, with meekness and fear; 16 having
a good conscience, that when they defame you as evildoers,
those who revile your good conduct in Christ may be ashamed.
17 For it is better, if it is the will of God, to suffer for doing
good than for doing evil. NKJV**

Being willing to suffer doesn't mean that the persecution will necessarily stop (Isaiah 57:1), but those who trouble you will suffer everlasting destruction (verses 6-9 below), unless of course they repent and turn.

**2 Thessalonians 1:4-9
4 so that we ourselves boast of you among the churches of
God for your patience and faith in all your persecutions and
tribulations that you endure, 5 which is manifest evidence
of the righteous judgment of God, that you may be counted
worthy of the kingdom of God, for which you also suffer; 6
since it is a righteous thing with God to repay with tribulation
those who trouble you, 7 and to give you who are troubled rest**

with us when the Lord Jesus is revealed from heaven with His mighty angels, 8 in flaming fire taking vengeance on those who do not know God, and on those who do not obey the gospel of our Lord Jesus Christ. 9 These shall be punished with everlasting destruction from the presence of the Lord and from the glory of His power, NKJV

Those who continue in their faith, through the persecutions and tribulations will be "counted worthy of the Kingdom of God" (verses 4-5 above), but those who do not obey the Gospel, and do not come to know God, will be "punished with everlasting destruction" (verses 8-9 above).

Every Christian needs to know that, since that in itself can help us decide whether or not we want to be in the group that suffers now, or in the group that suffers later.

Our enemies will reap the trouble that they bring upon us. Those who hate the righteous shall be condemned, according to the Word of the Lord, written in Psalm 34:21. That means that those who oppose the truth, and hate us because we speak God's Word will be condemned (2 Timothy 3:8).

However, we must do good to them here on earth, and by doing so we will heap burning coals of fire on their heads (verse 20 below). We can be overcome by evil, or we can overcome evil with good, the choice is ours (verse 21 below).

Romans 12:17-21
17 Repay no one evil for evil. Have regard for good things in the sight of all men. 18 If it is possible, as much as depends on you, live peaceably with all men. 19 Beloved, do not avenge yourselves, but rather give place to wrath; for it is written, "Vengeance is Mine, I will repay," says the Lord. 20 Therefore "If your enemy is hungry, feed him; If he is thirsty, give him a drink; For in so doing you will heap coals of fire on his head." 21 Do not be overcome by evil, but overcome evil with good. NKJV

Every Christian needs to know about suffering if we plan on ceasing from sin in our life, and sharing in Christ's glory. It's just a part of it. Many Christians today have no idea what is happening to them, and therefore, they may be on the verge of being overcome by evil.

If you know of someone who is trying to live a godly life, but is weighed down by the persecutions and trials, help them to understand these things. I watched my mom suffer without having anybody there that could explain these things to her, and perhaps that is why the Lord has taught me.

We have to speak in-line with the Word of God in order for our body to follow, and as soon as we start speaking with the Spirit of faith, there will be plenty of opposition, even from family members (Matthew 10:34-38). Therefore, there will be plenty of opportunities to suffer, or to draw back from the faith.

Therefore, if you decide to stop sinning here on earth, in accordance with what is promised in the Word of God, many will reject you, hate you, and speak evil of you. Some will even think that they are doing God's work by persecuting you. However, you will recognize them since they will reject what is written in the Bible, but they will accept the words of those who speak against the faith.

Matthew 10:22
22 And you will be hated by all for My name's sake. But he who endures to the end will be saved. NKJV

Knowing this ahead of time will help to prevent it from being a cause of stumbling when it happens (Galatians 5:15). Those who go with the crowd, or give in to peer pressure, may find it more difficult, but keep in mind that we must deny ourself in order to follow Jesus. He who endures to the end shall be saved.

Now what

We must be willing to suffer even if it comes through other Christians, in order to be done with sin (1 Peter 4:1-4 above). We are all called to do this in order that we would inherit a blessing, and Jesus left us an example to follow.

1 Peter 2:21
21 For to this you were called, because Christ also suffered for us, leaving us an example, that you should follow His steps NKJV

1 Peter 3:9
9 not returning evil for evil or reviling for reviling, but on the contrary blessing, knowing that you were called to this, that you may inherit a blessing. NKJV

Making someone aware that they have wronged us is one thing, and yes, we can approach those who have wronged us according to Matthew 18:15-17, but the unwillingness to suffer at the hands of others is something else.

There is a thin line between making someone aware of something, and complaining. Complaining can simply be the voice of one who is unwilling to suffer.

Therefore, if our conversation leads to arguing, slandering each other, or proclaiming things that we don't want to happen in the future while we are making someone aware that we have been wronged, then we have returned evil for evil. We should repent of that, and start over.

Returning evil for evil, or insult for insult, is counted as two wrongs, when we should always do what is right, which would be to bless those who persecute us (1 Peter 3:8). If we do not leave room for God's wrath, He will not avenge us (Romans 12:19 above).

Romans 12:14
14 Bless those who persecute you; bless and do not curse.
NKJV

Matthew 5:43-45
43 "You have heard that it was said, 'You shall love your neigh-bor and hate your enemy.' 44 But I say to you, love your ene-mies, bless those who curse you, do good to those who hate you, and pray for those who spitefully use you and persecute you, 45 that you may be sons of your Father in heaven; for He makes His sun rise on the evil and on the good, and sends rain on the just and on the unjust. NKJV

If we do not remain in love through the pressure, then our actions will be used to discredit our statements. Nobody will stop to check the scriptures to see if what we are saying is true, if they can find fault with us.

Yes, they will interrupt you, slap the table, curse you, and whatever else to stop you, so be ready. As much as it depends on you, live in peace with all men (Romans 12:18). It will be difficult because your body will not want to suffer, but keeping these things in mind before they happen will certainly help you go through them.

Luke 21:12-13
12 But before all these things, they will lay their hands on you and persecute you, delivering you up to the synagogues and prisons. You will be brought before kings and rulers for My name's sake. 13 But it will turn out for you as an occasion for testimony. NKJV

Everything I am telling you in this book has happened to me, and you will have to learn how to sit through it, remain calm, and wait for your turn to speak, because it will happen to you if you continue in your faith. If you return fire with fire, you will get caught up in the emotion of everything, and lose self-control because of your words. Then you won't be any different than the people you are trying to reach.

Now you should be able to see where you are headed. Persecutions are very much a part of the Christian life, and through these and various trials (sufferings), God is testing our faith and changing our character; what we do, and what we say.

2 Timothy 3:12
12 Yes, and all who desire to live godly in Christ Jesus will suf-fer persecution. NKJV

James 1:2-4
2 My brethren, count it all joy when you fall into various trials,
3 knowing that the testing of your faith produces patience. 4

But let patience have its perfect work, that you may be perfect and complete, lacking nothing. NKJV

Romans 5:3-4
3 And not only that, but we also glory in tribulations, knowing that tribulation produces perseverance; 4 and perseverance, character; and character, hope. NKJV

1 Peter 1:6-7
6 In this you greatly rejoice, though now for a little while, if need be, you have been grieved by various trials, 7 that the genuineness of your faith, being much more precious than gold that perishes, though it is tested by fire, may be found to praise, honor, and glory at the revelation of Jesus Christ NKJV

If your desire is to live a godly life, then trials and persecutions are on the way. You will know that you are headed in the right direction when they come.

If you remain a follower of this world, then the people of this world, who do not live by faith, will love you. That's not a good sign.

John 15:18-22
18 "If the world hates you, you know that it hated Me before it hated you. 19 If you were of the world, the world would love its own. Yet because you are not of the world, but I chose you out of the world, therefore the world hates you. 20 Remember the word that I said to you, 'A servant is not greater than his master.' If they persecuted Me, they will also persecute you. If they kept My word, they will keep yours also. 21 But all these things they will do to you for My name's sake, because they do not know Him who sent Me. 22 If I had not come and spoken to them, they would have no sin, but now they have no excuse for their sin. NKJV

If the people of this world, speak well of you, then ask yourself if you have lost your salt. God is not pleased with those who shrink back from living by faith (Hebrews 10:36-39).

Luke 6:26
26 Woe to you when all men speak well of you, For so did their fathers to the false prophets. NKJV

Father, in Jesus' name, forgive us for the sins that we have committed against You. We don't know how we should pray, but in Your abundant mercies hear us. In our ignorance we have spoken against Your Word, and have even taken our stand against it. Forgive us I pray, and now open our eyes that we may be able to see Your Word, and that it may live on the inside of us. Enable us to speak with the Spirit of faith, and take away the spirit of error from our mouth. Give us the grace needed to suffer through the trials we face. Without You, we are nothing. We love You, and we praise You, in the name of Jesus Christ. Amen!

Learn the verses that we have covered for yourself and refuse to speak against them. Until you are transformed (Romans 12:1-2) and born again through the Word of truth (1 Peter 1:22-25), speak what you know to be true and keep silent in the areas you do not yet understand.

Read the Word of God out loud constantly, and as you read, allow it to change you so that you will gain more understanding. (Hebrews 5:11-14, Psalm 111:10).

As long as you continue in your faith, and faith comes by hearing the Word of God, then you will remain holy in God's sight (Colossians 1:21-23). However, as soon as you stop hearing the Word of God in your ears, things will change for the worse.

Therefore, never stop reading it out loud, especially the New Testament, so that you can recognize the truth when you hear it. The measure you use will be measured to you (Mark 4:24, James 4:8). Those who are mature use the Word constantly, but baby Christians end up having to be taught all over again (Hebrews 5:11-14). Force yourself to hear the Word of God continually.

Always accept what is written, and never agree with or say amen to anything that is not written. There are tons of cute little sayings out there today in songs, and books that well-meaning Christians pick up and begin using without realizing the danger. Peace be with you.

If you have a question, please contact me.

www.HowToStopSinning.com

Alan's email alan@howtostopsinning.com

Lucie's email lucie@howtostopsinning.com

ഇ‍ൻ

14

Just Follow Jesus

ꟸ

Who wants to suffer? Raise your hand! Nobody wants to suffer, but as we have learned, it is a part of the Christian life that all of us are called to do (1 Peter 3:9, 2:20-21).

Even denying ourself is a form of suffering (Matthew 16:24-25, John 12:25-26). Therefore, we will suffer just by placing faith in Jesus Christ, and that is why many do not place faith in Him, but only believe that He exists. They don't want to suffer.

For example if we decided to follow Jesus and obey Matthew 6:14-15 and forgive everyone, our flesh would suffer (hurt, ache), but on the other hand, unforgiveness would not be able to control our life (Romans 6:16).

Someone asked, "But what if someone has really hurt us?" That would change the amount of suffering for those who decide to follow Jesus and forgive everyone, but the amount of suffering does not change what is promised. If we do not forgive, we will not be forgiven (Matthew 6:14-15), and there isn't a place in Heaven for those who do not forgive (Matthew 18:28-35).

Matthew 18:21-22
21 Then Peter came to Him and said, "Lord, how often shall my brother sin against me, and I forgive him? Up to seven times?"
22 Jesus said to him, "I do not say to you, up to seven times, but up to seventy times seven. NKJV

We all need forgiveness, and therefore, we all must forgive, since we reap what we sow (Galatians 6:7-10). Jesus also explained in the parable of the "Unforgiving Servant" that those who do not forgive people who wrong them, would not receive forgiveness from God our Father, even though they had previously been forgiven (Matthew 18:28-35).

Therefore, either we forgive, or we won't be forgiven, and if we forgive, we will suffer at the hands of other people. Our faith in Jesus Christ will eventually cause us to suffer, if we continue in our faith, and if we are willing to suffer in our flesh, we can indeed be done with sin (1 Peter 4:1-4), and receive the good that God has for us (Jeremiah 5:25).

Therefore, those who follow Jesus will suffer in their body, since they will be denying what their flesh wants them to do, but they will also not walk in darkness. Following Jesus is the cure for any sin problem, but it is hard on our flesh.

John 8:11-12
11 She said, "No one, Lord." And Jesus said to her, "Neither do I condemn you; go and sin no more." 12 Then Jesus spoke to them again, saying, "I am the light of the world. He who follows Me shall not walk in darkness, but have the light of life." NKJV

After the woman was caught in adultery, Jesus told her to stop sinning, and gave her the method in which she would accomplish it. "Whoever follows Me (Jesus) shall not walk in darkness." By simply taking the path that Jesus was taking, she could be freed from darkness, and so it is with us.

If we stop allowing our flesh to rule our life, we will not walk in darkness (verse 12 above). Imagine that. Can we remain in darkness and say that we have been following Jesus ever since we accepted Him as the Lord of our life? No, He does not lead us into darkness, but He is the way out of darkness.

The times that we remain in darkness are the times we choose "not" to deny ourself and follow Jesus. Many of those times can be summed up as the unwillingness to suffer at the hands of others. Add peer pressure, and the desire to fit in with the people of this world to that, and we will begin to see why Christians are still controlled by sin. We haven't died to the things that give us over to sin's control.

Long-time Christians, who are still caught up in darkness, got off track somewhere, since continuing in darkness is evidence of not following Jesus. How can we get back on track? We repent of the past and return to the Lord in accordance with what is written.

Some might argue that we already have redemption, the forgiveness of sins (Colossians 1:14 below), and praise God that we do. However, at the same time we have also been redeemed from our former way of life (1 Peter 1:18, Titus 2:14, below), and we were delivered from the power of darkness (Colossians 1:13 below). Therefore how is it that we are still caught up in it, if we are not using the forgiveness of sins as a license to remain in darkness?

Titus 2:14
14 who gave Himself for us, that He might redeem us from every lawless deed and purify for Himself His own special people, zealous for good works. NKJV

1 Peter 1:14-19
14 as obedient children, not conforming yourselves to the former lusts, as in your ignorance; 15 but as He who called you is holy, you also be holy in all your conduct, 16 because it is written, "Be holy, for I am holy." 17 And if you call on the Father,

who without partiality judges according to each one's work, conduct yourselves throughout the time of your stay here in fear; 18 knowing that you were not redeemed with corruptible things, like silver or gold, from your aimless conduct received by tradition from your fathers, 19 but with the precious blood of Christ, as of a lamb without blemish and without spot. NKJV

Colossians 1:13-14
13 He has delivered us from the power of darkness and con-veyed us into the kingdom of the Son of His love, 14 in whom we have redemption through His blood, the forgiveness of sins. NKJV

Father, in the name of Jesus Christ, have mercy upon all of us who are called by Your name. Forgive us for the sins that we have committed against You. Forgive us for not following You out of darkness, and for not forgiving others. Our fleshly desire to fit in with the people of this world has kept us under sin's control. Deliver us from the power of darkness that we may walk in Your ways, and become the people that You have called us to be. Amen.

It is obvious to me what's going on when someone quotes verse 14 of Colossians chapter one above, but they have no knowledge of verse 13. They are either using redemption as an excuse to continue in sin, or they are ignorant of what their Bible says.

Yes, we all need redemption, but at the same time, we can't ignore that we "have been" delivered from the power of darkness, and therefore, we should be coming out of it. We can't say that we have been living by faith in Jesus, and yet we are still remaining in darkness. It is far better to just say that we have not been living up to what we are called to do.

God calls us out of darkness (verse 9 below). We did not receive redemption, the forgiveness of sins, so that we should remain in darkness, but that we should come out. Jesus died for us in order to destroy the devil's work, and not so that we could continue in it (verse 8 below).

1 Peter 2:9
9 But you are a chosen generation, a royal priesthood, a holy nation, His own special people, that you may proclaim the praises of Him who called you out of darkness into His marvel-ous light; NKJV

1 John 3:8
8 He who sins is of the devil, for the devil has sinned from the beginning. For this purpose the Son of God was manifested,

that He might destroy the works of the devil. NKJV

Jesus delivered us from the power or the dominion of darkness, but the problem is that those who hate the light do not follow Him out. If you do not hate the light, repent of the past, and now follow Jesus in accordance with His teachings.

John 3:19-21
19 And this is the condemnation, that the light has come into the world, and men loved darkness rather than light, because their deeds were evil. 20 For everyone practicing evil hates the light and does not come to the light, lest his deeds should be exposed. 21 But he who does the truth comes to the light, that his deeds may be clearly seen, that they have been done in God." NKJV

Now wait a minute! You may not hate the light, and what you are doing may not be considered evil this day and age, but that's not necessarily the question either. The question is, are you following Jesus out of darkness in accordance with the written instructions? He who "does the truth comes to the light" (verse 21 above).

You may not be doing anything that is considered evil. Little old ladies don't rob banks on the weekend, but do they practice the truth (verse 21 above)?

Jesus paid our debt so that we could come out. Therefore, if we don't love darkness, and our deeds are not evil (verse 19 above), what other reason would we have to remain in it? We are either ignorant of this, or perhaps we haven't accepted Jesus Christ as the Lord of our life. Whatever it is, it doesn't change the message. Let us return to the Lord our God.

What matters to me is where people are going, and not where they have been. I'm writing this book to help those who want to come out of darkness, and worship God in truth and in Spirit (John 4:23-24).

I've already wasted enough time trying to reach people who want to remain in darkness, and use the Word of God as an excuse. Revelation 22:11 says to leave them alone, and that is what I will do. I now try to reach people who want to come out of darkness, but do not know the truth, or perhaps they have believed the false teachings of those who follow deceiving spirits, and the doctrine of demons (1 Timothy 4:1-2).

Revelation 22:11
11 He who is unjust, let him be unjust still; he who is filthy, let him be filthy still; he who is righteous, let him be righteous still; he who is holy, let him be holy still." NKJV

Therefore, it doesn't matter to me what sins you have committed, or what you are presently caught up in, as long as you are willing to repent of the past, believe what is written in the Bible, and start over. However, this time follow the instructions which have not changed in two thousand years, and still work just like they are written. That's the key to starting over.

Make sure that you have accepted Jesus as the Lord of your life. In other words, you have called on Him to save you, and you have declared Him Lord; "Jesus is Lord!"

Make sure that you have been baptized. I've met people who had been Christians for years, without being baptized. What was even more shocking to me was that some were actually told that they didn't have to get baptized. Would Jesus tell us not to get baptized (Mark 16:15-16, Matthew 28:18-20 below)? Therefore, would an ambassador of Jesus Christ instruct us to skip baptism?

If you don't believe that you need to be baptized, then answer this question. According to the following passage of scripture, if you do not receive baptism, what will you reject?

Luke 7:29-30
29 And when all the people heard Him, even the tax collectors justified God, having been baptized with the baptism of John. 30 But the Pharisees and lawyers rejected the will of God for themselves, not having been baptized by him. NKJV

The people, who did not receive John's baptism, rejected the will of God for their life (verse 30 above). However, when the people who had received John's baptism heard Jesus, they accepted God's Word, and they were able to declare that what they were hearing was right (justified, verse 29 above).

Jesus declared openly that the doctrine He was teaching belonged to God the Father Who sent Him (John 12:49), and if anyone chooses to do the will of God, then they would recognize, or know His doctrine.

John 7:16-18
16 Jesus answered them and said, "My doctrine is not Mine, but His who sent Me. 17 If anyone wills to do His will, he shall know concerning the doctrine, whether it is from God or whether I speak on My own authority. 18 He who speaks from himself seeks his own glory; but He who seeks the glory of the One who sent Him is true, and no unrighteousness is in Him. NKJV

It is certain that part of God's will for our life is for us to be baptized. It is a part of making disciples according to the Great Commission, and it is a part of the instructions given to the disciples according to Mark 16:15 below.

Matthew 28:19-20
19 Go therefore and make disciples of all the nations, baptizing them in the name of the Father and of the Son and of the Holy Spirit, 20 teaching them to observe all things that I have com-

manded you; and lo, I am with you always, even to the end of the age." Amen. NKJV

Mark 16:15-16
15 And He said to them, "Go into all the world and preach the gospel to every creature. 16 He who believes and is baptized will be saved; but he who does not believe will be condemned. NKJV

To sum things up, we will not accept God's will for our life if we do not receive John's baptism according to Luke 7:29-30 above, so let's ask ourself this question. Must we do God's will in order to enter the Kingdom of Heaven according to the Words of Jesus Christ, the One in Whom we trust?

Matthew 7:21
21 "Not everyone who says to Me, 'Lord, Lord,' shall enter the kingdom of heaven, but he who does the will of My Father in heaven. NKJV

We have to do the will of God in order to enter the Kingdom of Heaven, and people who do not receive John's baptism, do not accept the will of God for themselves. What does that tell us? I would say that we need to get baptized, ASAP. Wouldn't you?

Did Jesus receive John's baptism? Yes, he did (Matthew 3:13-16). Why not follow Him, and accept God's will? If we would just learn how to be like Jesus, we would notice a big difference in our life. What else would we do if we decided to follow Jesus?

Jesus did not ask us to build a boat, or to march around a building seven times. No, He simply commanded us to love one another. That's one disciple loving another disciple.

John 13:34-35
34 A new commandment I give to you, that you love one another; as I have loved you, that you also love one another. 35 By this all will know that you are My disciples, if you have love for one another." NKJV

Just as Noah built the ark by following God's instructions, we too will receive our hope by following Jesus' instructions. What is our hope? Christians hope for eternal life, and that life is through God's Son our Lord Jesus Christ, in the Kingdom of God our Father (Titus 3:7). Amen. Amen.

Faith in Jesus Christ will make us love one another, since that is what He has commanded His disciples to do. We know that we "have" to place faith in what Jesus has commanded us to do because those who do not follow those instructions, do not have eternal life abiding in them, according to the following verses.

1 John 3:14-15
14 We know that we have passed from death to life, because we love the brethren. He who does not love his brother abides in death. 15 Whoever hates his brother is a murderer, and you know that no murderer has eternal life abiding in him. NKJV

Those who do not obey Jesus Christ, do not have eternal life abiding (remaining) in them (verse 15 above). In this way, Jesus is the source of eternal salvation for those who obey Him.

Hebrews 5:9
9 And having been perfected, He became the author of eternal salvation to all who obey Him NKJV

Therefore, we can't just say that we believe in Jesus Christ, meaning we believe that He exists, but believing in Jesus Christ is the same as placing faith in the things He has said.

Being saved doesn't necessarily end with eternal salvation. We believe with the heart unto righteousness, and we confess unto salvation (Romans 10:10), but we have to continue believing unto the saving of the soul.

Hebrews 10:38-39
38 Now the just shall live by faith; But if anyone draws back, My soul has no pleasure in him." 39 But we are not of those who draw back to perdition, but of those who believe to the saving of the soul. NKJV

In other words, we can depart and turn away from what we have been given through unbelief (verse 12 below).

Hebrews 3:12
12 Beware, brethren, lest there be in any of you an evil heart of unbelief in departing from the living God; NKJV

Yes, contrary to popular opinion, we can neglect our salvation, and fall away from the faith (Hebrews 2:3).

Hebrews 2:1-3
1 Therefore we must give the more earnest heed to the things we have heard, lest we drift away. 2 For if the word spoken through angels proved steadfast, and every transgression and disobedience received a just reward, 3 how shall we escape if we neglect so great a salvation, which at the first began to be spoken by the Lord, and was confirmed to us by those who heard Him, NKJV

The righteousness of faith involves speaking in-line with the faith on a continual basis (Romans 10:6-8). That's why the words "eternal life" are not mentioned in Romans chapter 10 or Ephesians chapter 2. Being saved is simply the beginning of our part, as we were saved and called for God's purposes (2 Timothy 1:9, Ephesians 2:10, John 15:16).

It takes the righteousness of God, which is through faith in Jesus Christ to all who believe (Romans 3:21-22), in order to enter the Kingdom of Heaven (verse 20 below). It takes calling on the name of the Lord Jesus, and believing in our heart that God raised Him from the dead in order to be saved into the Kingdom of Christ (Romans 10:9-13). Those are two different issues.

Matthew 5:20
20 For I say to you, that unless your righteousness exceeds the righteousness of the scribes and Pharisees, you will by no means enter the kingdom of heaven. NKJV

Our righteousness has to exceed that of the Pharisees in order to be able to enter the Kingdom of Heaven. We will go through many hardships before we reach that point (Acts 14:22, 2 Thessalonians 1:3-5).

God's righteousness is by faith in Jesus Christ (Romans 3:21-22), and Jesus commanded us to love one another (John 13:34-35). That's why we can say that those who love one another have passed from death to life, because that's evidence of having faith in Jesus, and believing (1 John 3:14-15 above).

Those who do not love one another, obviously have not placed faith in Jesus Christ, and consequently, they cannot be righteous by faith in Jesus. Faith in Jesus Christ will make us love one another (Galatians 5:6). It is the only thing that avails us (benefits us, rewards us).

Galatians 5:6
6 For in Christ Jesus neither circumcision nor uncircumcision avails anything, but faith working through love. NKJV

Again, simple faith in Jesus would make us forgive, deny ourself, come out of darkness, get baptized, and love one another, to name a few things. Obedience comes from faith, and we are supposed to be teaching Christians to obey Jesus according to the Great Commission anyway (Matthew 28:20). That's how we make disciples (Christ followers, Acts 11:26).

In fact, if we taught new Christians to obey Jesus Christ, what would the outcome be according to the following verses?

1 John 2:8-11
8 Again, a new commandment I write to you, which thing is true in Him and in you, because the darkness is passing away, and the true light is already shining. 9 He who says he is in the light, and hates his brother, is in darkness until now. 10 He who loves his brother abides in the light, and there is no cause

for stumbling in him. 11 But he who hates his brother is in darkness and walks in darkness, and does not know where he is going, because the darkness has blinded his eyes. NKJV

By simply obeying Jesus' command to love one another, there would be nothing on the inside of us that could make us stumble (verse 10 above). Think about that, and combine that with what God has promised according to 1 Corinthians 10:13.

1 Corinthians 10:13
13 No temptation has overtaken you except such as is common to man; but God is faithful, who will not allow you to be tempted beyond what you are able, but with the temptation will also make the way of escape, that you may be able to bear it. NKJV

God has made it easy for us. Not only has He delivered us from the power of darkness (Colossians 1:13), but He will not allow us to be tempted into sinning beyond what we are able to bear. Imagine that.

He will also provide a way out of the temptation. All we have to do is to learn to choose God's way out rather than choosing to sin, assuming that we are obeying Jesus so that there will be nothing on the inside of us that can make us stumble.

That is the position that all Christ followers (Christians, Acts 11:26) should be in from the start, but we're not, because we are not following Jesus. Why? Perhaps Jesus is not being taught, but whatever the reason, it can be summed up as this; God's people live in destruction because we don't know what we should know.

If we just taught people to obey Jesus, would there be anything on the inside of us that could make us stumble? No. Would anyone in the church remain in darkness, unless they wanted to remain in darkness? No.

Would there be such a thing as a "Christian addiction?" That's an oxymoron, since Christians are Christ followers, and there is no way that someone who follows Christ can have an "uncontrollable lust." Those who follow Jesus "shall not" walk in darkness (John 8:12 above).

That should be enough evidence to make you realize one of three things. Either we are not teaching people to place their faith in Jesus Christ, or many Christians today want to remain in darkness, or we need to start over and make sure that what we have come to believe, is actually what is written in our Bible. It's one or the other, because there is no such things as a Christ follower, who has an addiction.

There will always be some who want to remain in darkness, since the tares grow with the wheat (Matthew 13:30), but God's people are destroyed for lack of knowledge (Hosea 4:6). If the results are not right, we need to check to see if our instructions are right.

I can't help but to believe, that there are many Christians who are caught up in darkness simply because the truth is not being taught, or they sit under the teachings of those who follow deceiving spirits, and the doctrines of demons, which is happening today according to the Word of the Lord written in 1 Timothy 4:1-2.

If the things I have covered so far in this book sound strange to you, my wife and I want to help you. My friend, if someone does not have the ability to live the Christian life, that is a problem that can be resolved. They need to call on Jesus Christ to save them, get baptized, and believe what is written in the Bible. However, we cannot help people who do not accept the Word of God as truth, and we refuse to argue with them.

Those who obey Jesus, abide (remain) in the light (1 John 2:10 above), but those who hate their brother abide in darkness (1 John 2:11 above). The opposite of love is to hate. Darkness blinds the eyes of those who hate, even to the point of them not being able to see where they are going.

You may not be able to explain that to them because they can't see, and won't be able to see until they repent of the past and turn to follow Jesus. Many have become "alienated," or separated from the life of God, as it is written in some Bibles, due to their blindness.

Ephesians 4:18
18 having their understanding darkened, being alienated from the life of God, because of the ignorance that is in them, because of the blindness of their heart NKJV

Most Christians are somewhere in between those two situations, and that's not a problem, since darkness takes time to pass away (1 John 2:8 above). I really don't think that someone who is given over completely would want to know how to stop sinning, and purchase this book. However, make sure that you know which direction you are traveling in. Follow Jesus!

If you have a desire to do good, praise God. Just follow Jesus out of darkness, basically doing what He tells you to do. Love one another and there will not be anything on the inside of you that can make you stumble. We will discuss who to love, and how to love them in the next chapter.

The evidence of following Jesus is that sin would be decreasing, and not increasing. The remission (reduction, decrease) of sins is very much a part of the Gospel message, but this passage has been changed in every new Bible that I have checked so far, and I expect that trend to continue.

Luke 24:46-47
46 Then He said to them, "Thus it is written, and thus it was necessary for the Christ to suffer and to rise from the dead the third day, 47 and that repentance and remission of sins should be preached in His name to all nations, beginning at Jerusa-

lem. NKJV

My friend, if I were you, I would purchase a King James Bible, or a New King James Bible, like the one I am using in this book. No, I don't work for Thomas Nelson, the publisher, but I'm trying to help as many people as possible.

I have used many different Bibles over the past twenty years, and I like how some of the everyday verses are worded, which do not change the meaning of the scripture. However, it is the verses that most people don't know, that are changing at a rapid pace, in the newer Bibles. Therefore, the average Christian will not recognize the verses that have been changed in many Bibles today.

I know that the New King James Version Bible works just like it is written. If the instructions do not work like they are written, there is a problem.

Some might argue that they believe in Jesus and that is all they need for eternal life according to John 3:16. However, those who believe in Jesus come out of darkness as well.

John 12:46
46 I have come as a light into the world, that whoever believes in Me should not abide in darkness. NKJV

The person who wrote John 3:16 is the same person who wrote that verse, which is found in the same letter, and many of the other verses we have used in this book so far. Therefore, it should be obvious that his intention was not for us to simply believe there is someone named Jesus Christ, but to believe in Him, which means that we should believe what He has taught as well. Don't be tricked.

John never implied that we could just say "Jesus is Lord," and then remain as we were; living like the world around us. This is evident in what Jesus said in John 14:21-24 below.

John 14:21-24
21 He who has My commandments and keeps them, it is he who loves Me. And he who loves Me will be loved by My Father, and I will love him and manifest Myself to him." 22 Judas (not Iscariot) said to Him, "Lord, how is it that You will manifest Yourself to us, and not to the world?" 23 Jesus answered and said to him, "If anyone loves Me, he will keep My word; and My Father will love him, and We will come to him and make Our home with him. 24 He who does not love Me does not keep My words; and the word which you hear is not Mine but the Father's who sent Me. NKJV

When will Jesus make His home on the inside of us? Is it before or after we obey His teachings? Many people promise new Christians that as soon as they say "Jesus is Lord," this happens. Jesus says, "If" anyone loves Me, he will keep my Word, and We will come to him and make Our home in him (verse 23 above).

My friend, believe the Word of God.

We have already mentioned why the Apostle Paul was concerned about the Galatians. Miracles were happening among them, according to Galatians 3:5, so what could possibly be so wrong?

Galatians 4:19-20
19 My little children, for whom I labor in birth again until Christ is formed in you, 20 I would like to be present with you now and to change my tone; for I have doubts about you. NKJV

Paul had doubts about the Galatians because Christ had not been formed in them yet. They got saved, but there is no eternal life abiding (remaining) in those who do not obey Jesus (1 John 3:13-14), and He commanded us to love one another (John 13:34-35). Eternal salvation is for those who obey Jesus (Hebrews 5:9 above).

Christ in us, is our hope of glory (Colossians 1:27). The Apostle Paul prayed the same thing on behalf of the Ephesians, just as Jesus, Himself prayed for us today, that He would live in us (John 17:20-23 below).

Ephesians 3:17
17 that Christ may dwell in your hearts through faith; that you, being rooted and grounded in love NKJV

John 17:20-23
20 "I do not pray for these alone, but also for those who will believe in Me through their word; 21 that they all may be one, as You, Father, are in Me, and I in You; that they also may be one in Us, that the world may believe that You sent Me. 22 And the glory which You gave Me I have given them, that they may be one just as We are one: 23 I in them, and You in Me; that they may be made perfect in one, and that the world may know that You have sent Me, and have loved them as You have loved Me. NKJV

Jesus prayed that we would be one, just as He and the Father are One, and that we would be in Him and in God our Father (verse 21 above); "I in them, and You in Me" (verse 23 above).

Those who love Jesus keep His Word (John 14:23 above). If we believe in Jesus, the next thing to do is to obey His teachings, just as Noah followed God's instructions in building the ark (Genesis 6:22).

Those who love Jesus obey Him, and those who obey Him have nothing on the inside of them that can make them stumble. They may choose to stumble, but there is nothing in them that can make them stumble.

Now what

Why don't we follow Jesus? We don't like denying ourself. Self gets in the way. When we don't forgive people who wrong us, we are refusing to deny ourself. When we are impatient, we are refusing to suffer. When we don't love our brothers and sisters, it too is simply refusing to deny ourself.

Basically, our body wants to be in control, and sometimes we don't want to deal with the pain it can cause us for not allowing it to be, but we are called to suffer. All who belong to Christ, put their flesh to death (Galatians 5:24, Ephesians 4:20-24).

Galatians 5:24
24 And those who are Christ's have crucified the flesh with its passions and desires. NKJV

We put to death that part of us that always wants to be in control. Love is not self-seeking (1 Corinthians 13:5). Belonging to Christ is about putting our flesh to death. It's about denying what we feel like doing, and choosing to do what is right.

Now imagine being delivered from the power of darkness, and not being tempted beyond what we can say "no" to, and given a command to love one another, which would make us come out of darkness. What would our excuse be for saying no to that? As I have already mentioned, we can neglect our salvation (Hebrews 2:3).

We cannot say that we have followed Jesus, but we have remained in darkness (John 8:12). We can't even say that we believe Jesus and have remained in darkness (John 12:46). Somewhere we got off track, and we simply need to repent and start over. Maybe we do not know how to love one another, or who to love, which we will cover in the next chapter.

Father, in Jesus' name, have mercy on us. We need Your help to stay the course. Help us Lord, and forgive us for our sins. There are so many teaching different things today, and we are caught up in the pressures of this life. Deliver us I pray, and show us the right path. Save us and fill us with Your Word. Teach us through the power of Your Holy Spirit, and keep reminding us of the things that You have said. Make Your truth remain in us, and make us want to do what You want us to do. Fill us with the grace needed to do Your will. You are able, and You alone are worthy, in the name of Jesus Christ I pray. Amen.

If you have not been baptized into Christ Jesus, then get baptized. Why? The Bible says to, and that may be the reason why many are not "walking in the newness of life" (verse 4 below). By our baptism, we are agreeing to die with

Christ so that we can walk in the newness of life.

Romans 6:1-4
1 What shall we say then? Shall we continue in sin that grace may abound? 2 Certainly not! How shall we who died to sin live any longer in it? 3 Or do you not know that as many of us as were baptized into Christ Jesus were baptized into His death? 4 Therefore we were buried with Him through baptism into death, that just as Christ was raised from the dead by the glory of the Father, even so we also should walk in newness of life. NKJV

This is usually the point where someone will say that the thief on the cross wasn't baptized. However, we don't know if he was or not, and Jesus' covenant did not begin for us until His death anyway (Hebrews 9:16-17).

Many Christians have what I call the "thief on the cross faith" as if Jesus said that baptism was optional. No, it isn't optional, and Jesus didn't tell us to be like the thief either. Get the instructions right, and you won't have to guess as to whether or not everything is going to turn out right, but you will know for sure.

One day, I spent many hours in a round table discussion, listening to people go back and forth about the thief on the cross, while they totally ignored verse after verse on baptism. At the end of the day, one of the elders finally said, "Well, I guess we should be baptizing people." Praise God, halleluiah!

If I had not remained in love throughout this situation, they would have probably escorted me out before it was over. That one hour meeting, lasted all day. I'm sure that things like this will happen to you also. It's just a matter of time. Remember to remain in love, since knowledge puffs up, but love edifies (1 Corinthians 8:1). May God's grace be upon us. Amen.

I'm Alan Ballou; a servant. If you have any questions, please contact me.

www.HowToStopSinning.com

Alan's email alan@howtostopsinning.com

Lucie's email lucie@howtostopsinning.com

ℰⓍℭℛ

15

Who and How

If all we need to do is love one another, and follow Jesus, why is there little difference between the lives of those who attend weekly church services, and the people of this world? Christians seem to love one another in church, but they still have addictions, they commit adultery, they get divorced, they end up in jail, they curse, they slander, they steal, and pretty much do the same things that the people of this world do. Why isn't there a difference?

Anytime something that God has promised us, does not seem to work, double check the instructions. Years ago, I had accepted something as truth, but it didn't work. After that I went through a period of time where I didn't know what to think. My thoughts troubled me, as I pondered that the Word of God may not work like I believed that it would.

I wasn't reading scripture with scripture, and I had the wrong interpretation of some things, because of the Bible I was using at the time, and what I had come to believe. Don't misunderstand me, because I'm not saying that I know everything that I should know right now, or even that I am all that God has called me to be.

However, what I would like for you to know is that anytime something that God has promised to us according to His Word, doesn't seem to work like it is written in the New King James Version, double check the instructions. Besides that, read all of the verses that pertain to the subject in question; reading scripture with scripture.

For example, we have learned that if we love one another, there will be nothing on the inside of us that can make us stumble (1 John 2:10). We know that we have to believe that promise as Abraham believed, and we have to mix faith with it. Therefore, the following is what can happen if we set out to obey Jesus and love one another without reading scripture with scripture.

We go to church, smile, shake hands, hug, and whatever else, but nothing happens. We sing together, eat together, and even open the door for each other, but nothing happens. So we start giving up our regular seat for those who want to sit down, because we believe that this could be a form of suffering, but still nothing happens.

We volunteer to wash cars for the youth fund raiser, and still nothing. We're doing the best we can do, but still no change. We're still caught up in sins that lead to death, and we have no idea how to stop. Therefore, we use all of this as evidence to say in our heart that loving one another does not deliver us from darkness. Big mistake.

We believe in our heart unto righteousness (Romans 10:10). Therefore, God's Word is unquestionably true, but it is not working out for us, which means that it is time to double check the instructions to make sure that what we believe is actually what is written.

God says that if we obey Jesus, we would come out of darkness, and there would be nothing on the inside of us that could make us stumble (1 John 2:8-10). We know what Jesus wants us to do, but we have to read scripture with scripture.

Don't assume what love is, but read all of the scriptures that describe it, and allow the Bible to teach you. The Bible will explain itself, if you would read all of it. Everything you will ever need for this life is in it, and it will come through your knowledge of God (2 Peter 1:3).

1 Corinthians 13:4-7
4 Love suffers long and is kind; love does not envy; love does not parade itself, is not puffed up; 5 does not behave rudely, does not seek its own, is not provoked, thinks no evil; 6 does not rejoice in iniquity, but rejoices in the truth; 7 bears all things, believes all things, hopes all things, endures all things. NKJV

Love is patient (long suffering), and kind. It's not jealous, rude, proud, boastful, or self-seeking. It rejoices in the truth, and not in sin (iniquity). Love believes, hopes, and endures all things.

The last time we were rude, we fell out of love. The last time we rejoiced over someone's sin, we fell out of love, as well as the last time we did not rejoice in the truth, and so on.

Those are actions. We can say that we love someone, but as Christians we don't love with words, but with actions (1 John 3:18 below). Actually, it is possible to attend church all of our life, and hug everyone, every single weekend, and still not love any of them.

The last time we were impatient, we fell out of love. Imagine that. So hypothetically speaking, we can live Monday through Saturday in disobedience, and end up wondering why God's promise is not working, since we are hugging everybody at church on Sunday morning.

It does work, but it isn't working for us because we are not obeying Jesus. Obeying Jesus is going to take a lifestyle change, and not just a Sunday morning break.

Like I have said before, we're going to have to deny ourself in order to live the Christian life. I'm here to tell you about a path that is difficult on the flesh, but it's the only path that ends in life, and the Bible says that few find it (Matthew 7:13-14, Luke 13:22-28). If the path we are on does not require us to deny our flesh, then surely we are on the wrong path.

Father, in Jesus' name, have mercy on us. We had no idea what Your Word actually said, but we simply believed what we heard without testing it. Have mercy on us, and forgive us for the sins that we have committed against You. Wash us clean with the blood of Christ, that we may walk in Your ways, and that You may make Your home in us. Amen.

This is going to take practice, and that is why it says that the darkness is passing away, and the true light is already shining (verse 8 below).

1 John 2:8
8 Again, a new commandment I write to you, which thing is true in Him and in you, because the darkness is passing away, and the true light is already shining. NKJV

Obeying our command to love one another, will make darkness pass away, but it takes time to pass, as we practice the truth. However, we need to know that one of the quickest ways to fill our whole body with darkness is through our eyes.

Luke 11:34-35
34 The lamp of the body is the eye. Therefore, when your eye is good, your whole body also is full of light. But when your eye is bad, your body also is full of darkness. 35 Therefore take heed that the light which is in you is not darkness. NKJV

Therefore, if porn is your drug of choice, you need to learn all of the methods we have covered in this book that fight against sin, and put all of them into practice at the same time. God can deliver you from that as He has me, but if you are not careful, you can fill up with darkness faster than you will empty it out.

This is one of the reasons why separation from the real world can be an advantage for some people, since the opportunity to sin is drastically reduced. However, separation methods don't work for long, if we do not learn to live by faith before we return. They are mainly effective in stopping the snowball effect.

Porn is one of the many sins I was given over to, and so I know this will work in the comfort of your own home, but you will have to follow the instructions. That was over twenty years ago, and now I don't have a thought of it. That means it is not something that I have to wrestle with, because the Word of God has set me free (John 8:31-37).

The Lord has made me free, and He will make you free! Praise the Lord God almighty. When the Son sets you free from being a slave to sin, you will be free indeed (John 8:31-37).

Many Christians do not realize that there isn't a different solution for different types of sins. Human wisdom tells us to separate the alcoholics, and drug addicts from the homosexuals, adulterers, sodomites, and the slanderers, but the same solution for stopping sin is used for all.

We get saved, by calling on Jesus. We get baptized into His death, which is basically agreeing to die to the ways of this world with Him, in order that we will have the ability to walk in the newness of life. After that, we obey Jesus. Once we figure out what part of that solution we are missing, then we will know what is causing us to be given over to the sins listed above.

There is another passage of scripture that describes what love is, and by it we will know that the love of God is in us (verse 17 below), and that we belong to the truth (verse 19 below).

1 John 3:16-19
16 By this we know love, because He laid down His life for us. And we also ought to lay down our lives for the brethren. 17 But whoever has this world's goods, and sees his brother in need, and shuts up his heart from him, how does the love of God abide in him? 18 My little children, let us not love in word or in tongue, but in deed and in truth. 19 And by this we know that we are of the truth, and shall assure our hearts before Him. NKJV

Love is helping fellow disciples of Jesus Christ who are in need with the things that we have. That's how we know that the love of God is in us (verse 17 above). We don't love with word or tongue, but in deed and in truth (verse 18 above), and that's how we know that we belong to the truth (verse 19 above).

Faith in Jesus Christ will make us love one another by helping other Christians. If you have ever had the urge to help your Christian brother "in need," then that is the love of God that has been placed in you. Follow it!

1 Thessalonians 4:9
9 But concerning brotherly love you have no need that I should write to you, for you yourselves are taught by God to love one another NKJV

We have been taught by God to love one another. Nobody had to teach us, but God has poured His love into our heart by the Holy Spirit (verse 5 below). That's evidence of being saved (Titus 3:3-8).

Romans 5:5
5 Now hope does not disappoint, because the love of God has been poured out in our hearts by the Holy Spirit who was given to us. NKJV

Now that you know what love is according to God's Word, you should be able to see why you may not have the results you were expecting. The promises work, but again, God's people experience destruction because we don't know something (Hosea 4:6).

Being a friend of this world is not love toward God (James 4:4), but God's love in your heart is leading you to help His people. You can love in the way the world expects you to love, or you can follow God's instructions. Either way, God's method is the one that will bring the results that God has promised.

We need to remember this lesson so that whenever we learn a promise for healing, provisions, deliverance or whatever else, we will be careful to search out our definitions using scripture rather than assuming that what we grew up believing is in-line with God's Word. God's ways are not our ways (Isaiah 55:8-9, Romans 11:33).

We use different words this day and age to describe things, and so we rely on translations. Even so, the Bible can explain itself, if we read scripture with scripture.

I used to think that I had to hug people I didn't want to hug, because that is what I was taught. I was told that we might as well love each other now, since we would be spending eternity together, but that was not exactly the truth. Those who have everlasting life, hear God's Word, believe, and obey Jesus.

If what we have covered so far in this chapter seems strange to you, then we need to double check a few other things as well. The Bible says that we were "Created in Christ Jesus to do good works," which means that God saved us for the purpose of doing something good (verse 10 below).

Ephesians 2:8-10
8 For by grace you have been saved through faith, and that not of yourselves; it is the gift of God, 9 not of works, lest any-one should boast. 10 For we are His workmanship, created in Christ Jesus for good works, which God prepared beforehand that we should walk in them. NKJV

Saved people do good works. That's something that we needed to hear when we got saved, even though most of us didn't. However, it fits right in with what Jesus commanded us to do. We are not going to do good works in order to be saved, but we are going to do them because we were saved to do them. God has saved us for His own purpose (1 Timothy 1:9).

God prepared good works for us to do before we were born (verse 10 above). There are things that all of us can do, such as helping the least of God's people (Matthew 25:34-36, Galatians 6:10), and there are things that we are individually called to do, which we may not discover until we have renewed our mind with the truth (1 Peter 4:10, Romans 12:4-8).

Some people don't want to do good works (deeds), which makes me wonder about their salvation. If you do not want to do good works, cry out to the Lord Jesus to save you, and to place the love of God in your heart.

When we were saved, we were created in Christ to do good works (verse 10 above), and if at that time we experienced God's grace, we would be on fire (zealous) for good works (verse 14 below).

Titus 2:11-15
11 For the grace of God that brings salvation has appeared to all men, 12 teaching us that, denying ungodliness and worldly lusts, we should live soberly, righteously, and godly in the present age, 13 looking for the blessed hope and glorious appearing of our great God and Savior Jesus Christ, 14 who gave Himself for us, that He might redeem us from every lawless deed and purify for Himself His own special people, zealous for good works. 15 Speak these things, exhort, and rebuke with all authority. Let no one despise you. NKJV

When we came to the Lord, we were delivered from the power of darkness (Colossians 1:13), and redeemed from lawless deeds (verse 14 above). Grace itself teaches us to stop sinning, and to do good (verse 11-14 above).

I can see how people who have "not" experienced God's grace might not want to do good works, but I can't see anyone who has experienced grace not wanting to help God's people. Like I said, if you have no desire to help Christians in need, call on Jesus to save you, and to fill you with God's grace.

The good works we were created in Christ to do, benefit us by enabling us to come out of darkness (1 John 2:8-10). Praise God. Another benefit to this is written in the following passage of scripture.

Psalm 41:1-3
1 Blessed is he who considers the poor; The Lord will deliver him in time of trouble. 2 The Lord will preserve him and keep him alive, And he will be blessed on the earth; You will not deliver him to the will of his enemies. 3 The Lord will strengthen him on his bed of illness; You will sustain him on his sickbed. NKJV

It does not say that we won't get sick, but the Lord will strengthen us, and deliver us on our sickbed (verse 3 above). As I have mentioned, the righteous person may have many afflictions, but the Lord delivers him out of them all (Psalm 34:19). Praise be to the Lord God almighty!

Who are the righteous? Those who have faith in Jesus Christ and believe according to Romans 3:21-26, are righteous by faith. What will faith in Jesus Christ make a Christian do? If a Christian has faith in Jesus he will love other disciples (John 13:34-35).

Galatians 5:6
6 For in Jesus Christ neither circumcision availeth anything, nor uncircumcision; but faith which worketh by love. KJV

Faith in Jesus Christ will express itself through love (verse 6 above). How do we love one another according to the Word of God, except by helping our brother in need (1 John 3:16-19 above)? People, who speak with the spirit of error, want you to believe that hugging everyone and shaking hands with everyone is what Jesus commanded us to do, but the Bible is clear about what love is.

Therefore, we need to be careful to do good works, which God prepared in advance for us to do. In fact, the Bible says that we need to be careful to do them.

Titus 3:8
8 This is a faithful saying, and these things I want you to affirm constantly, that those who have believed in God should be careful to maintain good works. These things are good and profitable to men. NKJV

You already know why people speak against the faith; they cannot see the verses. They have been taken from them for one reason or another. Don't let it happen to you, since there is no guarantee that you will ever see these verses again, unless you are continually reading the Word of God; renewing your mind with the truth.

My friend, speak with the Spirit of faith and declare that you were "created in Christ to do good works," and that you should "maintain good works" (verse 8 above). Notice how often this should be confirmed (affirmed, stated) according to verse 8 above; constantly!

If we had known the verses concerning being saved and grace, we would already know about good works. The same is true concerning baptism. If we had received John's baptism, we would already know about good works.

What should we do? That's what the people asked John the Baptist, after coming out to be baptized by him. John came in the way of righteousness, or in other words, he came to show us the way of righteousness according to Matthew 21:28-32. Here is his message according to Luke 3:8-14.

Luke 3:8-14
8 Therefore bear fruits worthy of repentance, and do not begin to say to yourselves, 'We have Abraham as our father.' For I say to you that God is able to raise up children to Abraham from these stones. 9 And even now the ax is laid to the root of the trees. Therefore every tree which does not bear good fruit is cut down and thrown into the fire." 10 So the people asked him, saying, "What shall we do then?" 11 He answered and said to them, "He who has two tunics, let him give to him

who has none; and he who has food, let him do likewise." 12 Then tax collectors also came to be baptized, and said to him, "Teacher, what shall we do?" 13 And he said to them, "Collect no more than what is appointed for you." 14 Likewise the soldiers asked him, saying, "And what shall we do?" So he said to them, "Do not intimidate anyone or accuse falsely, and be content with your wages." NKJV

Basically, if a new Christian began with John's baptism, they would not have a problem believing Jesus, since they would already know about good works. John came to prepare the way for Jesus to live on the inside of us.

Bear fruits worthy of repentance (verse 8 above)! Basically John was saying to do what is right, and to share what we have with those in need (verse 11 above). That would be practicing righteous acts (doing what is right).

He who practices righteousness is righteous (1 John 3:7), but every tree that does not bear good fruit will be cut down and thrown into the fire (verse 9 above).

That was John's message, which agrees with what Jesus taught, according to John 15:1-6 (below), and Matthew 7:19. It also agrees with the Apostle Paul's message according to Acts 26:20. We have to bear fruits worthy of repentance, in order that righteous acts will control us (Romans 6:18).

John said that every tree, which does not bear good fruit will be cut down and thrown into the fire (verse 9 above). Then the people asked him what they needed to do? Jesus declared the same thing, according to His teachings.

John 15:1-6
1 "I am the true vine, and My Father is the vinedresser. 2 Every branch in Me that does not bear fruit He takes away; and every branch that bears fruit He prunes, that it may bear more fruit. 3 You are already clean because of the word which I have spoken to you. 4 Abide in Me, and I in you. As the branch cannot bear fruit of itself, unless it abides in the vine, neither can you, unless you abide in Me. 5 "I am the vine, you are the branches. He who abides in Me, and I in him, bears much fruit; for without Me you can do nothing. 6 If anyone does not abide in Me, he is cast out as a branch and is withered; and they gather them and throw them into the fire, and they are burned. NKJV

Jesus taught that if we did not bear the fruit, we would be taken away (verse 2 above), and the only way to bear fruit is to abide (remain) in Him (verse 4). He goes on to say that those who do not abide in Him would be cast out and thrown into the fire (verse 6 above).

Therefore, the only way to bear fruit, according to Jesus' teaching, is to abide in Him. How do we abide (remain) in Him? We have already discussed this, but it is so important to know. Therefore, every Christian should be able to answer that question. How do we abide in Jesus?

John 15:9-10
9 "As the Father loved Me, I also have loved you; abide in My love. 10 If you keep My commandments, you will abide in My love, just as I have kept My Father's commandments and abide in His love. NKJV

The only way to abide (remain) in Jesus is to obey His commandments, which means that the only way to keep from being cast into the fire is to obey His commandments. What are His commandments?

John 15:12-14
12 This is My commandment, that you love one another as I have loved you. 13 Greater love has no one than this, than to lay down one's life for his friends. 14 You are My friends if you do whatever I command you. NKJV

1 John 3:23-24
23 And this is His commandment: that we should believe on the name of His Son Jesus Christ and love one another, as He gave us commandment. 24 Now he who keeps His commandments abides in Him, and He in him. And by this we know that He abides in us, by the Spirit whom He has given us. NKJV

There is no way around it. We must love one another. Those who keep His commandments abide in Him (verse 24 above), and those who abide in Him bear much fruit, showing themselves to be His disciples (John 15:8). Those who bear much fruit come out of darkness (1 John 2:8-10), pass from death to life (1 John 3:14-15), and stop sinning (1 John 3:6).

What is meant by fruit? Is that like apples and pears? No, fruit is the same as the "good works" that God prepared in advance for us to do. Allow the Word of God below to explain itself, reading scripture with scripture.

Titus 3:14
14 And let our people also learn to maintain good works, to meet urgent needs, that they may not be unfruitful. NKJV

If you believe the Word of God, then you also believe that we need to maintain good works, so that we will not be unfruitful. Those good works include things like helping God's people in need (Philippians 4:16-17, 2 Corinthians 9:10-12), confessing the name of Jesus Christ (Hebrews 13:15-16), and basically doing what is right (Luke 3:8-14). Check the verses.

Without love, forget about it. Not only will we not be able to bear the right kind of fruit, but the Bible says that without love, we are absolutely nothing.

1 Corinthians 13:1-3
1 Though I speak with the tongues of men and of angels, but have not love, I have become sounding brass or a clanging cymbal. 2 And though I have the gift of prophecy, and understand all mysteries and all knowledge, and though I have all faith, so that I could remove mountains, but have not love, I am nothing. 3 And though I bestow all my goods to feed the poor, and though I give my body to be burned, but have not love, it profits me nothing. NKJV

Even if spiritual things are happening around us, we are required to love one another as we have described in this chapter. Even if we have the faith to move mountains, without love we are nothing (verse 2 above). Like I have said, don't chase signs and wonders, but look for the truth first, and let the signs follow (Mark 16:15-18).

The King James Version translates love as "charity" in 1 Corinthians 13, which is still in-line with scripture, since charity is helping people in need. Jesus expects His followers to give to charity. Giving "alms" means giving to charity.

Luke 11:41
41 But rather give alms of such things as you have; then indeed all things are clean to you. NKJV

Luke 12:33-34
33 Sell what you have and give alms; provide yourselves money bags which do not grow old, a treasure in the heavens that does not fail, where no thief approaches nor moth destroys. 34 For where your treasure is, there your heart will be also. NKJV

Some people quote Isaiah 64:6 out of context, saying that "All of our righteous acts are as filthy rags," and they would be, if we continued in sin, and needed to be saved according to the verse right before it (Isaiah 64:5). However, Jesus makes it clear, in the verses above, that alms-giving stores up treasure in Heaven that will surely reward us.

He also explains in great detail how we should help people in distress, according to the parable of the Good Samaritan, which also involves directly helping people in need (Luke 10:25-37). He says, "Go and do likewise."

Read the following verses out loud a few times so that you will be able to recognize those who speak according to the truth, and those who speak with the spirit of error.

John 5:28-29
28 Marvel not at this: for the hour is coming, in the which all that are in the graves shall hear his voice, 29 And shall come forth; they that have done good, unto the resurrection of life;

**and they that have done evil, unto the resurrection of damna-
tion. KJV**

What does Jesus think about those who do good, and those who do evil? If you are saved, you were created in Christ to do good works (Ephesians 2:10). As I have mentioned before, the face of the Lord is against those who do evil, point, blank, period (1 Peter 3:12). The choice is yours.

Read the following passage of scripture and know the value of righteous acts, and then you will also know that greed is the only reason why anyone would hide the truth about giving from you.

Ezekiel 18:21-24
**21 "But if a wicked man turns from all his sins which he has
committed, keeps all My statutes, and does what is lawful
and right, he shall surely live; he shall not die. 22 None of the
transgressions which he has committed shall be remembered
against him; because of the righteousness which he has done,
he shall live. 23 Do I have any pleasure at all that the wicked
should die?" says the Lord God, "and not that he should turn
from his ways and live?**

**24 "But when a righteous man turns away from his righteous-
ness and commits iniquity, and does according to all the
abominations that the wicked man does, shall he live? All the
righteousness which he has done shall not be remembered;
because of the unfaithfulness of which he is guilty and the sin
which he has committed, because of them he shall die. NKJV**

Are righteous acts valuable? They most certainly are, and what will happen to those who refuse to help the poor according to the following verses?

Proverbs 21:13
**13 Whoever shuts his ears to the cry of the poor Will also cry
himself and not be heard. NKJV**

Love or charity, as the King James Version describes it, is the first thing that Christians should be practicing, but these verses are downplayed today for obvious reasons. The love of money is the root of all kinds of evil (1 Timothy 6:10).

Under the Laws of Moses, the tithe was always food, and never given as money for constructing buildings and such, but it was always food given to feed people (Deuteronomy 14:22-23, 26:2, 2 Chronicles 31:4-6). No building or temple in the Bible was ever built with tithe money, but they were built only with offerings.

Therefore, if the tithe was collected and used for its intended purpose today, church-attending people who tithe would reap the benefits associated with helping God's people in need. Imagine that.

Again, allow the scriptures to explain the scriptures. The early church lived in equality among the believers.

2 Corinthians 8:13-15
13 For I do not mean that others should be eased and you burdened; 14 but by an equality, that now at this time your abundance may supply their lack, that their abundance also may supply your lack — that there may be equality. 15 As it is written, "He who gathered much had nothing left over, and he who gathered little had no lack." NKJV

Acts 4:32-35
32 Now the multitude of those who believed were of one heart and one soul; neither did anyone say that any of the things he possessed was his own, but they had all things in common. 33 And with great power the apostles gave witness to the resurrection of the Lord Jesus. And great grace was upon them all. 34 Nor was there anyone among them who lacked; for all who were possessors of lands or houses sold them, and brought the proceeds of the things that were sold, 35 and laid them at the apostles' feet; and they distributed to each as anyone had need. NKJV

I know that these verses may be a shock to you because they are not taught today. No, I'm not telling you to sell everything you have and place the money in an offering plate. There are plenty of godly people in the Bible who had material possessions, and even used their homes as a church.

Besides, I don't know of a place where equality among the brothers is practiced today (verse 14 above), or where there is a daily distribution of food among the Saints (the faithful in Christ, Acts 6:1). Do you?

I'm not looking for a donation from you, nor am I in need. However, I want you to know how to "love one another" in God's eyes, so that you may know what to do, and who to help in order to come out of darkness, stop sinning, and have the Lord heal you in your time of need. That's what this book is about, and I think it is probably obvious by now why church-attending people are not experiencing these results today.

Now what

Why is there little difference between those who attend weekly church services and the people of this world when it comes to sin? We're not obeying the message (1 Peter 2:8). It's just that simple. We ignore the parts that we don't like, and we have to twist other parts, in order to make them fit our message.

If we obeyed Jesus, we would come out of darkness, not have anything on the inside of us that could make us stumble, stop sinning, and be rescued in times of trouble, including being healed from sickness. However, we have rejected that, and even hide the verses from new converts.

If we have decided to do what is right, who are we going to love, and how are we going to love them? We are going to be helping our Christian brothers and sisters who are in need, in our own church, or in our own hometown from what we have to give.

That can be done through a local organization that helps the least of God's people with their needs, or that can be done directly by us. Either way, those are the instructions that bring the desired results.

Why does it need to be local? It doesn't have to be local, but as it is written, if anyone "sees" his brother in need, but has no pity on him, how does the love of God abide in him (1 John 3:17)? I guess we could see a Christian in need on TV, but you may be like me and not watch TV, or not believe what you see on TV.

According to Matthew 24:12, in the last days, wickedness or lawlessness will abound, and because of it, the love of most people will grow cold. In other words, scams will be on the rise. However, if the organization that you are supporting is local, you can visit and see for yourself what you are supporting to make sure that you are helping the least of God's people.

What should we give toward helping people? We can help them from our income, or from the things we have already accumulated, but we should never give something that we do not have to give (verse 12 below).

2 Corinthians 8:12
12 For if there is first a willing mind, it is accepted according to what one has, and not according to what he does not have. NKJV

Open your local phone-book and find the nearest Christian-based homeless shelter, or children's shelter. Find a local Christian-based soup kitchen, or any organization that helps Christians directly with basic needs, and go visit them. See who they are helping and how they are helping them. If what you see and hear is in-line with godly instructions, support that organization.

You may not be at a point in your life where you can give much of your hard-earned money, but I would start somewhere, and then grow from there (1 Thessalonians 4:10). God will even provide seed for those who are willing to sow (2 Corinthians 9:10). Just ask Him in faith without doubting.

There is one thing that I have noticed about people who don't have much money. They have plenty of time that they can give. Get involved! Volunteering is a form of helping. Either way, the measure we use, will be measured back to us.

Luke 6:38
38 Give, and it will be given to you: good measure, pressed down, shaken together, and running over will be put into your

bosom. For with the same measure that you use, it will be measured back to you." NKJV

The Laws of Moses required the people to give a tenth (Hebrews 7:5), but New Testament giving is based on the measure we use, and not through obligation, but as a matter of generosity (2 Corinthians 9:5). Abraham gave a tenth of the spoils, but it was not out of obligation (Genesis 14:20). God loves a cheerful giver.

I'm not asking you to stop supporting your local church. Those who preach the Gospel, should make their living from the Gospel, and those who reap spiritual things, should share their material things (1 Corinthians 9:11, 14).

However, make sure that you are hearing the Gospel, and make sure that the verses we have covered so far are not hidden from unsuspecting people. That's called deceit, and that is not of God.

Support whatever you want to support, but I am telling you what will work to stop sin, and promote healing in your body. Most of the time, decisions boil down to feelings, or faith, but know for sure that we reap what we sow (Galatians 6:7-10), and there is no partiality with God (Romans 2:11, Acts 10:34).

Know that if you decide to follow your feelings, the verses we have covered will not remain in you, and you may never hear them again (Mark 4:24-25). If you have been attending church services for years, and have not heard these verses, then obviously the chances of you hearing them again are very slim. May the Lord have mercy on you.

We're not just going to help people who are remaining in the faith. We're going to love everyone, but we are especially looking for people of faith, and the poor are rich in faith (James 2:5). Therefore, there is no way around it. We must love one another.

Galatians 6:9-10

9 And let us not grow weary while doing good, for in due season we shall reap if we do not lose heart. 10 Therefore, as we have opportunity, let us do good to all, especially to those who are of the household of faith. NKJV

Father, in the name of Jesus Christ, forgive us for not loving one another, as You have commanded us. Forgive us for not being all that You have called us to be, and now give us the grace needed to do Your will. Amen!

I'm Alan Ballou; a servant. If you have any questions, please contact me.

www.HowToStopSinning.com

ഇ൯ങ

16

The Good I Want To Do

ഇരുഗ

How can we obey Jesus to the point of coming out of darkness if the good we want to do, we cannot do? That's a good question.

However, does the Bible really say that the good we want to do we will never be able to do, and at the same time say that we were created in Christ to do good works according to Ephesians 2:10? That would be like a catch twenty-two. We need to double check the instructions.

Many proclaim that the good you want to do, you will never be able to do, and the evil you do not want to do, that you will continue to do, no matter how hard you try. Then they show people the following passage of scripture as proof.

Romans 7:18-19
18 For I know that in me (that is, in my flesh) nothing good dwells; for to will is present with me, but how to perform what is good I do not find. 19 For the good that I will to do, I do not do; but the evil I will not to do, that I practice. NKJV

Many have preached a sermon using those two verses alone, and left people thinking that they will never be able to stop doing the evil they may be presently caught up in. However, they have to avoid the remainder of Romans chapter seven in order to do it.

This is a good example why we need to read scripture with scripture. The seventh chapter of Romans was never intended to be used to say that we would never be able to stop sinning, but if we do not know what is in that chapter, then the verses above can be used to support a different viewpoint.

That is exactly what has happened to Christians who do not know enough of the truth themselves to recognize misinterpretations, which is one of the biggest hindrances for the ones who are trying to stop sinning. They are blown and tossed by the doctrines of men, spoken as if they are the commands of God (Ephesians 4:13-14, Matthew 15:9).

If you have been a Christian for any length of time, you have probably heard that the good you want to do, you will not be able to do, but the evil you don't want to do, that you will keep doing (Romans 7:18-19 above). That's like

Christianity 101 this day and age.

However, this is only true under certain conditions. Those conditions are rarely explained, and so most have accepted as fact that even if they want to continually do what's good, they will not be able to carry it out. So, why bother? They took the bait; hook, line, and sinker.

Let's take a closer look at the passage of scripture in Romans chapter seven. Notice the conditions as we add a few verses before and after verses 18 and 19.

Romans 7:15-20
15 For what I am doing, I do not understand. For what I will to do, that I do not practice; but what I hate, that I do. 16 If, then, I do what I will not to do, I agree with the law that it is good. 17 But now, it is no longer I who do it, but sin that dwells in me. 18 For I know that in me (that is, in my flesh) nothing good dwells; for to will is present with me, but how to perform what is good I do not find. 19 For the good that I will to do, I do not do; but the evil I will not to do, that I practice. 20 Now if I do what I will not to do, it is no longer I who do it, but sin that dwells in me. NKJV

The Apostle Paul said that "if" he was doing what he does not want to do, then it is no longer him, but "sin" dwelling in him that is doing it (verses 16-17 above). He says the same thing in verse 20 above.

If I do what I will not to do, it is no longer I who do it, but sin that dwells in me! If we only read verses 18 and 19, we will miss that information and then this passage can be used against the Word of God to say that we will never be able to stop doing the evil we do not want to do.

However, when we include verses 16, 17, and 20, it becomes clear that the Apostle Paul is saying, "if" he found himself in this situation, then it is "sin that dwells in" him that is making him do what he is doing. It doesn't say that he would always be in that position, but when it happens, then he could identify the problem as indwelling sin.

Sin made him do it, and under certain conditions, sin can make us sin also. Once we serve sin, we will become a slave to sin, and once we serve obedience, it will lead us into becoming a slave to righteousness (verse 16 below). That's how sin works.

Romans 6:16-18
16 Do you not know that to whom you present yourselves slaves to obey, you are that one's slaves whom you obey, whether of sin leading to death, or of obedience leading to righteousness? 17 But God be thanked that though you were slaves of sin, yet you obeyed from the heart that form of doctrine to which you were delivered. 18 And having been set free

from sin, you became slaves of righteousness. NKJV

What the Apostle Paul is describing in Romans chapter seven, is a safeguard for those who follow the teachings covered in Romans chapter 6. A person who becomes a slave to righteousness will indeed be "set free from sin" (verse 18 above).

If we offer ourself to obedience, obeying the doctrine of Jesus from the heart, we will be set free from sin (verses 17-18 above). If we continue to offer ourself to sin, we will be a slave to sin. Either way, we will be a slave to whichever one we offer ourself to (verse 16 above).

Therefore, there are certain people who cannot do good. Even if they give to support the right message, or to a Christian organization that practices the truth, they will ruin their gift by violating Matthew 6:1-4, because they do not obey Jesus. Indwelling sin will always prevent them from doing the good they want to do. We will discuss the solution for that, later in this chapter.

Only those who obey the doctrine of Jesus Christ will be able to bear the right kind of fruit (John 15:4-6). Those who do not practice righteousness are not of God.

1 John 3:10
10 In this the children of God and the children of the devil are manifest: Whoever does not practice righteousness is not of God, nor is he who does not love his brother. NKJV

Therefore, those who obey Jesus will be set free from indwelling sin, but those who do not obey Jesus will still have sin as their master. The only way to bear the right kind of fruit is to remain in the vine (John 15:6). The only way to remain in the vine is to obey Jesus' commands (John 15:10).

He commanded us to love one another, and believe in His name (John 15:12, 17, 1 John 3:23). Those who abide in Jesus, stop sinning (1 John 3:6), but what would happen if unsuspecting Christians, who never test what they hear, were never taught that? What if they never read their Bible for themself? May the Lord send His Word to heal us all. Amen.

Here is the important part to remember about Romans 7:15-20. He is talking to those who "will to do good, but cannot carry it out." Basically, he is talking to Christians who have experienced grace, and now have a desire to obey Jesus, as we have discussed in previous chapters. This doesn't even apply to those who do not want to do good.

People who speak against "being created in Christ to do good works" have no idea how close to death they are (Ephesians 2:10), since their own words will lead their body away from the truth (James 5:19-20, Proverbs 15:9-10). They will not want to do good.

The sacrifices of people without God are made to demons, as I have already mentioned (1 Corinthians 10:20). In other words, they may not have a problem with giving, but they support false teachings (1 Timothy 4:1-2), or they support worldliness among Christians.

They cannot give in accordance with faith in Jesus Christ, unless they sound the trumpet in order to receive their reward in this life (Matthew 6:1-4), rather than storing up treasure in Heaven (Luke 12:33). Those who do not abide in Jesus cannot possibly bear the right kind of fruit (John 15:4-6).

If you will to do good, but cannot carry it out, and you have not followed the teachings of Romans chapter six, then here is the solution, which is also found in Romans chapter seven. Apart from the Law, sin is dead.

Romans 7:8
8 But sin, taking opportunity by the commandment, produced in me all manner of evil desire. For apart from the law sin was dead. NKJV

Apart from the Law, meaning the Laws of Moses, sin is dead. In other words, sin will not be able to control you if you die to the Laws that came through Moses. The Apostle Paul made that clear back in Romans chapter 6, which happens to be the verses that precede Romans 6:16-18 above.

Romans 6:14-15
14 For sin shall not have dominion over you, for you are not under law but under grace. 15 What then? Shall we sin because we are not under law but under grace? Certainly not! NKJV

Apart (separate) from the Law sin is dead. In other words, if we were not under the Law, indwelling sin would have no power over us, and we "would be able" to do the good we want to do.

In other words, we would be able to obey Jesus Christ (under grace), if we were not under the Laws of Moses (under the Law, verse 14 above). However, if we noticed that we could not do the good "we want to do," then we "should recognize" that it is sin on the inside of us that is controlling us, meaning that we were back under the Law.

Apart from the Law, sin is dead! Say that several times so that you can remember it and quote it the next time a well-meaning Christian quotes Romans 7:18-19 in a way that implies that you will never be able to stop sinning.

Tell him that instead of trying to keep the Laws of Moses in order to be righteous (Romans 2:13), you are switching to the righteousness of God through faith in Jesus Christ, which is what is making you do good works, so that you can be set free from sin. Tell him that you are offering your body to Jesus, under grace, and consequently, sin shall not have dominion over you (verse 14 above).

However, sin will have dominion over those who remain under the Laws of

Moses (verse 14 above). Therefore, the only people among Christians who will never be able to stop sinning, no matter how diligently they try are those who remain under the Law, rather than dying to the Law, and serving under grace.

Consequently, Law-based churches will always be filled with people who cannot stop sinning. No wonder they boldly say that Christians cannot stop sinning, and interpret the verses in such a way as to quiet their conscience. May the Lord have mercy on them.

Now what

You already know why some people cannot see these verses; they speak against them (1 Timothy 6:20-21). Therefore, those who use Romans 7:18-19 as an excuse to say that Christians cannot stop sinning, will not be able to see the verses we have covered in this chapter, and that's why they interpret Romans chapter 7 as they do.

Unfortunately, those who use Romans 7 as an excuse to say that they will not be able to do the good that they want to do are correct, if they are referring to themself. Their mouth prevents them from doing it, since the tongue controls the body. However, they speak with the spirit of error. May the Lord have mercy on them.

Those who speak with the Spirit of faith, proclaim that they will obey Jesus, and consequently, they will come out of darkness, and stop sinning by abiding in Him, Lord willing. We know He is willing because that is in-line with the Word of God. Praise God, halleluiah!

If this is the first time you can see these verses we have covered in this chapter, and in the past you have used Romans 7 as an excuse, then simply repent, and turn. Start over, being careful never to speak against the verses again. Force yourself to speak with the Spirit of faith (2 Corinthians 4:13, Romans 10:6-8). May the Lord have mercy on you as He has me.

Father, in Jesus' name, forgive us for misinterpretations. We didn't know, and we trusted those who did not know Your Word. We now choose You, and Your ways above anything. Therefore, give us eyes that can see, and ears that can hear Your Word. Cause Your Word to live on the inside of us that we may stay on the paths that You have marked out for us, and bring glory to Your holy name. Amen.

I'm a firm believer in fifteen second prayers at any time during the day depending on the situation. I believe that we should repent of things while they are on our mind, which will help us keep a clear conscience.

The Bible says to "Pray without ceasing" (1 Thessalonians 5:17). Therefore, don't wait until the end of the day to pray, especially if you do not know anything about controlling your thoughts, which we will cover later (2 Corinthians 10:3-5,

Matthew 15:15-20).

Don't fool yourself, thinking that a daily devotional and a quick prayer over a morning cup of coffee is all you need. You need a daily diet of the pure Word of God from the New Testament, out loud in your ears, and I'm not talking about five minutes, but more like first place in your life.

I use an iPod with an audio version of the Bible on it, and I keep it playing most of the day. Praise God. Some people have mentioned that we can't really focus on what we are hearing that way, and that is correct. However, the Word of God playing in the background is far better than anything else we can listen to. Nothing else even comes close.

The Bible says that "There will be false teachers among us" today (verse 1 below), and that "Many will follow them" (verse 2 below). The only way to be sure that we are not taken for a ride by a false teacher is to know the truth for ourself (Ephesians 4:13-14).

2 Peter 2:1-3
1 But there were also false prophets among the people, even as there will be false teachers among you, who will secretly bring in destructive heresies, even denying the Lord who bought them, and bring on themselves swift destruction. 2 And many will follow their destructive ways, because of whom the way of truth will be blasphemed. 3 By covetousness they will exploit you with deceptive words; for a long time their judgment has not been idle, and their destruction does not slumber. NKJV

Money is the root of all kinds of evil, and so if someone is going to lie to you, it will usually boil down to receiving your money. According to Acts 20:29-32, false teachers draw people away from the truth in order to make their own followers (disciples) rather than making disciples of Jesus Christ.

It is not a degree or a title that makes one approved by God to teach, but those whom the Lord sends, simply speak in accordance with His Words.

Jeremiah 23:22
22 But if they had stood in My counsel, And had caused My people to hear My words, Then they would have turned them from their evil way And from the evil of their doings. NKJV

John 3:34
34 For He whom God has sent speaks the words of God, for God does not give the Spirit by measure. NKJV

An ambassador does not speak for himself, but he speaks for the one who sent him. Listen to the words. If what you are hearing is against the doctrine of Jesus Christ, then can the speaker possibly be speaking for Jesus? That's the proof that the Lord has sent someone to speak, regardless of their background, how they look, or there worldly title. If they do not speak according to the Word, there is no light in them (Isaiah 8:20).

Therefore, if the Word is not living in them, don't expect to get God's guidance out of them (Matthew 12:34-35). God's people need to hear God's Word.

I'm Alan Ballou; a servant. If you have a question about something in this book, ask me, and Lord willing, I will answer you in accordance with what is written.

My wife Lucie and I hold seminars wherever we are welcomed with small and large groups, and even from house to house. We do not charge anyone, but serve all who call on us for help.

www.HowToStopSinning.com

Alan's email alan@howtostopsinning.com

Lucie's email lucie@howtostopsinning.com

ജ൫

What we do right now with our time and money is exactly what we would do with more time, and money. He who is faithful with little, is also faithful with much (Luke 16:10).

The wrong way will always seem right to those who do not know the truth for themself (Prov 14:12).

Just about anything can be used for good, or to promote evil. If you have a twitter account, and would like to receive godly reminders, with the verses included, please consider joining me. @AlanBallou

IF GOD'S PEOPLE EXPERIENCE DESTRUCTION FOR
LACK OF KNOWLEDGE, THEN THE POWER TO AVOID
THAT DESTRUCTION IN OUR LIFE IS THE WORD OF
GOD LIVING ON THE INSIDE OF US.

Alan Ballou

17

Law and Spirit

ᏅᏓᏅᏃ

If we gave a Bible to a new Christian and asked him to read Romans chapter seven without telling him what to think, he would be able to see that he needs to die to the Law in order to be able to serve in the Spirit.

> **Romans 7:4-6**
> **4 Therefore, my brethren, you also have become dead to the law through the body of Christ, that you may be married to another — to Him who was raised from the dead, that we should bear fruit to God. 5 For when we were in the flesh, the sinful passions which were aroused by the law were at work in our members to bear fruit to death. 6 But now we have been delivered from the law, having died to what we were held by, so that we should serve in the newness of the Spirit and not in the oldness of the letter. NKJV**

He won't know what "the Law" is, and you may be in the same boat for now, but he will know that in order to be a part of the "bride of Christ" (verse 4 above), and in order to "serve in the newness of the Spirit," he must become dead to the Law (verse 6 above).

What would happen if a new Christian never learned that? He may even join a Christian organization that is Law-based, since many are Law-based, and consequently, these verses will never be mentioned.

That means that he will remain under sin, and be taught that the good he may want to do, he will not be able to do, which will prove true for him. Sin is only dead apart from the Law (Romans 7:8).

Get this! Sinful passions are aroused by the Law, so that those who are under the Law bear fruit unto death (verse 5 above). That may be a shock to you, but the Law was added so that sin would increase, not decrease (Romans 5:20).

We have to die to the Law in order to be delivered from the effect that it will have on us (verse 6 above). How do we die to the Law when Jesus, Himself said that it is not going anywhere until Heaven and earth pass away (Matthew 5:17-18)?

It doesn't go away, but it has to be fulfilled, and we fulfill (fully meet the requirements of) it through faith in Jesus Christ. Therefore, through faith we establish, or uphold the Law (Romans 3:31).

That doesn't mean that we are now going to start stoning people who work on the Sabbath day as the Law requires (verse 15 below, Numbers 15:32-36), but as long as we continue in our faith, and live according to the Spirit, we will fully meet the righteous requirements of the Law (Romans 8:4, Colossians 1:21-23).

Exodus 31:15
15 Work shall be done for six days, but the seventh is the Sabbath of rest, holy to the Lord. Whoever does any work on the Sabbath day, he shall surely be put to death. NKJV

In other words, Christians (Christ followers) do not follow the Law by the letter, but we fulfill the Law through love, and consequently, we serve in the newness of the Spirit (Romans 7:6 above). We simply follow Jesus.

For example, Jesus healed a man on the Sabbath and told him to pick up his mat and walk (John 5:5-9). Did Jesus do according to what is written in the letter of the Law, or did He fulfill the Law? Love is the fulfillment of the Law (Romans 13:8-10 below).

Another example would be the woman caught in adultery. The Laws of Moses say that a man and a woman caught in adultery, shall be put to death (Leviticus 20:10 below).

Leviticus 20:10
10 'The man who commits adultery with another man's wife, he who commits adultery with his neighbor's wife, the adulterer and the adulteress, shall surely be put to death. NKJV

Did Jesus follow the letter of the Law, or show mercy toward the woman caught in adultery, according to John 8:10-11 below?

John 8:10-11
10 When Jesus had raised Himself up and saw no one but the woman, He said to her, "Woman, where are those accusers of yours? Has no one condemned you?" 11 She said, "No one, Lord." And Jesus said to her, "Neither do I condemn you; go and sin no more." NKJV

Jesus did not condemn the woman, and neither will we. Those who follow Jesus will fulfill all of the Laws of Moses through love rather than by trying to keep every single command.

As I have mentioned, if we would just teach people to follow Jesus, there would be major differences in the church today. All of a sudden, church-attending people would come out of darkness, stop sinning, and start doing good to those who are in need.

Actually, I believe that there are Christians in every church that practice this through the Spirit, but they may not be able to explain it with scripture (1 John 2:27). I have met some godly people from just about every denomination, who practice the truth, from Pentecostals, to Baptists, to Catholics, and all in between. Praise God, halleluiah!

Jesus commanded us to love, and love is not only the fulfillment of the Laws of Moses, but love fulfills any other law as well (verse 9 below). That means that just by simply obeying Jesus, in the way that we have described in previous chapters, we will fully meet all of the requirements of the Laws of Moses, and any other spiritual law.

Romans 13:8-10
8 Owe no one anything except to love one another, for he who loves another has fulfilled the law. 9 For the commandments, "You shall not commit adultery," "You shall not murder," "You shall not steal," "You shall not bear false witness," "You shall not covet," and if there is any other commandment, are all summed up in this saying, namely, "You shall love your neighbor as yourself."   10 Love does no harm to a neighbor; therefore love is the fulfillment of the law. NKJV

If you love your neighbor as you love yourself, you will fulfill the Law and the prophets (verse 10 above, Galatians 5:13-15, Matthew 7:12). What you would have men do for you, do likewise to them. In fact, that will fulfill any commandment (Romans 13:9 above). Imagine that.

How do you do that exactly? Simple, if you like to eat, feed your neighbor. Love your neighbor "as you" love yourself, or simply obey Jesus, as we have previously discussed.

However, what would happen if you donated money on a regular basis, but that money was not used to love anyone? Many people give today, thinking that they are doing what Jesus commanded us to do, but we need to make sure that what we support is in keeping with faith in Jesus Christ.

Give what you want to give to and support whatever you want to support, but if you do not give in the way that we have discussed, in keeping with faith in Jesus Christ, then you are not abiding in Christ.

If we want to stop sinning, and avoid the diseases brought about by the curses which come on those who disobey the Laws of Moses (Deuteronomy 28:58-63), we must fulfill the Law through love (Romans 13:8-10 above). That's worth checking to see where your money is going.

One man asked how he could love someone if he didn't love himself. The Bible says that "No man ever hated himself," but that he nourishes his body (Ephesians 5:29). Therefore, if you find someone who says that they do not love themself, ask them if they have stopped eating.

We may not love ourself very much, but we can love our neighbor as we love ourself. Therefore, if we like to eat, we should help to feed our neighbor (local), who is in need, by supporting our local soup kitchen, food bank, or the like. If we like having a roof over our head, then we should support our local Christian-based homeless shelter. That will fulfill the Law.

The parable of the Good Samaritan is a good example of loving your neighbor as you love yourself (Luke 10:25-37). As I mentioned, New Testament giving is all about helping people, but especially the least of God's people (Galatians 6:10).

Jesus said that whatever we do for the least of His brothers, we do for Him (Matthew 25:40), and He identified His brothers as those who hear the Word of God, and do it (Luke 8:19-21, Mark 3:32-35). Just as Abraham gave a tenth to the high priest, I suggest giving a tenth (tithe) directly to Jesus in this way.

That's how you will fulfill the Law, and once you fulfill the Law, you will receive the blessings associated with keeping it, instead of the curses associated with disobedience (Deuteronomy 28:1-68). That's the cure for many diseases that people are seeking today. In this way, faith in Jesus Christ heals all of our diseases (verse 3 below).

Psalm 103:1-4
1 Bless the Lord, O my soul; And all that is within me, bless His holy name! 2 Bless the Lord, O my soul, And forget not all His benefits: 3 Who forgives all your iniquities, Who heals all your diseases, 4 Who redeems your life from destruction, Who crowns you with lovingkindness and tender mercies, NKJV

Jesus heals us, since faith in Jesus Christ fulfills the Law. If we fulfill the Law, we will receive the blessings for obedience rather than receiving the curses for disobedience, which include all kinds of sickness, and disease.

If we decided to follow the instructions in Romans 7:4-6 above, and die to the Law, in order that we could serve according to the Spirit, would the Holy Spirit lead us back under the Law?

Galatians 5:18
18 But if ye be led of the Spirit, ye are not under the law. KJV

Christians who are led by the Spirit, or I should say, who allow themself to be led by the Spirit (Romans 8:12-14), are not under the Laws of Moses.

2 Corinthians 3:17
17 Now the Lord is that Spirit: and where the Spirit of the Lord is, there is liberty. KJV

Jesus is the Spirit, and where the Spirit of the Lord is, there is liberty (verse 17 above). That freedom (liberty), which is described in 2 Corinthians 3:3-17, is indeed freedom from the Laws of Moses. Check the verses.

Many quote verses on healing, such as, "He took our infirmities," and "By His stripes we are healed," but they never mix faith with the message in order to receive healing from the Lord. The Spirit gives life to the body, but where the Spirit of the Lord is, there is freedom from the Laws of Moses.

If the Spirit of the Lord is the one leading us, then we are "not" going to be under the Law, but if we continue trying to be justified by Law, we will eventually fall away from grace.

Galatians 5:4-5
4 Christ is become of no effect unto you, whosoever of you are justified by the law; ye are fallen from grace. 5 For we through the Spirit wait for the hope of righteousness by faith. KJV

Yes, we can fall away from grace, if we attempt to be justified by observing the Law (verse 4 above). Nobody teaches this verse concerning grace, and you already know why; assuming you started reading at the beginning of this book (2 Timothy 4:3-4, 1 Timothy 4:1-2).

After accepting Jesus as the Lord of your life, if you turn back and attempt to be justified by Law, you will fall away from grace. Many today are in this condition and suffer sickness and disease because of it, as well as the other curses for disobedience, due to being under the Law (Deuteronomy 28:15-68), rather than fulfilling the Law through faith in Jesus Christ.

Those curses include diseases that were not even known to man, back when this was written (verse 61 below). I am sure that this describes diseases today that so many are desperately trying to find a man-made cure for, such as cancer, Alzheimer's disease, and the like, but the cure for all of them can be found by fulfilling the Laws of Moses through faith in Jesus Christ our Lord (Romans 13:8-10, James 2:8-10).

Deuteronomy 28:58-61
58 "If you do not carefully observe all the words of this law that are written in this book, that you may fear this glorious and awesome name, THE LORD YOUR GOD, 59 then the Lord will bring upon you and your descendants extraordinary plagues — great and prolonged plagues — and serious and prolonged sicknesses. 60 Moreover He will bring back on you all the diseases of Egypt, of which you were afraid, and they shall cling to you. 61 Also every sickness and every plague, which is not written in this Book of the Law, will the Lord bring upon you until you are destroyed. NKJV

I believe that simple repentance and turning to the Lord in accordance with what is written would empty the hospitals of Christians, who are presently under the Law, but don't realize it. This teaching could change healthcare in this country.

Praise God, halleluiah!

This isn't the only reason for illnesses, and diseases, but I'm sure that it is a major cause of them among Christians.

Now what

Again, if you would just obey Jesus, you would fulfill the Laws of Moses, and apart from the Law, sin is dead (Romans 7:8). That is just a different way of saying that if you obey Jesus, there would be nothing on the inside of you that could make you sin.

Reading scripture with scripture confirms it. With the right interpretation, the whole Bible fits together; Old and New Testament. Praise be to God. With this interpretation, there isn't a single verse in the Bible that we would have to dodge. Imagine that.

That means that if you repent of the past, and start obeying Jesus, you would be able to do good, and you would experience healing in your body, since the sickness brought on by disobeying the Law would leave. Glory be to the Lord God almighty!

However, if you worship in a place where the sign out front says that "It's all about Jesus," but inside the Laws of Moses are required of the people, then you are not free in Christ, but still under the Law, and subject to the curses for disobedience. As I have mentioned, sometimes our faith will only work away from the crowd we have been gathering with.

If the doctrine of Jesus Christ isn't welcomed (John 14:21-23, 15:4-6), then His followers aren't welcomed (2 John 1:9-11, Luke 10:16). In fact, our instructions are to not even welcome those who do not teach the doctrine of Jesus (2 John 1:10).

Those who remain under the Law can't help but sin. Sinful passions are aroused by the Law so that they bear fruit unto death (Romans 7:5).

They do not know the truth, and that is why it is so easy for them to speak in direct opposition to the faith by declaring that Christians cannot stop sinning. They have tried, with all their might, but they didn't follow the instructions.

Now they cannot see the verses, since they continually speak against them (1 Timothy 6:20-21), and they reject the verses when they are corrected, for that very reason (Mark 4:24-25). May the Lord have mercy upon them.

Father, in the name of Jesus Christ, have mercy on all of us, and send Your Word to heal us. Open the eyes of those who read this book, and give us all an understanding in these things. Forgive us for speaking against the faith, and give us all a moment of clarity, that we may choose Your ways, and turn so that You would heal us. Amen.

The more that sin increases, the worse off Christians who are under the Law become, because the strength of sin is the Law (1 Corinthians 15:56). In other words, the more we trespass the Law, the more power sin has over us to control us, and this is the reason many well-meaning preachers make the 6 o'clock news. Unbeknownst to them, they fell away from grace (ability).

They are really not any different than we are, and we are not any better than them, but those who try to keep part of the Law, rather than follow the instructions and die to it, become obligated to keep the whole Law (Galatians 5:3), and end up being cursed.

Under the same circumstances, we (our flesh) would do the same things (1 Corinthians 10:13). Let us repent and return to the Lord our God.

Galatians 3:10-12
10 For as many as are of the works of the law are under the curse; for it is written, "Cursed is everyone who does not continue in all things which are written in the book of the law, to do them." 11 But that no one is justified by the law in the sight of God is evident, for "the just shall live by faith." 12 Yet the law is not of faith, but "the man who does them shall live by them." NKJV

Whoever does the works of the Law shall live by them (verse 12 above). When it says to die to the Law, it means all of it. Stop trying to be right with God by observing it, but be right with God through faith in Jesus Christ, and faith in Jesus will make us love one another. Consequently, that will fulfill the Law.

Those who are just, or justified in God's eyes, live by faith, and not by the Law (verse 11 above). It doesn't mean that we are any better than anyone else, but we have positioned ourself to receive what God has offered us, which is justification by faith.

We only have access to grace, through faith (Romans 5:2). Therefore, if we reject living by faith, there is no longer access to grace, and consequently, those who try to be justified by Law, fall away from grace (Galatians 5:4-5 above).

Faith is a condition of justification (Hebrews 10:37-39 below). The end of our faith is the salvation of our soul (1 Peter 1:9). No faith means no grace, and no grace means no salvation. The just live by faith.

My flesh isn't any different than your flesh. Given the opportunity, and under certain circumstances, any of us could end up in jail for life, but the Lord delivers the godly from temptations. Therefore, I have positioned myself so that God will deliver me, and I am teaching you to do the same. Praise the Lord God almighty!

2 Peter 2:9-11
9 then the Lord knows how to deliver the godly out of temptations and to reserve the unjust under punishment for the day of judgment, 10 and especially those who walk according to

the flesh in the lust of uncleanness and despise authority. They are presumptuous, self-willed. They are not afraid to speak evil of dignitaries, 11 whereas angels, who are greater in power and might, do not bring a reviling accusation against them before the Lord. NKJV

It is the Lord Who delivers the godly (the just) out of temptations, but He doesn't do the same for the "unjust" (verse 9 above). The just person isn't necessarily any better than the unjust, but he lives by faith in Jesus Christ. Therefore, none of us are any better than the next homeless guy walking down the railroad tracks, but if we live by faith, God will give us what He has promised to give a justified person.

Grab a hold of that, and never forget it. The "just shall live by faith." God is the One Who justifies the person who lives by faith in Jesus Christ (verse 26 below). Therefore, take the worst sinner in the world, and teach him to live by faith in Jesus Christ, and he will be the blessed of God!

Romans 3:23-26
23 for all have sinned and fall short of the glory of God, 24 being justified freely by His grace through the redemption that is in Christ Jesus, 25 whom God set forth as a propitiation by His blood, through faith, to demonstrate His righteousness, because in His forbearance God had passed over the sins that were previously committed, 26 to demonstrate at the present time His righteousness, that He might be just and the justifier of the one who has faith in Jesus. NKJV

Faith in Jesus Christ is what brings about justification from God. It's not a matter of falling short, but one of justification, and if we continue in our faith in Jesus, we will come out of darkness, stop sinning, and receive the blessings which come on those who fulfill the Laws of Moses through faith, which includes healing.

It's not by our own ability that we are able to live up to what we are called to do, but by our God-given ability (grace). We are justified by faith, because we believe as Abraham believed (Romans 4:20-24), and therefore we have access to grace (Romans 5:2).

God poured His love into our heart by the Holy Spirit (Romans 5:5), and we are allowing Him to use our body as a living sacrifice (Romans 6:12-14, 12:1-2), for His own purpose (2 Timothy 1:9, Ephesians 2:10, John 15:16). By following His lead, through His Spirit, He sanctifies our conduct (Romans 15:16), and heals our body (Romans 8:10-11, 1 Peter 2:24). Praise, glory, and honor, be to the Lord our God, now and forever more. Amen!

However, if we draw back, and stop living by faith in Jesus Christ, or if we reject faith in Him, He will take no pleasure in us (Hebrews 10:38-39 below). It's just that simple.

You might be thinking that we have been justified by His blood according to Romans 5:9. We have, and we could say that we have been justified by His grace (Titus 3:7). However, faith is a condition of justification according to Hebrews 10:37-39 (below). We have to continue in our faith.

Hebrews 10:37-39

37 "For yet a little while, And He who is coming will come and will not tarry. 38 Now the just shall live by faith; But if anyone draws back, My soul has no pleasure in him." 39 But we are not of those who draw back to perdition, but of those who believe to the saving of the soul. NKJV

Therefore, I will continue to live by faith in Jesus Christ, Lord willing, and I will teach others to live by faith, in order that the Lord my God will rescue them from temptations, and give them the grace needed to live the Christian life, as He has me. Amen.

Father, in Jesus' name, it is only because of You that any of us are still here. Your mercies fail not, and because of them we are not consumed. Have mercy upon us, and forgive us for the sins we have committed against You. Be with us, and show us every way out of temptations that we may not sin against You. Make Your Word live in us. Save Lord! Deliver us from the traps, and snares that we have gotten ourself entangled in. Show us Your salvation, and send Your Word to heal us. Amen.

If it is all about Jesus, then follow Jesus, and die to the Law! Live by faith in the Son of God, and watch your life change for the better. Peace be with you.

I'm Alan Ballou; a servant. If you have any questions, please contact me. My wife Lucie and I hold seminars with small and large groups, and even from house to house, wherever we are welcomed. We serve all who call on us for help. If we may be of service to you, please contact us.

www.HowToStopSinning.com

Alan's email alan@howtostopsinning.com

Lucie's email lucie@howtostopsinning.com

ℰᏅ

With the right interpretation, the whole Bible fits together like a hand in a glove. However, with the wrong interpretation, we have to dodge certain scriptures because they do not support what we are saying.

Alan Ballou

18

Abraham and Moses

ଚଠୡଔ

At the beginning of Romans chapter seven, we were instructed to die to the Law (Romans 7:4-6), and in verse 8 we were told why; because sin would continue to control us if we didn't. That's reason enough to want to die to the Law, but what is the Law, and how do we die to it?

Any command, decree, regulation, or rule that came through Moses is a part of the Laws of Moses, or better known as "the Law."

John 1:17
17 For the law was given by Moses, but grace and truth came by Jesus Christ. KJV

The Law was given by God to the people of Israel, through Moses. There are over six hundred laws that make up what is known as the Law, and they are all found in the books of Exodus, Leviticus, Numbers, and Deuteronomy.

Actually, there are many laws, and any rule or decree can be considered a law. However, when someone says "the Law," they usually mean the Laws that came through Moses.

I personally capitalize the word "Law" when I am writing about it, and when I mention a different law, then I will usually name it, such as the law of the Spirit, law of righteousness, Christ's law, etc.

We have already mentioned a few of the laws that make up the Laws of Moses in the previous chapter, and how Jesus fulfilled those laws. Add the Ten Commandments to those two we have already covered, and you will at least know twelve out of the six hundred and something laws, but you can learn them all from the books mentioned above.

A lady asked me why God would put a law in place that we would need to die to later. That didn't make any sense to her, and some of you may be thinking the same thing. Therefore, I want to explain it, since that type of reasoning could be used against dying to the Law.

We are supposed to imitate Abraham's faith, and so it would seem like we need to obey the Laws that came through Moses as well, instead of dying to them. After all, what's the difference between Abraham and Moses? Were they not both servants of God, and doesn't the Bible say to teach the Law (Matthew 5:17-19)?

Yes, we're going to teach people what the Law says, and to literally follow the Law. That's what Jesus said to do according to the verses below, but don't allow that to confuse you. Many false teachers use the following passage to hold people under the Law, but the Bible says that "They do not know what they are talking about" (1 Timothy 1:3-11). Check the verses.

Matthew 5:19
19 Whoever therefore breaks one of the least of these commandments, and teaches men so, shall be called least in the kingdom of heaven; but whoever does and teaches them, he shall be called great in the kingdom of heaven. NKJV

How can we teach people to follow the Laws of Moses, and at the same time, teach them to die to the Laws of Moses?

We are not teaching everyone to die to the Law, but only Christians (Christ followers), who believe. If a believer, was following the Laws of Moses to the letter, he would obey the prophet in whom Moses spoke about in Deuteronomy 18:18-19 (below), once He came, which Peter identified as Jesus Christ according to Acts 3:22-23 (below).

Deuteronomy 18:18-19
18 I will raise up for them a Prophet like you from among their brethren, and will put My words in His mouth, and He shall speak to them all that I command Him. 19 And it shall be that whoever will not hear My words, which He speaks in My name, I will require it of him. NKJV

Acts 3:22-23
22 For Moses truly said to the fathers, 'The Lord your God will raise up for you a Prophet like me from your brethren. Him you shall hear in all things, whatever He says to you. 23 And it shall be that every soul who will not hear that Prophet shall be utterly destroyed from among the people.' NKJV

Therefore, even if we could follow all six hundred and something laws that make up the Laws of Moses, we would turn and follow Christ, now that He has come, since Deuteronomy 18:18-20 is indeed a part of the Laws of Moses. Therefore, anyone under the Law should now obey Jesus wholeheartedly, or he will be destroyed (verse 23 above).

That is exactly what will happen to those who continue in the Law in order to be justified by it after accepting Christ Jesus as Lord, which we have already mentioned in the last chapter (Galatians 5:1-4). They will fall away from grace, and be destroyed.

With the right interpretation, the whole Bible fits together like a hand in a glove. Praise God. However, with the wrong interpretation, people have to dodge entire sections of scripture because it doesn't support what they teach.

Jesus was the prophet to come, and Peter revealed Him to the people. Yes, Jesus is a prophet, but God made Jesus both Lord and Christ (Acts 2:36).

Acts 2:36
36 "Therefore let all the house of Israel know assuredly that God has made this Jesus, whom you crucified, both Lord and Christ." NKJV

To say that we need to die to the Law, is just a way of explaining what we would already know, if we were actually keeping the Law to the letter. Therefore, Christ is the end of the Law, but only for those who believe in the way Abraham believed.

Romans 10:4
4 For Christ is the end of the law for righteousness to every one that believeth. KJV

Many do not believe, but they claim that they are not under the Law, and many do believe, but they choose to remain under parts of the Law.

Those who are without Law, practice lawlessness, which means that they do not hold to any law. They will perish (verse 12 below, Matthew 13:40-43).

Those who remain under the Law, will be judged by the whole Law, and not just the bits and pieces they choose to keep (verses 12-13 below). Only those who fulfill the Law through faith in Jesus Christ are righteous (Romans 3:21-22), and they shall enter the Kingdom of Heaven (Matthew 5:20), and escape judgment (John 5:24, Romans 4:7-8).

Romans 2:12-13
12 For as many as have sinned without law shall also perish without law: and as many as have sinned in the law shall be judged by the law; 13 (For not the hearers of the law are just before God, but the doers of the law shall be justified. KJV

If, and only if we could keep all six hundred and something laws, would we be declared righteous, as a "doer of the Law" (verse 13 above), but now Christ has become our righteousness, if we believe Him as Abraham believed God (Romans 4:20-24).

Whatever the Law says, it says to those who remain under it, and by it, the whole world has become guilty before God (verse 19 below), because none of us can keep all of its requirements.

Romans 3:19
19 Now we know that what things soever the law saith, it

saith to them who are under the law: that every mouth may be stopped, and all the world may become guilty before God. KJV

I wish I could use as many verses from the New King James Bible as I needed to use in this book, for those who may not be able to understand some of the King James language, but I can only use one thousand verses by permission.

The bottom line is that people who remain under the Laws of Moses will be judged by the Laws of Moses. However, how can anyone not receive wrath under the Laws of Moses, when they have previously accepted "Jesus as Lord" in keeping with the new agreement? In other words, if we recognize Jesus as Lord, how could we go back to the very thing that led us to Christ?

Therefore, if a person does not believe Moses, he will not believe Jesus either, and that is why so many churches today remain under the Laws of Moses. They don't believe Moses, which is obvious because they only follow the parts of the Law that benefit them. If they followed the Law to the letter, they would turn and follow Christ.

John 5:46-47
46 For if you believed Moses, you would believe Me; for he wrote about Me. 47 But if you do not believe his writings, how will you believe My words?" NKJV

If a person does not believe Jesus, then God's Word will not remain (abide) in him (John 5:38). Therefore, show me a person who rejects Kingdom teaching found in the New Testament (Luke 16:16), and I will show you someone who will turn back to the only teaching that he will have living in him, which is the Old Testament Law (1 Timothy 1:6-11).

This is why many today only preach out of the Old Testament. If this describes you, simply repent of the past, and correct the problem. We serve a merciful God.

Christ is the end of the Law for those who believe in order that we may be righteous by faith. Notice in Romans 10:4 above, it says "For righteousness."

Righteousness is still required in order to be blessed, and not cursed. Before faith was revealed through the Gospel, the only way to be righteous was to obey all of the commands contained in the Laws of Moses (Deuteronomy 6:25, Romans 2:13 above).

No one could obey all of the commands that make up the Laws of Moses, and therefore, everyone fell short of God's blessings for obedience, hence the saying, "we have all fallen short" (verse 23 below). However, now that Christ has come, a new way of obtaining righteousness is "revealed in the Gospel" (Romans 1:16-17); God's righteousness.

Romans 3:21-23
21 But now the righteousness of God without the law is mani-fested, being witnessed by the law and the prophets; 22 Even

the righteousness of God which is by faith of Jesus Christ unto all and upon all them that believe: for there is no difference: 23 For all have sinned, and come short of the glory of God; KJV

This new way of righteousness is through faith in Jesus Christ to all who believe (verse 22 above). Instead of trying to obey six hundred and something commands in order to be righteous (right with God), now all we need is faith in Jesus Christ, and to believe as Abraham believed (verse 22 above).

Therefore, the first reason we are going to obey Jesus Christ is that the Law commands us to, now that He has come. Jesus Christ commands us to love one another, which will fulfill the Laws of Moses, as well as any other law (John 13:34-35, Romans 13:8-10).

The second reason why we are going to obey Jesus is because no one can keep the Laws of Moses, and therefore, no one can be righteous by observing it (Romans 2:13). Therefore, no one can receive God's blessing for righteousness, except through faith in Jesus Christ, which means that only those who have faith in Jesus will make it into the Kingdom of Heaven, now that He has come (verse 20 below).

Matthew 5:20
20 For I say to you, that unless your righteousness exceeds the righteousness of the scribes and Pharisees, you will by no means enter the kingdom of heaven. NKJV

Righteousness is still required to enter into Heaven, but we cannot be righteous by observing the Law. Therefore, as Christians (Christ followers), we are going to seek God's righteousness first place in our life (Matthew 6:33).

This new way of righteousness is apart (separate) from the Law (Romans 3:21 above), and it comes through faith in Jesus Christ to all who believe (Romans 3:22 above). We already know that faith in Jesus will produce love, since He commanded us to love one another, and we already know how to love, which we discussed in chapter 15. Love comes from a pure heart, good conscience, and sincere faith, but some people stray away from that (1 Timothy 1:5-6).

Those who reject this, end up under the Law, or lawless, and we have already discussed what happens to both. Those who teach, and reject this, end up becoming teachers of the Law, but the Bible says that "They do not know what they are talking about" (1 Timothy 1:6-7).

Get this. The Law is not made for a righteous person (1 Timothy 1:9), but for anyone who does not conform to the Gospel (1 Timothy 1:10-11). In other words, the Law is for the people who are "not" going to make it into the Kingdom of Heaven. If we could be righteous through the Law, then Christ died for nothing (verse 21 below).

Galatians 2:19-21
19 For I through the law died to the law that I might live to God.
20 I have been crucified with Christ; it is no longer I who live,
but Christ lives in me; and the life which I now live in the flesh I
live by faith in the Son of God, who loved me and gave Himself
for me. 21 I do not set aside the grace of God; for if righteous-
ness comes through the law, then Christ died in vain." NKJV

Through the Law, we die to the Law (verse 19 above), so that we can live to God through faith in Jesus Christ. Righteousness is still required in order to receive God's blessings for obedience, but instead of trying to be righteous through obeying the Law, now we can be righteous through faith in Jesus Christ, assuming that we believe as Abraham believed.

That is what is meant by the term, "but now" in Romans 3:21 above. That is the good news of the Gospel. Our only hope of returning to the glory of God is through faith in Jesus Christ (Romans 5:2). We have all fallen short, but Jesus is our way of returning.

Therefore, the purpose of the Law was to lead us to Christ.

Galatians 3:24-25
24 Wherefore the law was our schoolmaster to bring us unto
Christ, that we might be justified by faith. 25 But after that faith
is come, we are no longer under a schoolmaster. KJV

In my own words, the Law brought God's standard of living to light (knowledge of sin). With the Law in place, we cannot look at God and say that He is just like us. Yes, we are made in His image, but His ways are much higher than our ways, and none of us can even come close to living up to His ways.

Therefore, through the Law we recognize what sin is to God, and we realize that we don't measure up to His standards. In other words, we have all fallen short. No flesh will be justified by trying to keep the Law, since we are incapable of keeping it anyway (verse 20 below).

Romans 3:20
20 Therefore by the deeds of the law there shall no flesh be
justified in his sight: for by the law is the knowledge of sin.
KJV

Therefore, we all need Jesus Christ to save us from God's wrath, which is due us for trespassing, or breaking His Law. We were reconciled to God by the death of His Son, and justified by His blood, and now we are being saved through Him (Romans 5:9-10).

Some might ask, how can the Law lead us to Christ, when the Law was hundreds of years before Christ died for our sins?

Although Christ died for our sins many years after Moses' time, the Gospel was preached to Abraham long before the Law was given. Actually, the Gospel came first.

Galatians 3:8-9
8 And the Scripture, foreseeing that God would justify the Gentiles by faith, preached the gospel to Abraham beforehand, saying, "In you all the nations shall be blessed." 9 So then those who are of faith are blessed with believing Abraham. NKJV

The Gospel was preached to Abraham in advance by the "Scripture," or the Word itself (verse 8 above), Who would later become Jesus (John 1:14 below). That may be hard to understand unless you just accept what it says (hearing with faith). In the beginning was "the Word."

John 1:1-4
1 In the beginning was the Word, and the Word was with God, and the Word was God. 2 The same was in the beginning with God. 3 All things were made by him; and without him was not any thing made that was made. 4 In him was life; and the life was the light of men. KJV

John 1:14
14 And the Word was made flesh, and dwelt among us, (and we beheld his glory, the glory as of the only begotten of the Father,) full of grace and truth. KJV

All of those verses are speaking about the Word. The Word, was with God, and was God, and all things were made through "Him." Life is in "Him," and He, the Word Himself, became flesh in the person we know as Jesus Christ, the Son of God. Perhaps this verse will help.

John 8:57-58
57 Then said the Jews unto him, Thou art not yet fifty years old, and hast thou seen Abraham? 58 Jesus said unto them, Verily, verily, I say unto you, Before Abraham was, I am. KJV

Jesus was alive and well, long before He became the "Son of man." Imagine that. He was known as the Word, or the Scripture, and He came to earth in the flesh (1 John 4:2-3). Praise God, halleluiah!

That's one of the downfalls of some people today. They believe in Jesus, but they do not accept that the "Word became flesh." The same "Word" that was in the beginning, and was God, and was with God, became flesh (John 1:14 above).

For those of us who believe every Word of God, now we can see how important the Word is. The Word is Jesus, and Jesus is the Word. Therefore, the following verses basically say the same thing.

John 3:36

36 He who believes in the Son has everlasting life; and he who does not believe the Son shall not see life, but the wrath of God abides on him." NKJV

John 5:24

24 "Most assuredly, I say to you, he who hears My word and believes in Him who sent Me has everlasting life, and shall not come into judgment, but has passed from death into life. NKJV

John 6:53-54

53 Then Jesus said to them, "Most assuredly, I say to you, unless you eat the flesh of the Son of Man and drink His blood, you have no life in you. 54 Whoever eats My flesh and drinks My blood has eternal life, and I will raise him up at the last day. NKJV

Now you can see why it is irrational to think that we can believe in Jesus, but reject the Word. To reject the Word, is the same as rejecting Jesus. Anyone who does not believe Jesus' Word, does not have Jesus (the Word) abiding in them (John 5:38). Let us return to the Lord our God that He may have mercy on us.

At this point, many people begin to see how other scriptures work together. All the scriptures fit together. For example, "you shall know the truth, and the truth shall make you free" (John 8:31-32). Knowing the truth is knowing Jesus, since the truth does not remain in those who do not believe it (John 5:38).

In other words, only those who believe Kingdom teaching, can retain Kingdom teaching, and those who have the teachings living on the inside of them, do not speak against it.

The truth, living on the inside of us, can make us free from being a slave to sin (John 8:35-36). It sanctifies us (John 17:17). It works, all by itself, on the inside of those who believe it (1 Thessalonians 2:13). It is alive, and it can judge our attitudes and thoughts from within (Hebrews 4:12). Faith comes by hearing Jesus (Romans 10:17)! Amen.

In the same way, reading the Word to the point of retaining it will set us free from all kinds of sins that lead to death (Romans 1:28-32). It won't remain in us, if we do not believe it, and keep it (Matthew 13:18-23). Therefore, "if" what we hear remains in us, we will remain in the Father, and in the Son (1 John 2:24, 1 Corinthians 15:1-2). Praise God!

The Scripture ("He") preached the Gospel to Abraham in advance, but it was only revealed, or made known to us in the New Testament, or through what is known to us as the Gospel message (Romans 1:16-17, Colossians 1:26). We're going to receive the Gospel as he did, and do what he did.

By faith Abraham obeyed (verse 8 below). Does that sound familiar? Obedience comes from faith. By faith he dwelt in the land (verse 9 below). Abraham lived by faith, and therefore, when God told him to go, he went (Genesis 12:1-4).

Hebrews 11:8-10
8 By faith Abraham, when he was called to go out into a place which he should after receive for an inheritance, obeyed; and he went out, not knowing whither he went. 9 By faith he sojourned in the land of promise, as in a strange country, dwelling in tabernacles with Isaac and Jacob, the heirs with him of the same promise: 10 For he looked for a city which hath foundations, whose builder and maker is God. KJV

The Lord God promised Abraham that he, and his descendants, would inherit the land forever (Genesis 12:7, 13:15). However, only those of faith are children of Abraham (verse 7 below), and children of Abraham, do the works of Abraham (verse 39 below).

Galatians 3:7
7 Therefore know that only those who are of faith are sons of Abraham. NKJV

John 8:39
39 They answered and said to Him, "Abraham is our father." Jesus said to them, "If you were Abraham's children, you would do the works of Abraham. NKJV

Now you can probably see why it is important to believe as Abraham believed. Here again, people who say that they do not believe this book (Word), or that book in the Bible (Word) have no idea what they are speaking against. Basically, they are saying that they do not want to be a child of Abraham.

The promise that Abraham would be heir of the world was not through Law, but through the "righteousness of faith." That should sound familiar too.

Romans 4:13
13 For the promise, that he should be the heir of the world, was not to Abraham, or to his seed, through the law, but through the righteousness of faith. KJV

The Seed mentioned in verse 13 above is Christ (Galatians 3:16), and therefore, if we belong to Christ, then we are Abraham's seed, and heirs with him of the promise that he will inherit the world (verses 13 above, and 29 below).

Galatians 3:29
29 And if ye be Christ's, then are ye Abraham's seed, and heirs according to the promise. KJV

Romans 8:17
17 And if children, then heirs; heirs of God, and joint-heirs with Christ; if so be that we suffer with him, that we may be also glorified together. KJV

We will share in the glory, if we are willing to share in the sufferings. That should sound familiar too. That basically means that we must be willing to deny ourself, and be willing to suffer for righteousness (Philippians 1:29, Matthew 5:10-11).

We should be fellow heirs and partakers in the promise made to Abraham (verse 6 below). This is what was hidden for so many years, but has now been revealed through the Gospel.

Ephesians 3:5-6
5 Which in other ages was not made known unto the sons of men, as it is now revealed unto his holy apostles and prophets by the Spirit; 6 That the Gentiles should be fellowheirs, and of the same body, and partakers of his promise in Christ by the gospel: KJV

A few verses down from the ones above, the Apostle Paul prayed for the Ephesians that Christ (the Seed) would dwell in their heart by faith (verse 17 below), and that was his concern with the Galatians as well (Galatians 4:19-20), which we have already covered.

Ephesians 3:17
17 That Christ may dwell in your hearts by faith; that ye, being rooted and grounded in love, KJV

We need the same thing. We need Christ, Who is the Seed, living in our heart through faith. That way we will be Abraham's seed, and heirs according to the promise (Galatians 3:29 above). Christ on the inside of us, is our hope of glory (verse 27 below).

Colossians 1:26-27
26 Even the mystery which hath been hid from ages and from generations, but now is made manifest to his saints: 27 To whom God would make known what is the riches of the glory of this mystery among the Gentiles; which is Christ in you, the hope of glory: KJV

Does any of this sound like the Gospel you have heard? Many preach a message that is unwritten today, but we are the ones who promote, and push that message. May the Lord have mercy on all of us.

Father, in Jesus' name, have mercy upon us. Forgive us for not being all that You have called us to be. Forgive us for not preaching Your Word. We didn't know, and we followed those who were before us. In Your loving kindness, please have mercy on us. Your compassions they fail not. We need You to save us. Open our eyes so that we can see Your Word that we may turn and follow You. Forgive us for our great transgressions, and wash us clean with the blood of Jesus Christ our Lord. Amen.

Christ on the inside of us, is our hope of glory (verse 27 above). I have asked you this before, but it is so important, so I will ask it again. When will Christ make His home on the inside of us according to His Word?

John 14:21-24
21 He who has My commandments and keeps them, it is he who loves Me. And he who loves Me will be loved by My Father, and I will love him and manifest Myself to him." 22 Judas (not Iscariot) said to Him, "Lord, how is it that You will manifest Yourself to us, and not to the world?" 23 Jesus answered and said to him, "If anyone loves Me, he will keep My word; and My Father will love him, and We will come to him and make Our home with him. 24 He who does not love Me does not keep My words; and the word which you hear is not Mine but the Father's who sent Me. NKJV

To love Jesus is to love the Word (verses 21 and 23 above). I know that we were saved, which means that we were seated with Christ in His Kingdom according to Ephesians 2:6, and Colossians 1:13, and we have redemption through His blood (Colossians 1:14, 1 Peter 1:19), but Christ in us is our hope of glory (Colossians 1:27 above).

Faith in Jesus Christ will deliver us from darkness, and enable us to bear the right kind of fruit. By obeying Jesus' commands, we will abide in Him, and those who abide in Him stop sinning (1 John 3:6). Therefore, loving one another can be used as evidence of an inheritance.

Read the following passage of scripture, and take note of what the righteous are doing, and what they will receive in the end.

Matthew 25:34-46
34 Then shall the King say unto them on his right hand, Come, ye blessed of my Father, inherit the kingdom prepared for you from the foundation of the world: 35 For I was an hungred, and ye gave me meat: I was thirsty, and ye gave me drink: I was a stranger, and ye took me in: 36 Naked, and ye clothed me: I

was sick, and ye visited me: I was in prison, and ye came unto me.

37 Then shall the righteous answer him, saying, Lord, when saw we thee an hungred, and fed thee? or thirsty, and gave thee drink? 38 When saw we thee a stranger, and took thee in? or naked, and clothed thee? 39 Or when saw we thee sick, or in prison, and came unto thee? 40 And the King shall answer and say unto them, Verily I say unto you, Inasmuch as ye have done it unto one of the least of these my brethren, ye have done it unto me.

41 Then shall he say also unto them on the left hand, Depart from me, ye cursed, into everlasting fire, prepared for the devil and his angels: 42 For I was an hungred, and ye gave me no meat: I was thirsty, and ye gave me no drink: 43 I was a stranger, and ye took me not in: naked, and ye clothed me not: sick, and in prison, and ye visited me not.

44 Then shall they also answer him, saying, Lord, when saw we thee an hungred, or athirst, or a stranger, or naked, or sick, or in prison, and did not minister unto thee? 45 Then shall he answer them, saying, Verily I say unto you, Inasmuch as ye did it not to one of the least of these, ye did it not to me. 46 And these shall go away into everlasting punishment: but the righteous into life eternal. KJV

Father, in Jesus' name, have mercy upon us and forgive us for the sins we have committed against You. Many have followed delusional teachings today, and are way off course. Have mercy on us, forgive us, and open our eyes in order that we may clearly see and choose to follow You in accordance with Your Word. Send Your Word to heal us. Save us Lord! Amen.

Now what

Those who continue in Law, now that Christ has come, will not be heirs with those who live by faith (verse 14 below). Living by the Law is a guarantee of sickness and disease, since none of us can keep it. Therefore, Law brings God's wrath (verse 15 below).

Romans 4:13-15
13 For the promise, that he should be the heir of the world, was not to Abraham, or to his seed, through the law, but through the righteousness of faith. 14 For if they which are of the law

be heirs, faith is made void, and the promise made of none effect: 15 Because the law worketh wrath: for where no law is, there is no transgression. KJV

As you can see, faith and the Law are totally separate from each other, and they do not mix. Those who live by the Law will not be heirs with those who live by the righteousness of faith (verse 14 above).

There are three things that I want you to see in the passage of scripture above. The first is that the promise that Abraham would be heir of the world was through the righteousness of faith, and not through the Law (verse 13 above). We covered the righteousness of faith, which included being careful to speak with the Spirit of faith (2 Corinthians 4:13), which is basically believing and then speaking in-line with what the Bible says (Romans 10:6-8).

Now you can probably see why I wanted to teach believing as Abraham believed, mixing faith with what is promised, getting the instructions right, speaking in-line with the faith, and faith in Jesus Christ before we covered this.

If those teachings have not remained on the inside of you, then you probably would have skipped this chapter by now, and especially if you are still caught up in the ways of this world, which will keep you from understanding spiritual things.

Therefore, please read through this book again, being careful to read all of the verses out loud, and accept them as truth. Some of this may be hard to understand, but it is something that we all need to know, since it will keep us from being led away (Ephesians 4:13-14).

The second thing I want you to notice from the passage of scripture above, is that those who are of the Law will not be heirs with those of faith (verse 14 above). I wanted to mention it again because so many mix Law and faith.

We cannot add Law to the covenant God made with Abraham by promise (verses 15 and 18 below). The inheritance depends on a promise, and not the Law (verse 18 below). Therefore, know that in the end, those who remain under the Law will be judged by the Law, and no one can keep the whole Law (Romans 2:12, 3:19).

Galatians 3:15
15 Brethren, I speak in the manner of men: Though it is only a man's covenant, yet if it is confirmed, no one annuls or adds to it. NKJV

Galatians 3:18
18 For if the inheritance is of the law, it is no longer of promise; but God gave it to Abraham by promise. NKJV

The third is that Law brings wrath, since there is punishment for those who disobey the Law. Even if someone could keep 573 of the rules and regulations associated with the Law, they would still receive punishment for disobedience since the Law doesn't come in parts, but as a whole.

Imagine how many Christians today are expecting to be heirs with Christ, but instead they will receive wrath because they didn't follow the instructions. My wife and I want to reach as many as possible before it is too late.

Many people mix Law with grace. In other words, they obey parts of the Laws of Moses, and part of what faith in Jesus Christ requires of us; big mistake. Disobeying one command of the Law is the same as breaking all of them (James 2:8-10). What we end up with is a house full of sinners, who hug on each other once a week.

We fulfill the Law, which is to fully meet all of its requirements, through faith in Jesus Christ (Romans 10:8-10), and we have to die to the Law in order to stop sinning (Romans 15:14, 7:8). Therefore, show me a house full of Christ followers, who love according to the instructions found in the Bible, and I will show you a place where those who are righteous by faith dwell.

Not to mention, that obeying Jesus and dying to the Law, will bring healing to our body. I have seen it happen over and over again.

Father, in Jesus' name, have mercy upon us. Forgive us for speaking against Your Word, and taking a stand against those whom You have sent. Open our eyes that we may be able to see the things that we cannot see now, and open our mind that we may understand the scriptures. Cause in us what is pleasing to You, and create in us a desire to know You in accordance with Your Word. Forgive us for speaking against the faith, and now show us Your salvation. Amen.

I'm Alan Ballou; a servant. If you have any questions, please contact me.

www.HowToStopSinning.com

Alan's email alan@howtostopsinning.com

Lucie's email lucie@howtostopsinning.com

&⟊⟋

19

Spirit Controlled

ઠ୦ଓଃ

Believe it or not, our body is controlled by spirits. That's how we were created. A body without a spirit is a dead body (James 2:26).

James 2:26
26 For as the body without the spirit is dead, so faith without works is dead also. KJV

Each of us has our own spirit (1 Corinthians 2:11), but that is not the only spirit within us. An individual can house many different spirits, and these spirits can transfer from one person to the next, depending on the things that we say, or simply participate in.

I know that probably sounds silly to you, but allow me to give you a few examples.

Acts 16:16-18
16 Now it happened, as we went to prayer, that a certain slave girl possessed with a spirit of divination met us, who brought her masters much profit by fortune-telling. 17 This girl followed Paul and us, and cried out, saying, "These men are the servants of the Most High God, who proclaim to us the way of salvation." 18 And this she did for many days. But Paul, greatly annoyed, turned and said to the spirit, "I command you in the name of Jesus Christ to come out of her." And he came out that very hour. NKJV

Here is a woman who had a spirit of divination, which she used as a fortuneteller (verse 16 above). Many today believe that people, who have this same spirit, are prophets of God. Big mistake. Prophets of God can reveal the future, but it is for the purpose of teaching, instructing, convincing, convicting, judging, and building up the people of God (1 Corinthians 14:3-4, 12, 29-31, 1 Corinthians 2:15, Galatians 6:1-2).

Fortunetellers, psychics, mediums, people who practice witchcraft, and the like, work through evil spirits, and the spirits of dead people, which is an abomination to the Lord (Deuteronomy 18:10-14, Leviticus 20:27). Those who practice such things have no inheritance (Galatians 5:20), and will be cast into the lake of fire (Revelation 21:7-8).

If you have ever seen these people operate, you will notice that they only know what a dead relative may know about the person they are working with, or perhaps if any money is coming their way through the world system controlled by the devil.

However, the secrets of your heart can be revealed to a prophet of God (1 Corinthians 14:24-25). Therefore, he may know things about you that your spouse doesn't even know. At a glance, it could be revealed to him, who you really are (Luke 7:39), for the purpose of admonishing (warning), edification, or encouragement (1 Corinthians 14:24-25, 29-31).

The Apostle Paul cast the spirit of divination out of the girl mentioned above, and it came out (verse 18 above). Therefore, the ability the spirit gave the girl was gone, but God's gifts and callings are irrevocable (Romans 11:29), and "should" be used to serve the church (1 Peter 4:10-11, Romans 12:6-8, 1 Corinthians 14:12).

When I first learned about demons, I would try to cast one out of everything that moved. One day I tried to cast an evil spirit out of a pit bull that had almost bit me. I screamed at that dog for about thirty minutes, until I realized that many people had come out of their homes to watch me like a circus act. Looking back, I am grateful that his chain, and collar held. Thank You, Jesus!

Sometimes spirits enable people to do things, and sometimes they disable people. For example, the following passage describes a woman who had a spirit of infirmity, which produced a disability in her body (verse 11 below).

Luke 13:10-16
10 Now He was teaching in one of the synagogues on the Sabbath. 11 And behold, there was a woman who had a spirit of infirmity eighteen years, and was bent over and could in no way raise herself up. 12 But when Jesus saw her, He called her to Him and said to her, "Woman, you are loosed from your infirmity." 13 And He laid His hands on her, and immediately she was made straight, and glorified God.

14 But the ruler of the synagogue answered with indignation, because Jesus had healed on the Sabbath; and he said to the crowd, "There are six days on which men ought to work; therefore come and be healed on them, and not on the Sabbath day." 15 The Lord then answered him and said, "Hypocrite! Does not each one of you on the Sabbath loose his ox or donkey from the stall, and lead it away to water it? 16 So ought

not this woman, being a daughter of Abraham, whom Satan has bound — think of it — for eighteen years, be loosed from this bond on the Sabbath?" NKJV

Like it or not, our body can be controlled by spirits for good, or for evil. Evil spirits, or unclean spirits are known as demons (Mark 7:25-26). The evil spirit in the passage of scripture above, which was controlled by Satan, caused this woman to be bent over for eighteen years (verse 16 above).

Jesus took control of the woman's body by speaking (verse 12 above), and then He freed her through a method known as the "laying on of hands" (verse 13 above), which is considered an elementary teaching (Hebrews 6:1).

However, Jesus didn't just cast evil spirits out of people. He also "performed cures" through faith (Luke 13:32), and that is what we have mainly focused on in this book, since that is what most people need in this country, and it can be done in the comfort of our home.

Praise God, that He has allowed me to conduct many healing seminars, as well as attend them, and one thing is very obvious. On average, less than twenty percent of the people in this country receive healing through authority alone (casting out demons, Luke 10:19). The remaining need to be cured through repentance, and turning (Acts 20:21, 26:20).

This is usually the point where someone says, "Jesus healed everybody!" Actually, Jesus was sent to the house of Israel, and He even ignored a non-Jewish woman, at first, who wanted Him to cast a demon out of her daughter (Matthew 15:26-28).

At the beginning of His ministry, Jesus declared that the Spirit of the Lord was upon Him to preach the Gospel, heal the sick, free those who were held captive, restore sight to the blind, give liberty to the oppressed, and to proclaim the acceptable year of the Lord (Luke 4:17-19). If you only read Acts 10:38, you will miss a few of those.

The next thing to keep in mind is that Jesus pronounced a curse on the towns that did not receive His message, spoken by His disciples (Luke 10:10-16), who were sent out to preach the Gospel, cast out demons, and perform cures (Luke 9:1). Jesus declared, *"If the mighty works which were done in you were done in Tyre and Sidon, they would have repented long ago."* (verse 21 below, Luke 10:13).

Matthew 11:20-24
20 Then He began to rebuke the cities in which most of His mighty works had been done, because they did not repent: 21 "Woe to you, Chorazin! Woe to you, Bethsaida! For if the mighty works which were done in you had been done in Tyre and Sidon, they would have repented long ago in sackcloth and ashes. 22 But I say to you, it will be more tolerable for Tyre and Sidon in the day of judgment than for you. 23 And you,

Capernaum, who are exalted to heaven, will be brought down to Hades; for if the mighty works which were done in you had been done in Sodom, it would have remained until this day. 24 But I say to you that it shall be more tolerable for the land of Sodom in the day of judgment than for you." NKJV

One preacher told me that nobody had to repent before Jesus healed them, and that may be true, but according to the verses above, there will be plenty on the last day who wished they had.

People were not being set free from evil spirits, and cured so that they could keep living like they were living. The disciples preached the Kingdom of God, and called people to repentance, just as Jesus did (Luke 5:32). Those who received healing, but rejected the message were cursed, and the same is true to this day.

Jesus also declared that whoever heard His disciples, heard Him, but whoever rejected them, also rejected Him and the one Who sent Him (Luke 10:16). The towns that rejected His Word would not make it to Heaven, but they would be brought down to Hades (Luke 10:15). Imagine that.

The message hasn't changed, but we only quote the parts of it that we want to hear. After healing a man, who had an infirmity for thirty-eight years, Jesus told him to stop sinning, or something worse would come upon him.

John 5:14

14 Afterward Jesus findeth him in the temple, and said unto him, Behold, thou art made whole: sin no more, lest a worse thing come unto thee. KJV

That's a part of the doctrine of Jesus Christ that we don't want to hear, but we all need to know it. When we can see the big picture, it becomes obvious that Jesus didn't heal people so that they could continue living like they were living. Calling people to repentance goes hand in hand with healing.

As I have mentioned, it is far better to accept and believe the Word of God, than to chase miracles, and especially miracles where the Word of God is not being preached (2 Thessalonians 2:9-12). Love the truth first, and then seek to be healed. That is if you do not receive healing just by simply repenting of the past and turning.

Yes, Jesus did heal everyone during that acceptable time, and there is an acceptable time for us as well (2 Corinthians 6:1-2), when we get saved, but if we reject the Word of God, we are no better off than those who are cursed. We have to hold on to the Word that was preached, unless we have believed in vain (1 Corinthians 15:1-2).

Therefore, if a Christian needs to have an evil spirit (demon) cast out of them, they should consider repentance as well, especially if they have been saved for some time, and have heard the Word of God, but have not lived up to it. However, I have met some Christians who act like repentance is an ugly word, due to the false doctrines they have come to believe.

The Lord wants all people to come to repentance (2 Peter 3:9), and God requires it of everyone (Acts 17:30). Repentance from dead works is an elementary teaching, that every Christian should know (Hebrews 6:1).

Even if an evil spirit is cast out of a Christian, and the house (their body) is swept clean, by the Word (John 15:3, Ephesians 5:26), if the Word is then rejected, what will keep their body from being filled again with evil spirits?

Luke 11:24-26
24 "When an unclean spirit goes out of a man, he goes through dry places, seeking rest; and finding none, he says, 'I will return to my house from which I came.' 25 And when he comes, he finds it swept and put in order. 26 Then he goes and takes with him seven other spirits more wicked than himself, and they enter and dwell there; and the last state of that man is worse than the first." NKJV

Now you can see why many people experience a moment of healing, but soon afterwards they are worse than they were before they received the laying on of hands. Therefore, attend any healing seminar you want, but if all they are doing is casting out demons, only about two out of every ten people, at the most, will experience any type of healing, and from those people, many will soon have what was cast out of them return (verses 24-25 above).

Why can evil spirits return? The people have not made their body a home for Jesus, and they still continue in the ways of this world (John 14:21-23), which we have covered. When many hear that, they will begin to say things like, "I have been a Christian for this many years," and the like, but that is only evidence against them if they do not accept the doctrine of Jesus Christ.

I would not tell anyone that I have been a Christian for twenty years, if I didn't know anything about the teachings of Jesus, and especially if I rejected parts of His teachings. It's far better to say that I haven't lived up to it, and then repent of the past, than to use time served, or our position in the church as evidence of heading in the right direction.

Father, in Jesus' name, have mercy on us. We are not yet what we are supposed to be. Give us the grace needed to do Your will, and cause in us what is pleasing to You. Forgive our sins, and save us from our ignorance. Amen.

The Word makes us clean, but if we do not believe Jesus, the Word will not remain in us (John 5:38), and the love of God is not in the person who loves this world (1 John 2:15). Therefore, those who cast evil spirits out of unsuspecting people, who have no desire to do the will of God, only make them worse in the end.

Christians are astonished when an evil spirit is cast out of someone, and it is a great crowd builder. All of a sudden, they can do something that they haven't been able to do for years. Praise God that they have regained control over a part of their body, but their joy may be short-lived.

Once the evil spirit returns with seven more spirits more wicked than himself, they will be worse than they were to begin with (verse 26 above). For this reason, we should not be in a hurry to lay hands on anyone (1 Timothy 5:22).

If you have made your body a home for the spirits of this world, then casting them out is not going to do you any good if you do not offer your body to God as a living sacrifice (Romans 12:1-2). That begins by leaving the world's ways behind, and renewing your mind with the truth, which we have discussed in previous chapters.

I always tell people in the hospital to read the Word of God out loud, like it is more important than eating, but some look at me as if I am crazy. We don't know the truth, and it would take weeks to teach someone who is full of false teachings. God's people are destroyed for lack of knowledge (Hosea 4:6).

Interview people six months after they have had an evil spirit cast out of them, and then you will be able to see what I am talking about. The ones who remain healed, turned in some way as to re-enter the process of being sanctified by the Spirit, living up to what they have attained (Philippians 3:16). We may not all be at the same place in our faith, and that is why I used the word "process" (procedure, course, method).

The ones who did not change spiritually, will be worse than what they were to begin with. They may even have died from the same disease they were healed of months before.

The devil cannot touch those who stop sinning (1 John 5:18), and the Holy Spirit gives life to the body of those in which He remains (Romans 8:10-11). Therefore, the teachings we have covered in this book, will work for the people who have not received permanent healing by having an evil spirit cast out of them, and for those who have been healed, and don't want their problems to return (John 5:14).

Why do many people from Third World countries receive healing? Those who have not heard the Gospel, receive and understand it (Romans 15:20-21), but once the truth is suppressed in those countries, then they will not be any different than we are today (Matthew 23:15). Give it some time, and watch the effectiveness diminish, since we are already in the "falling away," or the great rebellion" as it is written in some Bibles (2 Thessalonians 2:3).

How can you tell that we are in the falling away? If you listen closely to teachings today, you will notice that very few of the conditions written in the Bible are being mentioned, because people do not want to hear them (2 Timothy 4:3-4). Most of what you will hear are promises made to people who are not in the position to receive what is promised. The Bible calls it, "great swelling words of emptiness" (2 Peter 2:18, Jude 1:16, Colossians 2:8).

That is what is predicted to happen, and so it should not be a surprise to you (2 Timothy 4:3-4, 3:8). The truth is being suppressed today, and this will lead to the falling away of most church-attending people.

A disciple will be like his teacher (Luke 6:40). If I have not taught you according to God's Word, you will not be God-like through my teachings. Think about that. If I suppress the truth, and teach you to suppress the truth, then we will end up among the unrighteous (Romans 1:18), and there is no room in Heaven for the unrighteous (Matthew 5:20).

God's Spirit gives life to the body that He dwells in (John 6:63) because of righteousness (verse 10 below). There is no such thing as a righteous person who does not believe the Word of God, or that doesn't live by faith, which includes every Word of God (Romans 1:17, Hebrews 11). The Word is the evidence that we place our faith in.

Romans 8:10-11
10 And if Christ is in you, the body is dead because of sin, but the Spirit is life because of righteousness. 11 But if the Spirit of Him who raised Jesus from the dead dwells in you, He who raised Christ from the dead will also give life to your mortal bodies through His Spirit who dwells in you. NKJV

Therefore, as the Word of God is increasingly suppressed, more and more Christians will be in need of healing unless we learn righteousness (Isaiah 26:10). Faith in Jesus makes us practice righteousness, to the point of becoming slaves of righteousness (Romans 6:16-18).

Those who do not practice righteousness remain children of the devil (verse 10 below), and are not born of God (1 John 2:29).

1 John 3:7-10
7 Little children, let no one deceive you. He who practices righteousness is righteous, just as He is righteous. 8 He who sins is of the devil, for the devil has sinned from the beginning. For this purpose the Son of God was manifested, that He might destroy the works of the devil. 9 Whoever has been born of God does not sin, for His seed remains in him; and he cannot sin, because he has been born of God. 10 In this the children of God and the children of the devil are manifest: Whoever does not practice righteousness is not of God, nor is he who does not love his brother. NKJV

How can we be righteous if we do not practice righteousness (verse 7 above)? We are imputed righteousness because we believe as Abraham believed (Romans 4:20-24), but if we were children of Abraham, we would do the works of Abraham (John 8:39).

In other words, believing as Abraham believed will lead us to placing faith in what God said, and placing faith in what God says will lead to obedience (Romans 1:5). Obedience leads to the righteousness of faith (Romans 6:16, James 2:20-24).

That's why 2 Corinthians 5:21 has the word "might" in it. Some people say that they are the righteousness of God, and I don't have a problem speaking words of faith over my life, but at some point we have to follow the Holy Spirit if we want that statement to come true.

Galatians 5:5
5 For we through the Spirit wait for the hope of righteousness by faith. KJV

Those who allow themselves to be led by the Spirit will obey (Romans 8:12-14). However, sometimes, we get off to a good start, obeying the Spirit, but then we get off-track along the way, and follow the teachings of those who speak with the spirit of error.

Those who follow the Spirit, put to death their sinful nature (Romans 8:12-14, Galatians 5:24). However, those who follow the spirit of error, deceiving spirits, and the doctrine of demons, will never put their flesh to death (1 Timothy 4:1-2).

Christ followers are dying to sins, and living for righteousness. They will be healed. Glory be to God. Now you will probably have a better understanding of 1 Peter 2:24 (below).

1 Peter 2:24
24 who Himself bore our sins in His own body on the tree, that we, having died to sins, might live for righteousness — by whose stripes you were healed. NKJV

The body may be dead because of sin, but the Spirit of God can indeed give life to our body (Romans 8:11 above). As I have mentioned before, God can heal anyone He wants to. However, if we die to sins and live for righteousness, He will heal us according to His Word.

Angels are spirits as well. They are ministering (helping, caring) spirits sent by God to help those who will inherit salvation (Hebrews 1:14).

Hebrews 1:14
14 Are they not all ministering spirits sent forth to minister for those who will inherit salvation? NKJV

The following passage of scripture is an example of an angel in bodily form, but not all spirits sent by the Lord are in bodily form. Some can even enter the mind of enemies to control what they say (2 Chronicles 18:20-22). Check the verses.

Acts 12:5-9
5 Peter therefore was kept in prison: but prayer was made

without ceasing of the church unto God for him. 6 And when Herod would have brought him forth, the same night Peter was sleeping between two soldiers, bound with two chains: and the keepers before the door kept the prison.

7 And, behold, the angel of the Lord came upon him, and a light shined in the prison: and he smote Peter on the side, and raised him up, saying, Arise up quickly. And his chains fell off from his hands. 8 And the angel said unto him, Gird thyself, and bind on thy sandals. And so he did. And he saith unto him, Cast thy garment about thee, and follow me. 9 And he went out, and followed him; and wist not that it was true which was done by the angel; but thought he saw a vision. KJV

There are many more examples of spirits in the Bible, who control those in whom they possess (own, hold, retain), for good, evil, illness, health, or simply just to carry out the will of God.

The devil controls the people of this world through the "spirit of disobedience." However, he cannot touch those who do not sin (1 John 5:18-19), as I have already mentioned. God has no problem whatsoever with protecting us from the evil one (2 Thessalonians 3:3-4). Our sins are what give us over (1 John 5:18).

Once we serve sin, we become a slave to sin, but if we obey, we become a slave to righteousness (Romans 6:16). Therefore, once we sin, we will be controlled spiritually to sin again through the spirit of disobedience (verse 2 below).

Ephesians 2:2-3
2 in which you once walked according to the course of this world, according to the prince of the power of the air, the spirit who now works in the sons of disobedience, 3 among whom also we all once conducted ourselves in the lusts of our flesh, fulfilling the desires of the flesh and of the mind, and were by nature children of wrath, just as the others. NKJV

The spirit of disobedience, made all of us disobey at one time (verse 3 above). It still controls the people of this world, and the sons of disobedience today (verse 2 above), making them "fulfill the desires of their flesh and of their mind" (verse 3 above).

I call it the spirit of disobedience because those who are controlled by it, disobey. Many times in the Bible, spirits are named by what they do; Spirit of truth, spirit of infirmity, evil spirit, deceiving spirit, etc. The Bible calls it the prince of the power of air, or the spirit who works in the sons of disobedience (verse 2 above). Therefore, I describe it as the spirit of disobedience.

The spirit of disobedience will make us bear fruit unto death. That's what we were doing before God saved us, and that is what the "sons of disobedience" are doing today, since the good they may want to do, they will not be in the position to carry it out because they disobey the message.

We were all controlled in that way at one time; fulfilling the desires of our body (flesh), and our mind in accordance with the ways of this world (verse 3 above). That sums up what the people of this world are doing, but they do not know that it is a spirit that is making them do it.

What will a person, who is controlled by the Holy Spirit, do? When Jesus was anointed with the Holy Spirit what did He do?

Acts 10:38
38 how God anointed Jesus of Nazareth with the Holy Spirit and with power, who went about doing good and healing all who were oppressed by the devil, for God was with Him. NKJV

Among other things, He went about doing good, and that is exactly what we will do if we are controlled by the Holy Spirit, Who puts the love of God in our heart.

Romans 5:5
5 Now hope does not disappoint, because the love of God has been poured out in our hearts by the Holy Spirit who was given to us. NKJV

When the Holy Spirit places the love of God in our heart, we will love one another, which is the evidence that the love of God is in us (verse 17 below). In doing so, the Holy Spirit helps us achieve what Jesus commanded us to do (John 13:34-35, 14:16).

1 John 3:17
17 But whoever has this world's goods, and sees his brother in need, and shuts up his heart from him, how does the love of God abide in him? NKJV

How does the love of God abide (remain) in a person's heart if they have this world's goods, and see their brother in need, but do not have compassion on him? It doesn't. People of this world are not going to do good, unless there is something in it for them in return (Luke 6:32-34, Matthew 6:1-4).

When I was first controlled by the Spirit, I didn't know what was happening to me. I literally started chasing homeless people on the street, trying to buy their lunch, and stopping on the interstate to help perfect strangers replace flat tires. I was looking for any, and every opportunity to help someone (Galatians 6:9-10).

If I saw someone walking, I would give them a ride. I almost got mugged doing that, but the Lord rescued me. God, Who called us to work for His own purpose (2 Timothy 1:9), is the same God who can protect us from evil (2 Thessalonians 3:3). Praise be to the Lord our God forever, and ever. Amen.

All I wanted to do was to help someone and to read my Bible. That's all I had any interest in doing. I stopped participating in many other activities which I had enjoyed before, such as playing tennis, because I no longer had any interest in them.

I was washed, and renewed by the Holy Spirit (Titus 3:5). Therefore, the desires living in me that fulfilled what the spirit of disobedience was making me participate in were gone. He healed me of my oppression (domination), and made me free in Christ to do His will. Praise God, halleluiah!

However, I didn't know what was going on. I was beginning to think that something was wrong with me, since so many people told me that it was not normal to just stop hanging out with friends, and leaving everything I had previously enjoyed in life. I couldn't explain it either, but I was very happy with what I was doing.

A definite sign that the love of God is "not" in us, is that we love this world (verse 15 below). In other words, if there is no difference between how we live, and how the people of this world live, then we are definitely being controlled by the spirit of disobedience.

1 John 2:15
15 Do not love the world or the things in the world. If anyone loves the world, the love of the Father is not in him. NKJV

That doesn't mean that we didn't get saved. However, for one reason or another, we have returned to, or even remained under the control of the spirit of disobedience, which makes us fulfill the desires of our flesh (body) and of our mind (Ephesians 2:3 above).

If you have suddenly stopped doing the things of this world, and have randomly begun helping people you would not normally help, without receiving anything in return, then you have experienced a good dose of God's grace. Grace itself teaches us to deny worldly desires (verse 12 below). Many Christian don't realize this.

Titus 2:11-15
11 For the grace of God that brings salvation has appeared to all men, 12 teaching us that, denying ungodliness and worldly lusts, we should live soberly, righteously, and godly in the present age, 13 looking for the blessed hope and glorious appearing of our great God and Savior Jesus Christ, 14 who gave Himself for us, that He might redeem us from every lawless deed and purify for Himself His own special people, zealous for good works. 15 Speak these things, exhort, and rebuke with all authority. Let no one despise you. NKJV

He redeemed us from the lawless deeds that we used to participate in, and made us zealous (on fire) for good works (verse 14 above). That is what the Holy Spirit, Who places the love of God in our heart, will make us do (Titus 3:3-7, Romans 5:5).

Be careful, because we can be talked out of doing what we are supposed to be doing. Actually, we can even reach a point spiritually that we think that we are all God wants us to be, and leave good works behind, but listen to this warning that Jesus gave to the church at Ephesus, who did not continue in the first works, which are the deeds they did at first.

Revelation 2:1-5
1 Unto the angel of the church of Ephesus write; These things saith he that holdeth the seven stars in his right hand, who walketh in the midst of the seven golden candlesticks;

2 I know thy works, and thy labour, and thy patience, and how thou canst not bear them which are evil: and thou hast tried them which say they are apostles, and are not, and hast found them liars: 3 And hast borne, and hast patience, and for my name's sake hast laboured, and hast not fainted.

4 Nevertheless I have somewhat against thee, because thou hast left thy first love. 5 Remember therefore from whence thou art fallen, and repent, and do the first works; or else I will come unto thee quickly, and will remove thy candlestick out of his place, except thou repent. KJV

As you can see, it is easy to get so caught up in spiritual stuff, and forget about, or diminish the good works that the Spirit is leading us to do, which is for our benefit. Only a slave to righteous acts is set free from sin (Romans 6:15-18).

Now you can see how a church full of people, who are doing what is right, may even remain under sin. Their good works (acts of righteousness) have diminished, and if we continue in sins, all of our righteous acts become filthy rags (Isaiah 64:5-6).

Isaiah 64:5-6
5 You meet him who rejoices and does righteousness, Who remembers You in Your ways. You are indeed angry, for we have sinned — In these ways we continue; And we need to be saved. 6 But we are all like an unclean thing, And all our righteousnesses are like filthy rags; We all fade as a leaf, And our iniquities, like the wind, Have taken us away. NKJV

The Lord loves those who pursue righteousness (Proverbs 15:9). He rejoices over those who do righteousness, and remember His ways, but He is angry with those who continue in sin (verse 5 above). Yes, the face of the Lord is against those who do evil (1 Peter 3:12). Acts of righteousness are not an excuse to continue in sin. Our sins (iniquities) take us away (verse 6 above).

Now what

I heard one preacher ask, "How many good works is enough?" As many as it takes to remain under the leadership of the Holy Spirit, without grieving Him (Ephesians 4:30), insulting Him (Hebrews 10:29), or resisting His leadership (Acts 7:51). I would say that amount would be enough. Wouldn't you?

It's not a matter of how many good works, but are we being led by the Holy Spirit? If we are led by the Spirit, He determines how much, when, where, how, and so on. We just follow, since those who are led by the Holy Spirit, are the true sons of God.

Romans 8:14
14 For as many as are led by the Spirit of God, they are the sons of God. KJV

When people continually speak against the faith, the parts they speak against will not remain in them, which we have already discussed (1 Timothy 6:20-21). Salvation is a gift, but not like an earthly gift. Salvation is a gift that we have to do something with.

Can we neglect our salvation, instead of working it out through obedience according to Hebrews 2:3 and Philippians 2:12? Yes, we can. Can we receive the grace of God in vain according to 2 Corinthians 6:1? Yes, we most certainly can. Can we believe in vain according to 1 Corinthians 15:1-2?

Consequently, according to the Word of God, we can have salvation, receive grace, and believe, all to no avail. Who would want you to believe otherwise? Accept and believe what the Bible says, and reject those who follow deceiving spirits until they repent.

Our concern should be if a person is being led by the Holy Spirit (Galatians 5:25), and not necessarily what the Holy Spirit is making them do, or how much they are doing. We should be encouraging Christians to "be careful to maintain good works," according to the Word of the Lord written in Titus 3:8, and Titus 3:14, rather than questioning their actions as if they are headed in the wrong direction.

Titus 3:8
8 This is a faithful saying, and these things I want you to af-firm constantly, that those who have believed in God should be careful to maintain good works. These things are good and profitable to men. NKJV

Christians who do not practice righteous acts, are the ones who are headed in the wrong direction (verse 10 below). Those are the ones that we need to try and reach with the truth, just as Jesus warned the Ephesians in Revelation 2:1-5 above.

1 John 3:10

10 In this the children of God and the children of the devil are manifest: Whoever does not practice righteousness is not of God, nor is he who does not love his brother. NKJV

I have noticed over the past few years that when someone starts doing what the Holy Spirit wants all of us to do, that's when a seemingly spiritual person comes along and says something like, "You can't earn your salvation," as if that is what we are trying to do. That is correct, we can't earn our salvation, but at the same time, we can't refuse to follow the Holy Spirit either (Hebrews 3:7-19).

The Word of God tells us to be careful to maintain good works (verse 8 above), and that is what we are doing. Therefore, we're living by faith, and not by a man's doctrine. We are not keeping up with the amount, because we want our reward from Heaven, and not from men (Matthew 6:1-4).

However, if someone insists on an amount, tell them that "He who has been forgiven much, loves much" (Luke 7:47). Maybe then, they will want to receive the grace of God, and be led by the Holy Spirit, rather than by deceiving spirits (1 Timothy 4:-12).

Our instructions do not say to keep up with the amount of good works. If we are still caught up in sins that lead to death, then obviously there may be a problem with the amount, or perhaps we are not mixing faith with Matthew 6:1-4, which means that the good works we are doing are being used for our own glory.

If our faith isn't producing the right results, we need to examine ourself to make sure that we are in the faith (2 Corinthians 13:5). We need to double-check the instructions.

Those who obey Jesus come out of darkness (1 John 2:8-10), pass from death to life (1 John 3:14-15), abide in Jesus (John 15:10), and consequently, they stop sinning (1 John 3:6). Glory be to God! The proof that we are doing what we are supposed to be doing is in the results, and not in the amount.

Therefore, how many good works is enough? We will know that it is enough when we fulfill the Laws of Moses (Romans 13:8-10), in order that we will be a part of the bride of Christ (Romans 7:4-8). Those who are led by the Holy Spirit, will not be under the Laws of Moses (Galatians 5:18).

We will know that it is enough when we stop stumbling, and consequently, we will receive a rich welcome into the eternal Kingdom of our Lord and Savior (2 Peter 1:10-11). The predicted results should reveal the correct amount, since these things require that we love in the way we have previously described. Let us return to the Lord our God in accordance with His Word.

My question in return is, "How can a person be sealed with the Holy Spirit, and be guaranteed an inheritance if they reject the truth, that is written in the Bible?" We can only be "sealed in the Holy Spirit" after we "hear" the truth contained in the Gospel and "believe" it (verses 13-14 below).

Ephesians 1:13-14
13 In Him you also trusted, after you heard the word of truth, the gospel of your salvation; in whom also, having believed, you were sealed with the Holy Spirit of promise, 14 who is the guarantee of our inheritance until the redemption of the purchased possession, to the praise of His glory. NKJV

There is no such thing as a person who is guaranteed an inheritance, that doesn't believe God's Word, and there is no such thing as a righteous person who does not believe God as Abraham believed (Romans 4:20-24). Holding to the teachings is a part of the Gospel message that we should be preaching (2 Thessalonians 2:13-15, 3:14, 1 Corinthians 15:1-2, John 8:31-32).

Therefore, if the Bible says that we need to "Be careful to maintain good works" (verse 8 above), but because of greed, someone decides to reject that and speak against it, can he possibly be led by the Holy Spirit? No, that's evidence of a deceiving spirit being in the lead. Preach the Word (2 Timothy 4:1-4)!

The Spirit, Who is the truth (John 6:63), is not going to lead us into speaking against Himself. That would be a deceiving spirit doing that, which many will follow in the last days (1 Timothy 4:1-2).

Did Abraham believe part of what God said, or everything He said? Did he take a stand against what God said? Children of Abraham do the works of Abraham, and the children of the devil, do the works of the devil (John 8:37-47).

A person who does not believe God, cannot be following the Holy Spirit's lead. Therefore, show me someone who speaks against the verses written in the Bible, and I will show you someone who needs to repent, turn, and follow the right Spirit. Let us repent and return to the Lord our God.

Father, in the name of Jesus Christ, our hope is in You. Through Your mercies we are not consumed. Great is Your faithfulness. Through Your great compassion, and according to Your abundant mercies, forgive us our sins. We have not known Your Word, and we have placed it aside. Have mercy on us. Forgive us for following the spirit of disobedience, and now cause in us what is pleasing to You through the power of Your Holy Spirit. Let Your grace rain down upon us that we may now walk in Your ways, to the glory of Your holy name. Amen.

I'm Alan Ballou; a servant. If you have any questions, please contact me.

www.HowToStopSinning.com

so)cs

The entire Christian life is lived by faith from start to finish (Romans 1:17). In other words, we were saved through faith, and now we are expected to continue in our faith, to the point of living by faith.

Alan Ballou

20

If By the Spirit

⟅⟆

To begin with, we called on the name of our Lord Jesus Christ to save us, and believed in our heart that God raised Him from the dead (Romans 10:9). Praise God, halleluiah!

By simply confessing that Jesus Christ is the Son of God, God will abide in us and give us the help we need (1 John 4:15). He, Himself will teach us to love one another (1 Thessalonians 4:9).

When God had mercy on us in Christ, He poured out the Holy Spirit upon us (verse 6 below). There is no other way that a person of this world can be freed from the power of darkness, and stop the spirit of disobedience from controlling him, except through calling on the name of Jesus Christ our Lord (Acts 4:12).

Titus 3:3-7
3 For we ourselves were also once foolish, disobedient, deceived, serving various lusts and pleasures, living in malice and envy, hateful and hating one another. 4 But when the kindness and the love of God our Savior toward man appeared, 5 not by works of righteousness which we have done, but according to His mercy He saved us, through the washing of regeneration and renewing of the Holy Spirit, 6 whom He poured out on us abundantly through Jesus Christ our Savior, 7 that having been justified by His grace we should become heirs according to the hope of eternal life. NKJV

According to God's mercy, He justified us by His grace (verse 7 above). Therefore, God enabled us to accept Jesus as Lord (John 6:44). He purchased us (1 Corinthians 6:20), and made us alive in Christ, even while we were dead (Ephesians 2:1).

The blood of Jesus Christ, not only redeemed us from the transgressions (sins) committed under the first covenant (Hebrews 9:15), but He also redeemed us from the way we were living before we were saved (1 Peter 1:18, Colossians 1:13-14).

Therefore, we have been purchased, saved, delivered, redeemed, given the faith we need (Ephesians 2:8), and given the help we need in order to live the life we have been called to live. Glory to God, halleluiah! Our part is simply to continue in what He has given us (Colossians 1:21-23, Romans 11:22), but we are not forced to continue.

Notice that verse 7 above says that "We should become heirs." God poured out His Spirit on us, so that with His help, we would put to death the misdeeds of the body, rather than continue living in sin (verse 13 below).

The wage that sin pays is death, but the gift of God that we have been given is eternal life in Christ Jesus our Lord (Romans 6:23). We can do one, or the other, but if by the Spirit, we put to death the deeds of our body, we will live (verse 13 below).

Romans 8:12-14
12 Therefore, brethren, we are debtors — not to the flesh, to live according to the flesh. 13 For if you live according to the flesh you will die; but if by the Spirit you put to death the deeds of the body, you will live. 14 For as many as are led by the Spirit of God, these are sons of God. NKJV

We are debtors to live according to the Holy Spirit (verse 12 above). In other words, we should allow the Holy Spirit to lead us into living a holy life. We were not saved from our former way of life, so that we could remain that way, but that we should walk in the new way (Romans 6:4-6, 1 Peter 2:9).

We owe our life to Jesus. One died for all that those who live should no longer live for themself, but for Him who died (2 Corinthians 5:15). That's a total commitment, and not a "make time for Jesus every now and then" sort of thing.

If we allow ourself to be controlled by the Spirit, we will put to death the deeds of our flesh (verse 13 above), and receive the righteousness that is by faith in Jesus Christ, through the Spirit (Romans 3:21-22, Galatians 5:5, James 2:20-24).

How are we going to do that? We are going to continue in the faith that we were given. The entire Christian life is lived by faith from start to finish (Romans 1:17). In other words, we were saved through faith, and now we live by faith.

We were given the faith we needed to be saved (Ephesians 2:6), but we are not forced to live by faith after we are saved. However, we are expected to continue in the faith that we have been given (Romans 12:3), in order to remain holy in God's sight (Colossians 1:21-23).

If we continue to live by the faith we were given, then we will grow it (2 Thessalonians 1:3), abound in it (2 Corinthians 8:7), increase it (Romans 10:17, 2 Corinthians 10:15), and pursue it, now that we are saved (1 Timothy 6:11, 2 Timothy 2:22), to the point of continually living by faith (Romans 1:17).

The just, or the righteous person, as it is written in some Bibles, will live by faith. In other words, the people who are justified, and those who remain justified in God's eyes, live by faith (Hebrews 10:37-39, Galatians 2:20, 3:11, 2

Corinthians 5:7).

If we refuse to live by faith, or continue in our faith after we are saved, we will end up with weak faith (Romans 14:1-3), dead faith (James 2:14-17), or even shipwrecked faith (1 Timothy 1:18-19), all the while thinking that everything is okay. This can especially happen if we are in a group of Christians, who teach us that it is okay to ignore our conscience.

When some of us hear "gift of God," we immediately think in terms of a worldly gift, and we use philosophy in our interpretation of what receiving a gift means, in order to explain it. That's not the case with those who live by faith. Faith includes the evidence of things not seen (Hebrews 11:1). Therefore, we gladly receive the gift of God, but we also allow the Word of God to explain what we are supposed to do with it.

Salvation is a gift, but salvation is a gift that we have to do something with. We can neglect our salvation, according to Hebrews 2:3. That means that we can throw it away, or refuse to work it out so to speak, as it is written in Philippians 1:12. Know that for yourself, because false teachers will never mention it.

If we continue in our faith, then we will follow the Spirit. If we follow the Spirit, then we will obey Jesus Christ.

Jesus commanded us to love one another (John 13:34-35), which is not optional, and when the Holy Spirit places the love of God in our heart, that is exactly what we will do. The same Jesus we called on to save us, has informed us that He actually chose us, and has appointed us to do something for Him (verses 16-17 below).

John 15:16-17
16 You did not choose Me, but I chose you and appointed you that you should go and bear fruit, and that your fruit should remain, that whatever you ask the Father in My name He may give you. 17 These things I command you, that you love one another. NKJV

We didn't just decide to come to Jesus one day, but God enabled us to come to Him (John 6:44), for His own special purpose (2 Timothy 1:9). Think of it this way. We were plucked, so to speak, out of death, and made alive in Christ to love whom He wants us to love, in a way that He wants us to love them.

Afterwards, He will give us what we ask the Father in His name (verses 16-17 above). Imagine that.

To recap, we were dead, and we called on Jesus Christ to save us. God made us alive, put His love in our heart, gave us the faith we need in order to live the Christian life, and He gave us a Helper to help us. At that point, all we had to do was obey Jesus. What happened?

If you were like me, then you didn't know any of this when you accepted Jesus as the Lord of your life because it's not being taught. That's probably the reason why you are reading this book. Praise God!

Now that we know the truth, we need to know a few things about love. Love comes from a pure heart, good conscience, and sincere faith (verse 5 below).

1 Timothy 1:3-5
3 As I urged you when I went into Macedonia — remain in Ephesus that you may charge some that they teach no other doctrine, 4 nor give heed to fables and endless genealogies, which cause disputes rather than godly edification which is in faith. 5 Now the purpose of the commandment is love from a pure heart, from a good conscience, and from sincere faith, NKJV

Therefore, if we are going to continue obeying what Jesus commanded us to do, then we are going to need to develop an uncontaminated heart, a blameless conscience, and a genuine faith.

In other words, we're going to fill our heart with the pure Word of God, as the Spirit leads us into all truth (John 16:13), unless of course we refuse to follow the Spirit. We're going to keep our conscience clear before God (1 Peter 3:21), allowing His Word to be the judge of our life (Hebrews 4:12), unless of course we reject parts of the Word of God.

We're going to do whatever it takes in order to remain in the faith (Colossians 1:21-23). However, we have to fight the good fight of faith, or wage the good warfare, in order to remain in the faith, which includes keeping a clear conscience toward God.

1 Timothy 1:18-19
18 This charge I commit to you, son Timothy, according to the prophecies previously made concerning you, that by them you may wage the good warfare, 19 having faith and a good conscience, which some having rejected, concerning the faith have suffered shipwreck NKJV

Therefore, if we are going to obey Jesus, now that we have been given everything we need to do so, we are going to fight against the desires of our flesh, which have been used in the past to satisfy the spirit of disobedience. We are going to remain in the faith at all cost, and we are going to repent if we do not remain in it. It's just that simple.

For example, the Word of God tells us to forgive everyone (Matthew 6:14-15). If that verse is living on the inside of us (pure heart), then we are "not" going to deny that it exists or reject it (clear conscience toward God), but we are going to do whatever we need to do in order to forgive everyone (genuine faith).

If Matthew 6:14-15 is not living in us, then as we renew our mind with the truth, we will forgive everyone. The Spirit will lead us into all truth, so it's just a matter of time, if we continue in our faith. When we eventually read that verse, and decide not to forgive, the Spirit will convict us of sin (John 16:8).

Consequently, we will no longer have a good conscience, which means that we will no longer be able to remain in love, which means that we will no longer be able to bear the right type of fruit (John 15:4-6). At this point, we need to repent, and ask God our Father to forgive us for our sin (or sins), in the name of Jesus Christ. If we confess our sins, He will forgive us and cleanse us from all unrighteousness (1 John 1:9).

Father, in Jesus' name, You alone are worthy of praise, glory, and honor, forever and ever. Have mercy upon us. Forgive us for the sins that we have committed against You, and wash our conscience clean from acts that lead to death, that we may serve You with a clear conscience this day, in the mighty name of Jesus Christ. Amen!

That is how the Christian life is supposed to work. Maybe you didn't know that before now, or perhaps you have some issues that you need a little help with, but either way, learn what we have just covered for yourself. My wife and I will help you, Lord willing, but we cannot learn the scriptures for you.

Now that we know we need a clear conscience, how do we get one? We repent of the past, and ask God our Father, in the name of Jesus Christ, to wash our conscience clean with the blood of Jesus! Amen.

Hebrews 9:13-14
13 For if the blood of bulls and goats and the ashes of a heifer, sprinkling the unclean, sanctifies for the purifying of the flesh, 14 how much more shall the blood of Christ, who through the eternal Spirit offered Himself without spot to God, cleanse your conscience from dead works to serve the living God? NKJV

The blood of Jesus Christ washes our conscience clean from acts that lead to death. Praise God, halleluiah! Blessed be the Lord God almighty, Who is able!

We get all that old junk (sins) cleansed out of our mind with the blood of Jesus, and then we serve God with a clean and clear conscience (Hebrews 10:2). Praise God.

When I minister to Christians, who are caught up in sins that they cannot get out of their head, I have them pray Psalm 51 daily, out loud, and on their knees, until their conscience is clear. This is the prayer that David used after being with Bathsheba. If this describes you, pray all of it, except the last two verses.

After we obtain a clear conscience, we need to fight to keep it clear. Sinful desires make war against us, in our mind (1 Peter 2:11).

For example, sins like adultery don't have to be physical (verse 28 below), but it can also be committed in the mind. However, it will eventually lead to some form of physical action, since once we sin, we become a slave to our sinful nature (Romans 6:16). Just about any body part can be used as an instrument of unrighteousness, or righteousness, depending on who we choose to serve (Romans 6:13).

Matthew 5:27-30
27 "You have heard that it was said to those of old, 'You shall not commit adultery.' 28 But I say to you that whoever looks at a woman to lust for her has already committed adultery with her in his heart. 29 If your right eye causes you to sin, pluck it out and cast it from you; for it is more profitable for you that one of your members perish, than for your whole body to be cast into hell. 30 And if your right hand causes you to sin, cut it off and cast it from you; for it is more profitable for you that one of your members perish, than for your whole body to be cast into hell. NKJV

Saved people are alive from the dead (Colossians 2:13). In other words, we were dead in our trespasses and sins in which we used to live according to the ways of this world (Ephesians 2:1-3).

Since God has made us alive in Christ, we should "not" return to live like the people of this world, but offer our body parts to God as instruments of righteousness, unless we want to be dead again (2 Peter 2:20-22).

Therefore, instead of looking at things that promote desires, such as sexual desires, we have been given the power to say "no" and to offer our eyes to God as an instrument of righteousness (Romans 6:1-7).

How do we do that? If we offer our eyes to God as an instrument of righteousness, then we would start using our eyes to read scripture as much as possible, and reduce or cut out altogether watching anything that is not godly. If your right eye causes you to sin, stop it (verse 29 above).

Remember that whatever we offer ourself to, it will in turn be what can control us for good or for evil (Romans 6:16). It's either things of the Spirit, or things of the flesh. There isn't anything wrong with playing checkers, but if that prevents us from following the Spirit during the day, then it is against us. If our right hand causes us to sin, stop it (verse 30 above).

Some Christians believe that all they need is more grace, which we all do, but even grace teaches us to say no to ungodly lusts (Titus 2:11-14). We should cry out to the Lord our God, that we may receive more grace in our time of need (Hebrews 4:16), but we also need to be careful not to receive grace in vain (2 Corinthians 6:1). Therefore, as we receive grace, let us offer our hands, our feet, and our whole body as instruments of righteousness (Romans 6:13).

If our left foot causes us to sin, then we need to confess our sins, ask for more grace, and somehow use that left foot as an instrument of righteousness. The same goes for our ears, arms, and any other body part.

Righteousness can control us, just as sin can control us (Romans 6:20-22). Therefore, that same right eye, or left foot that has been leading us into sin, needs to be offered to God as an instrument of righteousness. Volunteering to help Christians who are in need would be a good example.

Whatever body part is causing the problem, needs to be dealt with ASAP, in order to always keep a clear conscience before God, being careful not to reject what is written. In other words, we should always allow the Word of God to be the judge of our attitudes and thoughts (Hebrews 4:12).

Hebrews 4:12
12 For the word of God is living and powerful, and sharper than any two-edged sword, piercing even to the division of soul and spirit, and of joints and marrow, and is a discerner of the thoughts and intents of the heart. NKJV

The Apostle Paul, attempted to always keep a clear conscience toward God, and we should do the same (Acts 24:16). Love will only come from a pure heart, good conscience, and sincere faith (1 Timothy 1:5 above).

As the Word is increasing on the inside of us, assuming that we are in the process of renewing our mind with the truth (Romans 12:1-2), we will begin to hear verses in our conscience. This should be used like a tool to change our behavior as we go throughout our day.

Therefore, rather than repenting of things after they happen, we will eventually use the Word of God, living on the inside of us, to "prevent sin" from happening. Any sin that we can prevent, will start in our mind as a desire or a lust.

The reason I'm mentioning the sins that we "can" prevent is because if we are not free from indwelling sin, or if we have been given over to sin's control, by serving our sinful nature, with our eyes, hands, or feet, then we will not be able to stop the sins that come as a result of those conditions, which we have covered.

Once we sin, we become a slave to sin, but if we obey, we will become a slave of righteousness, or righteous acts (Romans 6:15-18). We have already discussed those things throughout this book, and I would advise you to keep reading the verses until they are living on the inside of you.

When we are free from sin's control, then we are ready to fight sin before it starts in our mind. At this point, God will not allow us to be tempted into sinning beyond what we can stand up against (1 Corinthians 10:13).

Therefore, we have to learn how to choose God's way out of the temptation before we choose sin, and that can only be accomplished in our thoughts (verse 14 below). That's another reason for keeping a clear conscience.

James 1:14-15
14 But each one is tempted when he is drawn away by his own desires and enticed. 15 Then, when desire has conceived, it

gives birth to sin; and sin, when it is full-grown, brings forth death. NKJV

Sin begins with a conceived desire in our thinking, which can come long before we ever act physically upon whatever it is we were thinking about. Therefore, in order to stop sin completely, we will have to tackle it while it is still a fresh thought in our thinking.

Therefore, we don't just entertain the thoughts that pop up in our mind (Galatians 5:17), but we sift through them, and cast down imaginations, and anything that sets itself up against the knowledge of God, while it is still a thought (verse 5 below).

2 Corinthians 10:3-5
3 For though we walk in the flesh, we do not war after the flesh: 4 (For the weapons of our warfare are not carnal, but mighty through God to the pulling down of strong holds;) 5 Casting down imaginations, and every high thing that exalteth itself against the knowledge of God, and bringing into captivity every thought to the obedience of Christ; KJV

That's how Christians are supposed to fight. We cast down imaginations, and take every thought captive, checking to see if it is in-line with faith in Jesus Christ. If it is not in-line with obedience to Christ, we cast it out (verse 5 above).

Usually, if I end up doing something that I don't want to do, it is because I did not have my mind set on the things above. Either I started my day without the right mindset, because something occupied my thoughts, or I let my mind drift during the day, because I was caught up in the busyness of life, or the pressures brought on by the situation I was in. Those things can be resolved, but it takes much prayer (Luke 22:40), practice, and grace.

If we do not have the ability to take our thoughts captive, then we need more grace (ability). That is assuming that we have been following the teachings we have already covered, such as not conforming to this world, dying to self, speaking our faith, dying to the Laws of Moses, and baptism to name a few.

People who have not been baptized will not have the ability to live the new life (Romans 6:4). Nor will those who remain under the Laws of Moses (Romans 7:4-8), as well as many other things that we have already covered.

The reason this chapter is near the end of this book is because we will not be able to put these things into practice, if we are not ready for them. Therefore, please start this book from the beginning, or read this book again, being careful to read the verses out loud.

If you do not have the ability to take your thoughts captive, and you are practicing what we have already covered, then this is what you need to know. If you can keep your mind set on the things above, you will "not" fulfill the desires of your sinful nature (verse 16 below). In other words, if you could keep your mind on the things above, all day long, you would not sin that day, and the next, and for as long as you keep your mind on the things above.

That's pretty simple, but like I said, it takes being in the position to be able to do it, and then it takes prayer, practice, and grace.

Galatians 5:16
16 I say then: Walk in the Spirit, and you shall not fulfill the lust of the flesh. NKJV

If we are not under sin's control already because we have sinned (Romans 6:16), then our mindset determines if we are going to sin or not in the near future. That means that the things we participate in, and the things that we allow to occupy our mindset, can dictate the direction of our life.

How would the world system occupy your thoughts if you died to this world's ways? It couldn't. How could peer pressure force you to follow this world's expectations, if you were willing to suffer? It couldn't. If your eyes and hands were slaves to righteous acts, how would they force you to sin? They couldn't.

You see, if you cannot walk in the Spirit, it will be because you have not followed some of the things we have discussed in the book, which amounts to the unwillingness to die to the flesh. The things of this world can choke the Word that is living in you, and make it unfruitful (Matthew 13:22, Mark 4:18-19).

In other words, if we are caught up in doing the things that the people of this world are doing, which amounts to following the spirit of disobedience, then we will not obey Jesus. However, if we keep a clear conscience toward the things of God, we would obey Jesus first and foremost, and allow His Word to judge our attitudes and thoughts (Hebrews 4:12 above).

All sin starts with a desire in our thinking (James 1:13-15). Just as the spirit of disobedience wants us to keep our mind set on the things of this world, the Holy Spirit, wants us to keep our mind on the things above (verses 5-8 below).

Romans 8:5-8
5 For those who live according to the flesh set their minds on the things of the flesh, but those who live according to the Spirit, the things of the Spirit. 6 For to be carnally minded is death, but to be spiritually minded is life and peace. 7 Because the carnal mind is enmity against God; for it is not subject to the law of God, nor indeed can be. 8 So then, those who are in the flesh cannot please God. NKJV

Those who live (walk) according to the flesh set their mind on the things of the flesh, and those who live according to the Spirit, the things of the Spirit (verse 5 above). If our mind stays set on the things above, we cannot possibly choose to follow our sinful nature through the spirit of disobedience. In this way, by the Spirit, we put to death the desires (lusts) of our sinful nature (Romans 8:12-14,

Galatians 5:24).

To be worldly (carnally) minded is death (verse 6 above), and those with a worldly mindset are hostile (enmity) toward God (verse 7 above). Imagine praying and asking God to bless you, and to show you favor when you have been hostile toward Him for years, and have cast His ways behind you.

Most Christians have no idea that they have even fallen away from the truth. When Christians fall away, they stop repenting of the things that they need to repent of (Hebrews 6:4-6). They don't necessarily stop going to a place called church, but they no longer repent. Let us repent and return to the Lord our God.

Father, in Jesus' name, You alone are the giver of life. Have mercy on us. We didn't know Your Word, and so we didn't know Your ways. Forgive us our sins, and forgive us for grieving Your Holy Spirit. According to Your great compassion, let Your grace rain down upon us, that we may walk in Your ways. Send Your Word to heal us. Amen!

The Holy Spirit wants us to keep our mind on the things above, but the spirit of disobedience, the things of this world. That means that we are going to study the Bible more than what we have been doing in the past. We're going to seek those things above, and abandon (forsake) the things of this world.

Colossians 3:1-2
1 If then you were raised with Christ, seek those things which are above, where Christ is, sitting at the right hand of God.
2 Set your mind on things above, not on things on the earth. NKJV

Isaiah 55:7
7 Let the wicked forsake his way, And the unrighteous man his thoughts; Let him return to the Lord, And He will have mercy on him; And to our God, For He will abundantly pardon. NKJV

The simple difference between a person who walks in the Spirit, and one who follows the spirit of disobedience, is what they keep their mind set on. Therefore, those who follow the Holy Spirit of God will not be able to follow the spirit of disobedience, and vice-versa, since their paths are opposite (Galatians 5:17, Romans 8:9).

This can be a hard teaching if you have never heard this before, but be careful not to reject it, since you may never see it again (Mark 4:24-25). Why did Jesus call Peter, Satan?

Matthew 16:23
23 But He turned and said to Peter, "Get behind Me, Satan! You are an offense to Me, for you are not mindful of the things of

God, but the things of men." NKJV

Do you think that Jesus would not treat us the same way if we continued keeping our mind on the things of this world, since He is the same now, and forever (Hebrews 13:8)?

Now you can see the difference between a worldly Christian, and one who keeps his mind on the things of God. The worldly Christian definitely has something to repent of, but most of them have no idea that they are hostile toward God (Romans 8:7), since they never hear these verses taught.

Who are the enemies of the cross of Christ? Who would you consider to be an enemy of what Jesus has done for us?

Philippians 3:17-19
17 Brethren, join in following my example, and note those who so walk, as you have us for a pattern. 18 For many walk, of whom I have told you often, and now tell you even weeping, that they are the enemies of the cross of Christ: 19 whose end is destruction, whose god is their belly, and whose glory is in their shame — who set their mind on earthly things. NKJV

Enemies of the cross of Christ keep their mind on earthly things (verse 19 above). Imagine attending church all your life and never learning that. Imagine being in a place full of people who are called Christians, but none of them repent of their worldly mindset, and even promote a worldly mindset in church gatherings. Let us return to the Lord our God.

The righteous requirements of the Law will only be fulfilled in the person who walks according to the Spirit, and "not" according to the flesh (verse 4 below). Many people pull promises out of Romans chapter eight and promise them to anyone who will listen, but the word "us" below, identifies those who are right with God (righteous). They walk according to the Spirit, which means that they keep their mind on the things above (Romans 8:5-8 above).

Romans 8:4
4 that the righteous requirement of the law might be fulfilled in us who do not walk according to the flesh but according to the Spirit. NKJV

Christians, who keep their mind on the things above, will be able to fulfill the righteous requirements of the Law. Those who do not keep their mind on the things above, will not be able to love their neighbor as they love themselves. The good that they want to do, they will not be able to do, because they serve their fleshly mindset, which keeps them given over to it, in order to fulfill its desires.

Apart from the Law, sin is dead, but if we do not fulfill the Law through faith in Jesus Christ by remaining in love, we are automatically back under the Law, and are convicted as a transgressor (James 2:8-13). Like I said, worldliness, and the cares of this life will choke the Word and make it unfruitful (Matthew 13:20-22).

If the Word in us is unfruitful, we cannot remain (abide) in the vine, and those who do not remain in the vine, cannot stop sinning. This would be the point of needing more grace (ability) in order to continue in our faith.

However, those who keep their mind on the things above, will fulfill the Law, and consequently, they will receive the blessings associated with keeping it. They shall be the blessed of God. All the promises that we hear people quote out of the Bible for blessings will apply to them, and any of the curses for disobedience, such as sickness and disease, that they used to be under, will be healed.

As we continue in righteous acts, they will control us for good, and not for evil (Romans 6:16-21). Grace only reigns in righteousness (Romans 5:21), and the righteous requirements of the Law are met in the person who walks according to the Spirit, and not according to the flesh (Romans 8:4 above).

That's not the case for the unrighteous. Just as grace reigns in righteousness, sin reigns in death (Romans 5:21). Therefore, those who keep their mind on the things of the flesh remain in death, and need to repent (Romans 8:6 above).

With the mind we serve the law of God, but with the flesh, the law of sin (Romans 7:25). May the Lord have mercy on all of us.

If we obey the Spirit, He will lead us into being righteous by faith (verse 16 below, Galatians 5:5). However, if we choose sin, then sin will control us to sin again, and eventually, it will lead to death (James 1:15).

Romans 6:15-18
15 What then? Shall we sin because we are not under law but under grace? Certainly not! 16 Do you not know that to whom you present yourselves slaves to obey, you are that one's slaves whom you obey, whether of sin leading to death, or of obedience leading to righteousness? 17 But God be thanked that though you were slaves of sin, yet you obeyed from the heart that form of doctrine to which you were delivered. 18 And having been set free from sin, you became slaves of righteousness. NKJV

Continuing in sin means that sin will control us, and eventually put us to death (verse 16 above). If we obey, by choosing God's way out of every temptation (1 Corinthians 10:13), then we will become a slave to righteousness (verse 16 above), and be set free from the control of sin (verse 18 above). Again, die to sins, live for righteousness, by His stripes we are healed (1 Peter 2:24).

For Christians, who are free in Christ, it's all about which one we offer ourselves to; sin leading to death, or obedience leading to righteousness (verse 16 above). Our instructions are, "Do not let sin reign in your body" (verse 12 below), and in order to do that, we continually offer our members (our hands, feet, eyes, body parts) as instruments of righteousness (verse 13 below).

Romans 6:11-13
11 Likewise you also, reckon yourselves to be dead indeed to sin, but alive to God in Christ Jesus our Lord. 12 Therefore do not let sin reign in your mortal body, that you should obey it in its lusts. 13 And do not present your members as instruments of unrighteousness to sin, but present yourselves to God as being alive from the dead, and your members as instruments of righteousness to God. NKJV

It really is all about who we offer our members (body parts) to (verse 13 above). Do not present your members as instruments of unrighteousness to sin, but as instruments of righteousness to God. We actually do one or the other, all day long, whether we realize it or not, but if we offer ourselves to obedience through the Spirit, we will put to death our sinful nature (Romans 8:12-14, Galatians 5:24-25).

We willingly become slaves to righteousness in order that our conduct will be controlled by righteousness, rather than being controlled by sin. Only a slave to righteousness is set free from sin (Romans 6:18 above).

Therefore, show me someone who does not practice righteousness, and I will show you someone who is caught up in all kinds of sins. They may not be noticeable things, but they are there.

I heard one scoffer say, "God doesn't expect us to be robots!" No, He expects us to become His slaves with the fruit of righteousness, resulting in eternal life (verse 22 below). Those who allow Him to lead them into doing that, are His Sons (Romans 8:14 above), but robots are electronic machines that make decisions based on how they are programed. They do not have the Spirit.

Therefore, it is true, God doesn't expect us to be robots. However, He expects us to be set free from sin, and to be His slaves, with our fruit unto holiness, and the end result of eternal life (verse 22 below). Robots do not go to Heaven, but if by the Spirit we put to death the misdeeds of the body, we will live forever (Romans 8:13 above, verse 22 below).

Romans 6:20-22
20 For when you were slaves of sin, you were free in regard to righteousness. 21 What fruit did you have then in the things of which you are now ashamed? For the end of those things is death. 22 But now having been set free from sin, and having become slaves of God, you have your fruit to holiness, and the end, everlasting life. NKJV

Who is set free from sin with the end result of eternal life according to verse 22 above? Slaves of God are. Should I teach people something different, just because they don't want to hear it? No, those who belong to God, hear God's Word (John 8:47). Those who reject God's Word, have heard that which will judge them on the last day (John 12:47-48).

If we live according to the flesh, and remain a slave to sin, we will die. Once our sinful nature is fully grown, it will put us to death (James 1:15). However, by becoming God's slave we will live forever (verse 22 above).

Father, in Jesus' name, Forgive us, and lead us in the way everlasting. Amen!

Now what

Just like Martha was caught up in all the preparations that had to be made, while Mary was listening to the Word of God spoken by Jesus, so it is today (Luke 10:38-42). People who are given over to a worldly mindset are caught up in what the world is doing through television, radio, newspapers, cell phones, tablets, and whatever will soon be invented for that specific purpose.

Have you not noticed that the world system keeps us so busy with things that "have" to be done, just like Martha was? More of the same is on the way, simply because that is the direction in which the world is headed.

Why did the Lord destroy man from the face of the earth with the flood?

Genesis 6:5
5 And God saw that the wickedness of man was great in the earth, and that every imagination of the thoughts of his heart was only evil continually. KJV

It wasn't just because of wickedness, but He also knows our thoughts (Psalm 139:4). Every imagination of the thoughts of man's heart was continually on evil. Imagine how close we are to that today, and even in the house of God?

People who are controlled by the Holy Spirit keep their mind set on the things above, and not on earthly things. They are not only holy in conduct, but they are looking for opportunities to help people, and especially people of faith (Galatians 6:9-10).

Acts of righteousness are controlling them to do even more acts of righteousness. They are being controlled by righteousness (Romans 6:20), and therefore, they are set free from sin (Romans 6:18).

Our mindset and desires reveal where we are headed, and control how we live. In fact, you can learn to listen to people speak, and know what is in their near future, since words control our days, and out of the abundance of the heart, the mouth will speak (Matthew 12:34).

What are "things" above? The Word of God is from above. It is Spirit, and it describes the things that we are to set our mind on.

John 6:63
63 It is the Spirit who gives life; the flesh profits nothing. The words that I speak to you are spirit, and they are life. NKJV

Philippians 4:8-9
**8 Finally, brethren, whatever things are true, whatever things
are noble, whatever things are just, whatever things are pure,
whatever things are lovely, whatever things are of good report,
if there is any virtue and if there is anything praiseworthy —
meditate on these things. 9 The things which you learned and
received and heard and saw in me, these do, and the God of
peace will be with you. NKJV**

There are many things that we can set our mind on that are considered
"things above." However, if we have not renewed our mind to the point of being
transformed, then what we mostly need is to keep our mind on the Word of God.

As I have said many times, read the Word out loud daily. Read at least 10 or
15 chapters a day, and especially from the New Testament. Read it to the point of
retaining it in your heart (Romans 1:28-32). That in itself will place life in your
body (verse 63 above).

I have watched many people receive healing, deliverance, and many of
the things that they needed, simply because they started reading the Bible out
loud on a daily basis. Even homeless people with prison records obtained good
employment, all within a few weeks, by doing the same thing. All they did was
repent of the past and began doing what all Christians are supposed to be doing
to begin with, and the Lord had mercy on them. Praise God.

We serve a merciful God, Who is full of compassion, and slow to anger.
Praise be to the Lord our God forever. Amen.

Renewing our mind is not the only thing that Christians are supposed to be
doing, but that is where many people need to start, because that is where they
stopped soon after they got saved. We have already covered many different things
that we should be doing in this book according to faith, and therefore, reading
the Word of God out loud may not be everyone's problem.

However, if you started this book from the beginning, then I'm sure that
you know which areas you need to start working on. If my wife and I can be of
assistance to you, please let us know.

Walking in the Spirit is very simple, but it will take much practice, since we
may already be filled with all kinds of desires and false doctrines created while
we walked according to the spirit of error, as well as the doctrines of deceiving
spirits taught today (1 Timothy 4:1-2). Ask God our Father to cleanse your conscience, and fill you with His grace (ability) in the name of Jesus Christ. Amen.
That way you can start over with a clean slate, but be careful to forgive everyone.

Whatever is necessary for you, in order to follow what is written in the
Bible,is what you need to do. Everybody is different and just about any gadget
today can be used for good or for evil.

I'm not saying that you will have to get rid of your smart phone, TV, or whatever you use during the day, but you should decide what you need to cut out of your life based on your success; keeping your mind on the things above.

There is absolutely nothing wrong with a game, but playing games can only grow our flesh, and make our desire for the things of the flesh more abundant (John 3:6). That's how it is with things of the flesh, or any worldly activity that we participate in. I'm not saying don't play a game, but I am asking you to recognize the time you are spending doing it, and to keep the things of God first place in your life.

There is no such thing as a godly person who doesn't take the time needed to be godly. As we draw near to Him, He will draw near to us (James 4:8). Think about that.

Once we learn how sin works, and what we are supposed to be doing as Christians to prevent it, then the question becomes, "How long can we walk in the Spirit?" That will determine how long we can go without sinning.

If we are walking in the Spirit, how long can we go without allowing a deceiving spirit to create a desire large enough that would make us turn to follow it? If we are willing to suffer in our flesh no matter what comes up, then we can be done with sin from now on (1 Peter 4:1-4). Therefore, this depends on what we are willing to give up (Luke 14:25-35).

In order to stop sinning completely, you must not allow anything to get you off track, no matter what comes up. It can be done, but there is a cost (Luke 14:25-33).

For Christ followers there isn't a desire large enough that could "make us" turn, since God will not allow us to be tempted beyond what we can bear, and when we are tempted, He will also provide a way of escape. However, life itself comes with its own circumstances, and worldly situations that we must deal with (Luke 14:25-33), but if we turn back, we choose to turn.

Father, in the name of Jesus Christ, help us. We need Your help in order to be able to live the Christian life. We want to be filled with Your Spirit, and we want You to lead us out of the mess we have made. Lead us into all truth by the power of Your Holy Spirit. If we have been filled in the past, we beg You to forgive us for grieving Your Holy Spirit, and now fill us that we may walk in Your ways, and become what You have called us to be. In the mighty name of Jesus Christ we pray. Amen.

I'm Alan Ballou; a servant. If you have any questions for me or my wife Lucie, please contact us.

www.HowToStopSinning.com

ℰᏇ

21

Refusing Him Who Speaks

ಬಂಬ

When the Holy Spirit places God's love in our heart, and we do what He is leading us to do, then we will be sowing to please the Spirit. Consequently, we will fulfill the Laws of Moses, come out of darkness, and receive all of the good that God has planned for us (Jeremiah 5:25).

If we sow to please our flesh, which is the opposite of sowing to please the Spirit, we will reap corruption, but by sowing to please the Spirit, we will "reap everlasting life" (verse 8 below).

Galatians 6:7-10
7 Do not be deceived, God is not mocked; for whatever a man sows, that he will also reap. 8 For he who sows to his flesh will of the flesh reap corruption, but he who sows to the Spirit will of the Spirit reap everlasting life. 9 And let us not grow weary while doing good, for in due season we shall reap if we do not lose heart. 10 Therefore, as we have opportunity, let us do good to all, especially to those who are of the household of faith. NKJV

That's a verse on everlasting life that we will rarely hear, because it does not match what most people have come to believe. It is certainly evident that we are in the very last days, when the Word of God doesn't match what is accepted and proclaimed by the majority of Christians. Nevertheless, those who will reap everlasting life, sow to please the Spirit.

Don't stop doing good (verse 9 above)! We will reap if we do not give up. That too is far from what most preach, but those are our instructions. As we have discussed, it is God's will that we do good (1 Peter 2:15), and only those who do the will of God will be able to enter the Kingdom of Heaven (Matthew 7:21).

By that one passage of scripture, you should be able to recognize that the vast majority of church-attending people have taken a stand against what the Bible says. Verse 7 begins with, "Do not be deceived!"

You decide for yourself as to whether or not God's Word is true, but as for me and my house, we believe every word, and therefore, we will continue to allow

God's Word to judge our attitudes and thoughts (Hebrews 4:12).

The biggest problem for Christians is unbelief, which we discussed in the first chapter of this book. We don't see it as unbelief, but there is no other way to explain holding to a few verses on one page in our Bible, and totally ignoring the verses on the next page. Jesus called it straining out a gnat, and swallowing a camel (Matthew 23:24).

Love for God is that we keep His commandments without them becoming burdensome (1 John 5:3). In other words, love for God, is to keep doing what He wants us to do, without it becoming a problem for us (verse 9 above, and 3 below).

1 John 5:2-4
2 By this we know that we love the children of God, when we love God and keep His commandments. 3 For this is the love of God, that we keep His commandments. And His commandments are not burdensome. 4 For whatever is born of God overcomes the world. And this is the victory that has overcome the world — our faith. NKJV

Some Christians have been taught that if they have to do anything after they are saved, it isn't of God. It should be obvious to you by now that teachings like that are false. In the last days, many will follow deceiving spirits (1 Timothy 4:1).

Those who love God keep His commandments (verse 2 above). The children of God, love the children of God, by keeping God's commandments, and by doing so, whoever is born of God overcomes the world (verse 4 above).

If we are doing what we are supposed to be doing as Christians, which we have discussed, we would overcome the world, assuming we do not give up. In other words, if we were loving who we are supposed to love, in the way we are supposed to love them, and were avoiding the things that we are instructed to avoid, the end result would be what is promised. Don't give up!

Do not join the vast majority of people headed in the wrong direction. Why? It is written that it will happen, and so it is happening. Take another look at Luke 13:24-28 below. Notice that it starts with "Strive to enter!" That means to make every effort to enter the right gate.

Luke 13:24-28
24 Strive to enter in at the strait gate: for many, I say unto you, will seek to enter in, and shall not be able. 25 When once the master of the house is risen up, and hath shut to the door, and ye begin to stand without, and to knock at the door, saying, Lord, Lord, open unto us; and he shall answer and say unto you, I know you not whence ye are:

26 Then shall ye begin to say, We have eaten and drunk in thy presence, and thou hast taught in our streets. 27 But he

shall say, I tell you, I know you not whence ye are; depart from me, all ye workers of iniquity. 28 There shall be weeping and gnashing of teeth, when ye shall see Abraham, and Isaac, and Jacob, and all the prophets, in the kingdom of God, and you yourselves thrust out. KJV

Many will seek to enter, but will not be able (verse 24 above). He is not talking about people who have not been saved, but people who are expecting to be able to remain in the Kingdom, but they will be thrust out (verse 28 above, Matthew 7:21-23). Do non-Christians call Jesus, "Lord," but never come to know Him, as we have previously discussed in chapter 7?

How do we come to know Jesus? We come to know Him by obeying His commands (1 John 2:3), putting off our old ways, renewing our minds, and putting on the new person (Ephesians 4:20-24). We cannot do any of those things before we get saved, but only after. However, that's doing something after we are saved.

You can allow worldly Christians to talk you out of doing those things if you want to, but know that the workers of iniquity (sin) are the ones who will be cast out of the Kingdom, according to verse 27 above. Therefore, don't be tricked. "Strive to enter" the right gate; the one that few find according to the Words of Jesus Christ (verse 14 below).

Matthew 7:13-14
13 "Enter by the narrow gate; for wide is the gate and broad is the way that leads to destruction, and there are many who go in by it. 14 Because narrow is the gate and difficult is the way which leads to life, and there are few who find it. NKJV

How can you recognize the difference between the two gates. First of all, the teachings we have covered in this book will be suppressed by those who enter the wide gate. The unrighteous always suppress the truth (Romans 1:18).

Also, Christians who take the wrong gate, do not teach the doctrine of Jesus Christ, or teach that we must obey Him at all, because that would be telling people what to do, and they don't want to be told what to do.

One lady told me that telling people what to do was legalism. Telling people what to do, in order to restrict freedom of choice is legalism. Strict dress codes, and any disputable matter that is "not" written in scripture is legalism. However, preaching the doctrine of Jesus Christ, and what His disciples have instructed us to do, is far from legalism. Calling the doctrine of Jesus legalism is just an excuse to practice lawlessness.

Some people say that I preach Law. Praise God. I do preach Law, just as Jesus asked us to do according to Matthew 5:17-19, but for the purpose of leading people to Christ (Galatians 3:24). Have you noticed that ninety-nine percent of the verses I use are from the New Testament?

I used to spend hours trying to explain the Laws of Moses and Christ's law, through emails, and social media. I have dedicated three chapters of this book to explaining our relationship with the Law, and now I am done arguing with unbelievers, who cannot possibly understand it due to their unbelief.

Am I under the Laws of Moses? No, Lord willing, I am not. Am I under Christ's law? Yes I am, and so was the Apostle Paul, and those he taught according to the Word of the Lord, written in 1 Corinthians 9:21 below.

1 Corinthians 9:19-21
19 For though I am free from all men, I have made myself a servant to all, that I might win the more; 20 and to the Jews I became as a Jew, that I might win Jews; to those who are under the law, as under the law, that I might win those who are under the law; 21 to those who are without law, as without law(not being without law toward God, but under law toward Christ), that I might win those who are without law; NKJV

Was the Apostle Paul under Christ's law? Yes he was. Christ commanded us to love one another, which includes forgiving people, feeding people, as well as many other things associated with love according to the Bible. You can call that legalism if you want, but the Bible calls it Christ's law.

We all have the freedom to choose, and I choose to be under Christ's law. That means that I am free from the Laws of Moses, but through love, I serve the people of God, just as I am instructed to do by the Word of God.

Galatians 5:13-15
13 For you, brethren, have been called to liberty; only do not use liberty as an opportunity for the flesh, but through love serve one another. 14 For all the law is fulfilled in one word, even in this: "You shall love your neighbor as yourself."   15 But if you bite and devour one another, beware lest you be consumed by one another! NKJV

People who practice lawlessness do not hold to any teachings. In other words, they do not hold to the Laws of Moses, or the doctrine of Jesus Christ (Christ's law). According to them, telling people what to do is legalism.

Get this. Those who practice lawlessness will not be able to enter the Kingdom of Heaven (Matthew 7:21-23, 13:41). They are in the Kingdom now, and so we have to love them, but in the end, they will be removed.

Matthew 13:40-43
40 Therefore as the tares are gathered and burned in the fire, so it will be at the end of this age. 41 The Son of Man will send out His angels, and they will gather out of His kingdom

all things that offend, and those who practice lawlessness, 42 and will cast them into the furnace of fire. There will be wailing and gnashing of teeth. 43 Then the righteous will shine forth as the sun in the kingdom of their Father. He who has ears to hear, let him hear! NKJV

So now, where will those who practice lawlessness end up according to the Word of Jesus Christ in verse 41 above? Would you like to join them?

In the last days lawlessness will abound (Matthew 24:12). Therefore, it is expected that churches that promote lawlessness are going to grow by leaps and bounds. Basically, they will provide a place where people can go, who are seeking some sort of spirituality, but they do not want to hear the things we have covered in this book (2 Timothy 4:3-4, 3:1-5).

My friend, look around. That is already happening today, and many of the basic teachings of the faith have been suppressed in order to make the listener-friendly message sound as if it fits God's Word. They are actually teaching people to say, "That's legalism," when someone tells them that we have to do something after we are saved. Instead of Bible classes, they are teaching people how to respond to those who teach what the Bible says.

Programs that support worldly solutions for health, provisions, and deliverance, are even right inside the house of God. In other words, they have replaced God's advice for this world's advice, which is also predicted (2 Timothy 3:1-5).

These things will happen, but we do not have to be a part of it, or support the wicked work of those who fall away to perdition, which is the destruction of the soul (Hebrews 10:37-39, 2 Peter 3:7). Let us return to the Lord our God!

Father, in the name of Jesus Christ, we're sorry. Have mercy on us. Forgive us for refusing Him Who speaks, and replacing Him with worldly solutions. Have mercy on us and receive us back under Your wings as You have ever since we were young. Forgive us of our great transgressions. You alone can save. Rescue us from our sins, and wash us clean with the blood of Jesus again. Give us the grace needed to do Your will. For You alone are worthy of praise, glory, and honor forever, and ever, Amen.

Everyone who is going to reap eternal life, sows to please the Spirit (Galatians 6:8 above). Don't be left behind. Therefore, we should be looking for opportunities to do good (Galatians 6:10 above). That is how the Christian life is designed to work, and through doing what we are supposed to be doing, we will be made holy in our conduct.

Sanctification (holiness) in conduct is through the Spirit (Romans 15:16-18), and the washing of water by the Word (Ephesians 5:25-26). That is very much a part of the true Gospel message (verses 13-14 below). We have to be born of water and Spirit in order to enter the Kingdom of God (John 3:5).

Many have rejected this and only lead people into being saved, which is expected in the last days (2 Thessalonians 2:9-12). However, eternal salvation is for those who "obey Jesus" (Hebrews 5:9), and He commanded us to love one another (John 13:34-35).

2 Thessalonians 2:13-15
13 But we are bound to give thanks to God always for you, brethren beloved by the Lord, because God from the beginning chose you for salvation through sanctification by the Spirit and belief in the truth, 14 to which He called you by our gospel, for the obtaining of the glory of our Lord Jesus Christ. 15 Therefore, brethren, stand fast and hold the traditions which you were taught, whether by word or our epistle. NKJV

God has chosen us for salvation through the sanctifying work of the Spirit, and belief in the truth (verse 13 above). Notice in verse 14 above, that the Apostle Paul says that we were called to this through the Gospel that he preached, and it should be a part of the Gospel we preach, but we are a long way from that.

Father, in Jesus' name, have mercy on us. Open our eyes, and turn us from darkness to light. Send Your Word to heal us, that we may walk in Your ways, and bring glory to Your holy name. Amen.

Yes, while we were still enemies, Christ died for us (Romans 5:8), and now that we are justified by His blood (past tense), we are "being" saved (future tense) through His life (Romans 5:9). Now that we have been reconciled to God through Christ's death (past tense), again we are "being saved" (future tense) through His life (Romans 5:10).

In other words, now that we have redemption (verse 14 below), and have been delivered from the power of darkness (verse 13 below), we have been given the right to share (be partakers) in the inheritance of the saints (verse 12 below).

Colossians 1:12-14
12 giving thanks to the Father who has qualified us to be partakers of the inheritance of the saints in the light. 13 He has delivered us from the power of darkness and conveyed us into the kingdom of the Son of His love, 14 in whom we have redemption through His blood, the forgiveness of sins. NKJV

We have been qualified to be partakers in the inheritance (verse 12 above). That's what we received when we were saved, but that doesn't mean that we are forced to continue in our faith. Therefore, as the Holy Spirit leads us into all truth, we have to continue to believe to the saving of the soul (verse 39 below).

Hebrews 10:39
39 But we are not of them who draw back unto perdition; but of them that believe to the saving of the soul. KJV

Those who do not believe, cannot possibly be sealed with the Holy Spirit. However, hearing the Word of truth, combined with believing guarantees our inheritance after we are saved, and baptized into Christ Jesus (Ephesians 1:13-14).

Therefore, those of us who are led by the Spirit of God, are the sons of God, and we wait patiently for our adoption (future tense); the redemption of our body (Romans 8:23-25). Those who do not continue believing the Word of God as they are lead into all truth by the Spirit, are in danger of falling away to perdition (verse 39 above).

What does that tell you about those who reject the teachings we have covered in this book? We are supposed to be making disciples of Jesus Christ, which requires that we teach people to obey the doctrine of Jesus (Matthew 28:19-20).

Therefore, we don't just lead people into being saved, but we teach and admonish (warn) them concerning the doctrine of Jesus Christ, and the inheritance as well. We teach them to seek God's Kingdom, and His righteousness first place in their life (Matthew 6:33). We teach sanctification in conduct, through faith and the Spirit, and we teach people these things after they are saved and baptized into Christ Jesus our Lord.

The Apostle Paul was sent to turn us from darkness to light, and from the power of Satan, to the power of God, in order that we would receive forgiveness of sins, and sanctification by faith (verse 18 below).

Acts 26:18
18 to open their eyes, in order to turn them from darkness to light, and from the power of Satan to God, that they may receive forgiveness of sins and an inheritance among those who are sanctified by faith in Me.' NKJV

The forgiveness of sins is not the end of our journey, but the beginning. We need that, and we also need an inheritance, which requires sanctification (verse 18 above, Hebrews 12:14, Acts 20:32).

Everything the Apostle Paul taught and did was to make the people he ministered to obedient (Romans 15:18). That's in-line with the Great Commission, which is to make disciples of Jesus Christ (Matthew 28:19-20), and that is what we should be teaching.

He didn't just get people saved, using a sinner's prayer, but he made sure that they were sanctified by the Spirit (verse 16 below), by reminding them of it, after they were saved (verses 15-16 below).

Romans 15:15-16
15 Nevertheless, brethren, I have written more boldly to you

on some points, as reminding you, because of the grace given to me by God, 16 that I might be a minister of Jesus Christ to the Gentiles, ministering the gospel of God, that the offering of the Gentiles might be acceptable, sanctified by the Holy Spirit. NKJV

The Apostle Paul was working and striving, warning everyone with a Gospel that would make the people he was ministering to "sanctified" (verse 16 above), or "perfect in Christ Jesus" (verse 28 below).

Colossians 1:28-29
28 Him we preach, warning every man and teaching every man in all wisdom, that we may present every man perfect in Christ Jesus. 29 To this end I also labor, striving according to His working which works in me mightily. NKJV

By submitting to God, and resisting the devil through faith (James 4:7, 1 Peter 5:8-9), our conduct will be made holy (sanctified), by faith in Jesus Christ (Acts 26:18 above). Faith in Jesus Christ will make us love one another (John 13:34-35), and when God pours His love into our heart by the Holy Spirit, that is exactly what we will do.

However, instead of dying to sin and living for righteousness through faith in Jesus Christ, we can refuse to hear the Word of God, and turn away (verse 25 below). That's the option that many have taken today, but that's not a wise decision.

Hebrews 12:25
25 See that you do not refuse Him who speaks. For if they did not escape who refused Him who spoke on earth, much more shall we not escape if we turn away from Him who speaks from heaven, NKJV

The Lord is the Spirit (2 Corinthians 3:17), and the Spirit is the Word (John 6:63). It is those who "hear" God's Word and believe that have everlasting life (John 5:24 below). Those who do not hear God's Word, do not belong to God (John 8:47), regardless if they meet once a week to sing songs to God, and talk about spiritual things.

We can't sing our way into the Kingdom of Heaven, but we must do the will of our Father in Heaven (Matthew 7:21). The will of God is our sanctification in conduct (verses 3-5 below).

1 Thessalonians 4:3-5
3 For this is the will of God, your sanctification: that you should abstain from sexual immorality; 4 that each of you should know how to possess his own vessel in sanctification

and honor, 5 not in passion of lust, like the Gentiles who do not know God; NKJV

The will of God is that we would "do good" (verse 15 below), and those who do the will of God, abide forever (1 John 2:17). Heaven is a place reserved for those who "do the will of God our Father" (Matthew 7:21). Don't get left behind!

1 Peter 2:15
15 For this is the will of God, that by doing good you may put to silence the ignorance of foolish men — NKJV

Eternal salvation is through the sanctifying work of the Spirit, and belief in the truth (2 Thessalonians 2:13-14 above). Do we believe the truth, or do we have a problem with it? In order to complete the Spirit's work in us, we are going to have to hold to the teachings (2 Thessalonians 2:15 above, 1 Corinthians 15:1-2, John 8:31-37).

Therefore, if we have received the Spirit of adoption, and call God "Father," then we should also allow ourselves to be led by the Spirit, which will require us to share in the sufferings of Christ at some point in our life (Romans 8:14-17). As I have mentioned, those who are led by the Holy Spirit, are sons of God (Romans 8:14).

All Christians can call themselves "sons of God," through faith in Jesus Christ (Galatians 2:26). However, those who have the hope of adoption living in them, also purify themself (1 John 3:1-3) with the washing of water, by the Word of God through the Spirit, to the point of sanctifying their soul (Ephesians 5:25-27, 1 Peter 1:22-25).

Ephesians 5:25-27
25 Husbands, love your wives, just as Christ also loved the church and gave Himself for her, 26 that He might sanctify and cleanse her with the washing of water by the word, 27 that He might present her to Himself a glorious church, not having spot or wrinkle or any such thing, but that she should be holy and without blemish. NKJV

Many use this passage of scripture for husbands alone, but it describes how Christ loves the church, and what He is expecting the church to be, "before" it is presented to Him in the end (verse 27 above, Romans 15:15-16 above). We should be holy (sanctified in conduct), by the washing of water by the Word (verse 26 above). We can't get there by refusing to hear the Word.

Some people use Hebrews 10:10 as if the blood does not agree with the Spirit, and the water, but they are mistaken (1 John 5:8). Yes, by one offering, through the blood of Jesus Christ, we have been sanctified, once and for all (Hebrews 10:10).

However, we can refuse to hear the blood, "which speaks" (Hebrews 12:24), and neglect the salvation that we have been given, if we do not pay careful attention to what we have heard (verses 1-3 below).

Hebrews 2:1-3
1 Therefore we must give the more earnest heed to the things we have heard, lest we drift away. 2 For if the word spoken through angels proved steadfast, and every transgression and disobedience received a just reward, 3 how shall we escape if we neglect so great a salvation, which at the first began to be spoken by the Lord, and was confirmed to us by those who heard Him, NKJV

In this way, Jesus has "perfected forever" those who are "being" sanctified (Hebrews 10:14), and He is not ashamed to be called their brother (Hebrews 2:11, Mark 3:35).

They are the ones who do not believe in vain (1 Corinthians 15:1-2). Nor do they receive the grace of God in vain (2 Corinthians 6:1), but they believe to the saving of the soul (Hebrews 10:39). Consequently, they will receive the inheritance (Acts 26:18). Praise be to the Lord our God forever and ever!

Those who refuse to hear the Word of God, trample the Son of God underfoot, and count the blood of the covenant, by which they were sanctified, a common thing, and insult the Spirit of grace (Hebrews 10:29). Therefore the Lord has said, "Vengeance is Mine!" The Lord will judge His people (Hebrews 10:30). Let us return to the Lord our God.

We will be punished if we neglect our salvation. Therefore, we must give more earnest (serious, intense) heed to the things we have heard (Hebrews 2:1-3). If we don't, we could drift away from the truth, and follow those who proclaim false doctrines.

After we have done the will of God, we will receive what is promised, but we must continue in our faith, and believe to the saving of our soul, or we will draw back to perdition, which is the destruction of the soul (Hebrews 10:36-39).

Therefore, hearing the Word of God and believing it, is evidence of everlasting life (verse 24 below). Avoiding the Word of God, and rejecting parts of it, is evidence of "refusing Him Who speaks" (Hebrews 12:25 above).

John 5:24
24 "Most assuredly, I say to you, he who hears My word and believes in Him who sent Me has everlasting life, and shall not come into judgment, but has passed from death into life. NKJV

The Word that Jesus spoke, was the Word that God gave Him to speak (John 12:49). "Jesus" is the name that is above every name, and that name was given to the Word made flesh (Philippians 2:9, John 1:14). The Words of Jesus, and the Words given to the disciples to speak by the Holy Spirit, are the Words of God (2 Peter 1:20-21, 2 Timothy 3:16).

Therefore, we cannot turn away from what is written in the Bible, and harden our heart against the Holy Spirit, Who is leading us (verse 15 below). In doing so, we will depart from God (verse 12 below).

Hebrews 3:15
15 while it is said: "Today, if you will hear His voice, Do not harden your hearts as in the rebellion." NKJV

Hebrews 3:12-13
12 Beware, brethren, lest there be in any of you an evil heart of unbelief in departing from the living God; 13 but exhort one another daily, while it is called "Today," lest any of you be hardened through the deceitfulness of sin. NKJV

If the Word we have heard from the beginning abides in us, then we will also abide in the Son and in the Father (1 John 2:24). However, whoever continues in sin, and does not abide in the doctrine of Christ, does not have God (2 John 1:9-11).

If and when the Spirit of God is dwelling in us, we cannot possibly be in the flesh, and those who do not have the Spirit of God dwelling in them, do not belong to Christ. Don't allow that to shock you, but let us return to the Lord our God, and He will have mercy on us.

Romans 8:9
9 But you are not in the flesh but in the Spirit, if indeed the Spirit of God dwells in you. Now if anyone does not have the Spirit of Christ, he is not His. NKJV

Father, in the name of Jesus Christ, have mercy on us. We don't know Your ways, because we have pushed Your Word aside. We have walked according to our own ways, and have even taught others to do so. Have mercy on us. Forgive us for this, and now open our eyes so that we will be able to see Your Word and retain it in order that it may live on the inside of us, and change us from the inside out. Place in us an overwhelming desire to know You according to Your Word. You alone are able to save. Save us Lord! Amen. Peace to all who are called by His name.

Grace is our God-given ability to serve Him, in the way that He expects us to serve Him; with reverence and godly fear (Hebrews 12:28-29). We should not use the grace of God as a license to continue in sin, and reject His Word after we are saved (Jude 1:4). May the Lord have mercy on us. Amen.

God is with those who have a contrite spirit, or a contrite heart, as it is written in some Bibles. Those who are contrite have a godly sorrow for sin, with a determination not to sin again (Psalm 34:18, 51:17, Isaiah 66:2, verse 15 below).

Isaiah 57:15

15 For thus says the High and Lofty One Who inhabits eternity, whose name is Holy: "I dwell in the high and holy place, With him who has a contrite and humble spirit, To revive the spirit of the humble, And to revive the heart of the contrite ones. NKJV

God will oppose those who are prideful, but He will give more grace to those who are humble (James 4:6, 1Peter 5:5). Those who do not have a godly sorrow for sin, may end up falling away. Let us call upon the name of the Lord Jesus, to give us a new heart that is receptive to His ways, that we may live. Amen.

If we confess our sins, He is faithful and just to forgive us, and cleanse us from all unrighteousness (1 John 1:9). In confessing our sins, we are agreeing with Him that we have done wrong, which is humbling ourself before Him. Therefore, God will give us the grace needed to live the Christian life that we are called to live.

Those who fall away from the faith, fall away from repentance (verse 6 below). In other words, they stop repenting of the sins that they commit, and their unrepentant heart makes them believe that God will automatically forgive them (Romans 2:4).

Hebrews 6:4-6

4 For it is impossible for those who were once enlightened, and have tasted the heavenly gift, and have become partakers of the Holy Spirit, 5 and have tasted the good word of God and the powers of the age to come, 6 if they fall away, to renew them again to repentance, since they crucify again for them-selves the Son of God, and put Him to an open shame. NKJV

However, if we find ourself in this position, God will not forget the love we have shown Him, if we have helped His people (verse 10 below). Ministering, or helping God's people is evidence of salvation, and that we have not fallen away completely (verses 9-10 below). Nevertheless, we are warned to continue in "things that accompany salvation" until the end (verse 11 below), and to not become sluggish (verse 12 below).

Hebrews 6:9-12

9 But, beloved, we are confident of better things concerning you, yes, things that accompany salvation, though we speak in this manner. 10 For God is not unjust to forget your work and labor of love which you have shown toward His name, in that you have ministered to the saints, and do minister. 11 And we desire that each one of you show the same diligence to the full assurance of hope until the end, 12 that you do not become

sluggish, but imitate those who through faith and patience inherit the promises. NKJV

This is happening today, and many are falling away from the faith because the truth is being suppressed. Therefore, many do not realize that the blood of Jesus cleanses those who walk in the light, but not those who walk in darkness (1 John 1:5-7). Those who walk in darkness need to confess their sins (1 John 1:9), ASAP, since they are in danger of being cursed (Hebrews 6:7-8).

I heard someone say that Hebrews 6:4-6 (above) doesn't apply to Christians. However, do non-Christians repent of their sins? Do they partake in the Holy Spirit, or the good Word of God (verses 4-5 above)? Do non-Christians put the Son of God to an open shame (verse 6 above)?

Let us return to the Lord our God so that He will have mercy on us and heal us. Amen. Jesus is not ashamed to be called the brother of those who are being sanctified (Hebrews 2:11, Mark 3:35), and now you know how to describe your brother in Christ. He does the will of God (Mark 3:35), and he hears the Word, and keeps it (Luke 11:28).

Now what

If you have been born of God, but you are not dying to sins, then perhaps you are fighting against the sanctifying work of the Spirit (2 Thessalonians 2:13-15). That means that you are rejecting parts of the Word of God.

Many follow doctrines that are not written in the Bible, and end up in this situation. However, if we have to reject the Word of God in order to follow teachings that are not written in the Bible, then what we have come to believe is ungodly.

As I have said, hearing the Word of God and believing it, is evidence of everlasting life (John 5:24 above, Ephesians 1:13-14). Avoiding what is written in the Bible is evidence of "refusing Him Who speaks" (Hebrews 3:12-13, 15 above).

The Holy Spirit is jealous for us to follow Him, and to submit to God's ways rather than choosing to follow the ways of the world around us, through the spirit of disobedience.

James 4:4-8
4 Adulterers and adulteresses! Do you not know that friendship with the world is enmity with God? Whoever therefore wants to be a friend of the world makes himself an enemy of God. 5 Or do you think that the Scripture says in vain, "The Spirit who dwells in us yearns jealously"? 6 But He gives more grace. Therefore He says: "God resists the proud, But gives grace to the humble." 7 Therefore submit to God. Resist the devil and he will flee from you. 8 Draw near to God and He will draw near to you. Cleanse your hands, you sinners; and purify your hearts, you double-minded. NKJV

You should be able to see why a friend of this world, makes himself an enemy of God. The spirit of disobedience leads us into following the ways of this world, and the more we do so, the more we will be controlled by that spirit (Romans 6:15-18), and consequently disobey the Gospel.

The instructions are to submit to God's ways, resist the devil, and he will flee from us (verse 7 above). Draw near to God, and he will draw near to us (verse 8 above). That means that we need to put off more of this world, which we have already discussed.

A double-minded person is wavering between opinions. We purify our heart through the Spirit, Who is the Word (1 Peter 1:22-25, Ephesians 5:25-26, John 6:63). Therefore, the more we learn how to walk in the Spirit, which includes casting any thought out of our mind, that doesn't line-up with the knowledge of God (2 Corinthians 10:3-5), the better off we will be.

If we submit to the Spirit of God, and resist the spirit of disobedience, the latter will eventually flee from us. We need to know that, since we must submit to God in order to live (verse 9 below).

Hebrews 12:9-13

9 Furthermore, we have had human fathers who corrected us, and we paid them respect. Shall we not much more readily be in subjection to the Father of spirits and live? 10 For they indeed for a few days chastened us as seemed best to them, but He for our profit, that we may be partakers of His holiness. 11 Now no chastening seems to be joyful for the present, but painful; nevertheless, afterward it yields the peaceable fruit of righteousness to those who have been trained by it. 12 Therefore strengthen the hands which hang down, and the feeble knees, 13 and make straight paths for your feet, so that what is lame may not be dislocated, but rather be healed. NKJV

If we do "not" submit to God's ways, we will experience chastening (discipline), even to the point of being lame (verse 13 above). If we continue in disobedience after being disciplined, and refuse Him Who speaks, then what is lame will become dislocated (verse 13 above). This is the reason why many Christians live with disabilities today.

That may be a hard pill to swallow, but God is very serious when it comes to us following His Spirit, rather than continuing with the spirit of this world. I'm just teaching what is written in verse 13 above, in which we need to believe like Abraham believed. If I suppress the truth, in order to sell more books, would I not be among the unrighteous (Romans 1:18)?

If God said it, Abraham believed it, and so it shall be with our faith. Therefore, let us return to the Lord our God, and submit to His ways in accordance with His Word. Let us not suppress the truth any longer, but turn toward Him, Who is able to deliver us, and provide what we need in order to do His will. Amen.

God's perspective is that no living man should complain about the punishment for his sins, but turn back to Him (verses 39-40 below).

Lamentations 3:38-41
38 Is it not from the mouth of the Most High That woe and well-being proceed? 39 Why should a living man complain, A man for the punishment of his sins? 40 Let us search out and examine our ways, And turn back to the Lord; 41 Let us lift our hearts and hands To God in heaven. NKJV

Chastening is discipline, discomfort, or hardship that leads to obedience. We're all different, and therefore the amount of discipline it would take for one person to obey, may be different from the next person, and so on.

Either way, God is serious about us being holy in conduct (Hebrews 12:10 above, 1 Peter 1:14-16). Why? Without holiness, no one will see the Lord (Hebrews 12:14). Therefore, how much discomfort would we need to experience in our life in order for us to be holy in conduct? That is what we can expect here on earth, if we are going to Heaven one day.

Those who are not holy, will not see the Lord (Hebrews 12:14). Millions and millions will be cast into outer darkness, even after making it into the Kingdom of Heaven, according to the following passages of scripture.

Matthew 8:11-12
11 And I say to you that many will come from east and west, and sit down with Abraham, Isaac, and Jacob in the kingdom of heaven. 12 But the sons of the kingdom will be cast out into outer darkness. There will be weeping and gnashing of teeth." NKJV

Matthew 22:10-13
10 So those servants went out into the highways and gathered together all whom they found, both bad and good. And the wedding hall was filled with guests. 11 "But when the king came in to see the guests, he saw a man there who did not have on a wedding garment. 12 So he said to him, 'Friend, how did you come in here without a wedding garment?' And he was speechless. 13 Then the king said to the servants, 'Bind him hand and foot, take him away, and cast him into outer darkness; there will be weeping and gnashing of teeth.' NKJV

Matthew 25:29-30
29 'For to everyone who has, more will be given, and he will have abundance; but from him who does not have, even what he has will be taken away. 30 And cast the unprofitable servant

into the outer darkness. There will be weeping and gnashing of teeth.' NKJV

Now my friend, see to it that you walk carefully, and cautiously (circumspectly), redeeming the time lost (verses 15-16 below). Surround yourself with things that help you to keep your mind set on the things above, and destroy, or get rid of the things that keep you from following the Spirit. Do not refuse Him Who speaks!

Ephesians 5:15-19
15 See then that you walk circumspectly, not as fools but as wise, 16 redeeming the time, because the days are evil. 17 Therefore do not be unwise, but understand what the will of the Lord is. 18 And do not be drunk with wine, in which is dissipation; but be filled with the Spirit, 19 speaking to one another in psalms and hymns and spiritual songs, singing and making melody in your heart to the Lord NKJV

Father, in the name of Jesus Christ. Save us from our sins! Forgive us for the sins we have committed against You, and forgive us for grieving Your Holy Spirit, Whom You caused to live in us. Give us the grace we need to be able to live the life You have called us to live, and forgive us for not allowing Your grace to change our character in the past. You saved us, and called us, even when we were dead. In Your loving kindness, rescue us from where we have fallen. Deliver us from the traps we have set for ourselves. Cause us to will and to act according to Your purposes. For You alone are able to do it. Amen.

Peace be with you. May the Lord bless you, and give you everything needed to do His will. May you abound in the hope, given by the power of His Holy Spirit, and may you walk in the ways that He has set before us. Amen.

Father, in the name of Jesus Christ, if I have spoken in accordance with Your Word, then may You bless those who hear, and judge between me and those who oppose what You have given me to speak. Amen.

I'm Alan Ballou; a servant. If you have any questions for me or my wife Lucie, please contact us. If we may be of service to you, free of charge, please let us know. We appreciate your prayers, and Lord willing, we will always pray for all people, but especially for those who enjoy this teaching. May the Lord bless you.

෨෬

About the Author

Alan Ballou is a servant, and called by the Lord to be a teacher.
He teaches on average two or three times a week, at church
events, small group meetings, homeless shelters, and from house
to house. He teaches on the web through his blog, and through
emails. He serves Christians, who contact him from all over the
world, in matters concerning deliverance, and healing, free of
charge.

Alan and his wife Lucie serve the Lord as a team in everything
they do. They make their home in the upstate of South Carolina.
If you have any questions about this book, or if you would like to
receive help concerning deliverance, or healing from the Lord,
please contact them by email.

For more information, video teachings, a contact form, or to
simply leave comments, please visit:

www.HowToStopSinning.com

Alan's email alan@howtostopsinning.com

Lucie's email lucie@howtostopsinning.com

ഇൽ

CPSIA information can be obtained
at www.ICGtesting.com
Printed in the USA
LVHW022222030121
675625LV00066B/5119

9 780989 196925